UNI-WISSEN

Andreas Müller-Hartmann
Marita Schocker-v. Ditfurth

Introduction to English Language Teaching

27.10.14

Klett Lerntraining

Bildnachweis:
Seite 77: aus: Patsy M. Lightbown and Nina Spada: How Languages are Learned, Oxford University
Seite 118: aus: Regina u. Gerd Riepe: Du schwarz – Ich weiß, Peter Hammer Verlag 1992

Bibliografische Information der Deutschen Nationalbibliothek
Die Deutsche Nationalbibliothek verzeichnet diese Publikation in der Deutschen Nationalbibliografie; detaillierte bibliografische Daten sind im Internet über http://dnb.d-nb.de abrufbar.

Auflage 3 2 1 | 2016 2015 2014
Die letzten Zahlen bezeichnen jeweils die Auflage und das Jahr des Druckes.

www.klett.de/uniwissen
Satz: Steffen Hahn GmbH Medienservice, Kornwestheim
Druck: AZ Druck und Datentechnik GmbH, Kempten
Printed in Germany
ISBN 978-3-12-939022-1

9 783129 390221

Contents

Introduction

Rationale of this book

Writing a book on the teaching and learning of English as a foreign language (EFL) is, for various reasons, a daunting task: The subject matter is complex as it covers a heterogeneous field where a number of factors come into play, involving different disciplines, research approaches, contexts of practice, learners and teachers, and social settings. Besides, there are quite a number of books on the teaching of English as a foreign or second language already on the market – so why write yet another one? As Medgyes (2002: 87) put it while reviewing one such book, "While suppressing a yawn, the reviewer begins to wonder what makes any of the titles unique and competitive. Aren't they mere clones of one another? (...A)ren't I supposed now to review a book which shares too many features with other titles to make it distinctly different?" So, what is it that makes our book distinctively different from other introductory textbooks on the teaching and learning of English as a foreign language?

The context: Teaching and learning EFL in Germany

Each of the books available at present is based on a particular philosophy of the teaching and learning of EFL. This is necessarily so, given the multitude of aspects to consider. Besides, each of these course-books has been produced for a particular 'EFL market' and does not therefore take into account the particularities of a specific teacher education or foreign language learning context. Our book, on the other hand, has been written for German student teachers of English as a foreign language in that it refers to approaches and materials which are particularly relevant for our context.

English as the language of instruction

Unlike other course-books, it is written in the target language. This is because we consider it to be a basic professional competence of EFL teachers to be able to join the European or international professional discourse in English. Besides, English is the means of instruction and communication in university-based methodology seminars, which is why the bulk of basic relevant readings has to be provided in English.

Research-based focus

Our methodology is research-based in that it draws insights about the teaching and learning of English from relevant research. It therefore hopes to contribute to the establishment of *Fremdsprachendidaktik* as an autonomous discipline.

Major issues of teaching and learning

A last distinctive feature of our book relates to our choice of contents and topics. It is based on three aspects of EFL teaching and learning which we consider to be particularly relevant today:

- Promoting intercultural communicative competence
- Developing learner- and learning-centred teaching in classrooms to delineate ways in which the social context of school affects language teaching and learning
- Supporting task-based learning

Organization of chapters

Each chapter follows roughly the same pattern: it introduces the main issues of a topic (including a survey of the historical development, if appropriate); it gives a summary of relevant research; it draws conclusions or illustrates examples of good classroom practice (we have included as many examples for materials and tasks from EFL classrooms as the space we were provided allowed); and it concludes by listing current trends and future perspectives. There is an end-of-book bibliography for students to get a survey of relevant current readings. In the bibliography we marked certain books (see: ◆) as recommended readings for students who wish to focus on specific topics in more detail (to prepare a topic for their exam, for example).

Intended readership

Our book may be used in various learning-to-teach scenarios. Student teachers may wish to prepare or read up on lecture-based methodology courses, or use it in accompanying tutorials. Lecturers may use it as a course book for their introductory methodology courses, and provide additional examples from practice (classroom tasks, lesson videos etc.) to illustrate what has been said. Or student teachers may wish to use it as a compendium to prepare their methodology exams, to choose a topic for their oral exams or to find relevant reading for a classroom research project they wish to do in their teaching practice.

Limitations

We are against top-down models of applied science in teacher education (Wallace 1991) which merely use classroom practice to exemplify academic research. Instead, we see language teachers not simply as consumers of theory, but as generators of theories based on their professional knowledge and their ongoing reflection on classroom teaching (Richards 2001). Theories should be developed not by people outside the classroom but by practitioners themselves (Freeman 2001). However, the limited length available for titles in this series made it impossible to present material in this way.

Glossary

We are not offering a glossary of basic theoretical terms as a tool for students. This is because there is an excellent dictionary for students to use for this purpose we would like to recommend instead. It explains very clearly those difficult theoretical terms (there are about 2000 entries) which students may encounter in the field: Jack Richards, Richard Schmidt, Heidi Platt, Marcus

SCHMIDT. *Dictionary of Language Teaching and Applied Linguistics.* 3rd. ed. Paperback Harlow: Pearson Education 2002.

Thanks

We would particularly like to thank KEITH MORROW and the editor of this series, ANSGAR NÜNNING, very much for their very thoughtful revision work. A word of thanks also goes to ANNETTE RICHTER who participated in the design of the general structure of the book. A number of colleagues provided helpful advice, among them KLAUS FEHSE, MECHTHILD HESSE, WERNER KIEWEG, MARKUS RITTER, JUTTA RYMARCZYK, and GISELA SCHMID-SCHÖNBEIN. We wish to thank all of them for their support.

1 CHAPTER Language Teacher Education: Defining the Knowledge Base

1 Introduction

Content and process of teacher education

We would like to begin this book on the teaching and learning of English as a foreign language by asking two basic questions:

1. What is the subject matter or content of foreign language teacher education? In other words: What is it that foreign language teachers need to know?
2. What is the process of teacher learning? In other words: How do people learn to teach?

To begin with a discussion of the knowledge base and how it may be acquired in teacher education may come as some surprise because other textbooks which deal with the same subject matter usually start differently: they place chapters concerned with the teaching of the basic skills at the beginning (CARTER/NUNAN 2001), they summarize what we know about how languages are learned (HEDGE 2000; CAMERON 2001) or they integrate these two aspects, offering some perspectives on what there is to learn – a foreign language – and on language learning itself (JOHNSON 2001).

Base teacher education on teaching

The reason why we feature the question of the knowledge base and teacher education so prominently is that when asked to write a compendium on the teaching and learning of English as a foreign language we felt we were in a dilemma: providing knowledge may give readers the idea that all it takes to become a good language teacher is relevant readings. But professional action in dynamic situations of practice (like in a classroom) has been characterized by features such as uncertainty, complexity, uniqueness, instability and value conflict (SCHÖN 1983). This is why teachers cannot be equipped adequately for their job just by reading relevant academic knowledge. Following SCHÖN and FREEMAN and JOHNSON (1998) we argue that the knowledge base must focus on the activity of teaching itself, on the teacher who does it, and on the contexts in which it is done. The starting point of this book is to highlight the fact that no knowledge whatsoever will ever contribute to the quality of learning foreign languages unless this knowledge becomes part of student teachers' ideas of their professional selves. Therefore we would like to make some basic remarks on teacher education to begin with.

2 The content of foreign language teacher education: What is there to learn?

a) A heterogeneous discipline

Different labels for one discipline

Second and foreign language learning and teaching is studied in different disciplines and therefore involves different labels. Within the scope of this book we cannot offer a comprehensive analysis of the various concepts used in different contexts, but we would like to present the most important ones (for a detailed description and further readings see BAUSCH et al 2003: 1–18).

Fremdsprachendidaktik* and *Sprachlehrforschung

In the German context the subject matter of foreign language teaching and learning is dealt with in two disciplines, *Fremdsprachendidaktik* and *Sprachlehrforschung*. What they have in common is that they focus on the teaching and learning of foreign languages in different institutional contexts for all age groups. To this day the professional community has not managed to agree on one label which includes the two, even though there are common concerns. As a very basic distinction one can say that the term *Fremdsprachendidaktik* was important in establishing a distinct discipline for the teaching of 'modern languages' as opposed to the methodology for the 'old languages' (the term dates back to the end of the 19th century). To this day the discipline is very much associated with the attempt to define what counts as relevant sister disciplines (*Bezugswissenschaften*, see below). *Sprachlehrforschung* on the other hand is a term that has been used since the beginning of the 1970s to establish a distinct discipline for the study of the teaching and learning of foreign languages, independent of related disciplines.

b) Establishing the teaching of English as a foreign language as a profession

Heterogeneous principles, research, standards, subject matter

The heterogeneity of the field is probably one of the reasons why those professionally concerned with the study of teaching and learning foreign languages cannot base their work on commonly agreed principles, research standards or clearly defined areas of relevant subject matter. Instead, the discipline may be characterised by what seem to be changing fashions over time. This state of affairs was criticised by MACKEY (1973: 255) as long as 30 years ago: *"It is likely that EFL [= The Teaching of English as a Foreign Language] will continue to be a child of fashion in linguistics and psychology until the time it becomes an autonomous discipline which uses these related sciences instead of being used by them."* Without an understanding of what these 'related sciences' are and without a degree of agreement on what counts as the appropriate principles for generating and applying knowledge for the study of language teaching and learning, our discipline will not qualify as a profession and will not gain academic autonomy. We would therefore like to contribute to the development of language teaching as a professional discipline not just by listing the relevant disciplines but also by discussing the appropriate procedures by which student teachers may develop the attitudes, the knowledge and the skills it takes to become professional foreign language teachers. To do so, we will offer a model which sees language teachers not just as consumers of ideas that have been developed outside language classrooms in related disciplines but views language teachers as generators of theories based on a reflection of their own language learning experiences and on an ongoing reflection of their classroom teaching.

c) Defining the knowledge base: A historical survey

Different views on language teaching and learning

LARSEN-FREEMAN attempted to give a historical survey of developments in the related 'sister disciplines' which she defined as linguistics, language acquisition (and views of language learners), language teaching methodology (what we in Germany call *Didaktik*) and resulting views on the role of language teachers.

Linguistics	Language Acquisition	Language Learner	Language Teaching	Language Teacher
Structural	Habit Formation (Behaviorism)	Mimic	Dialogues Pattern Practice Drills	Performer Model Conductor Cheerleader
Generative	Rule Formation (Cognitivism)	Cognitive Being	Inductive and Deductive Exercises	Knower
Social/ Functional	Interactionism	Social Being	Role Plays Information Gaps Problem-solving Tasks Cooperative Learning	Facilitator
Discourse/ Text/Corpus	Constructivism	Meaning-maker	Process Writing Language Experience Whole Language Content-based	Negotiator
Critical	Experiential	Political Being	Critical Pedagogy Participatory Approach Problem Posing	Advocate

Table 1.1: A Historical Review (LARSEN-FREEMAN 1998: 4)

Complexity of relevant factors

Simplified as this survey of developments undoubtedly is, it nevertheless demonstrates the many changes there have been in the last five decades in the way we view language teaching and learning. What we can learn from developments as a profession is best described in LARSEN-FREEMAN's (1998: 4) own words: *"(I)f I asked you which of these views is the correct one, you would no doubt respond that they all have some merit, but that none reflects the whole picture. Today we recognize that each of these areas is highly complex and multifaceted. Rather than search for the one right point of view, we must redirect the nature of our inquiry to search for wholeness – for more complete understanding of the many facets that comprise these basic constructs in our field. Being aware of the complexity has tremendous implications for how we train teachers."* Before we turn our attention to the practical consequences this complexity has on organising learning in teacher education, we will give a brief survey of the related disciplines as defined in BAUSCH et al (2003: chap. 3–11), which include Linguistics, Applied Linguistics, Second Language Acquisition, Philosophy of Education, Learning Theory and Psychology, Literary Studies, and Cultural Studies. Having said this, there is a problem in using English labels for some of these disciplines because some of the terms are not used in English. Languages divide the world up differently and in our field terms cannot be simply 'translated' – e. g. *Methodik/Didaktik* which do not have direct English equivalents.

d) A Survey of related disciplines

Linguistics

Linguistics describes languages as systems of human communication. It covers many different areas of investigation, for example sound systems (phonetics, phonology), the study of the basic meaningful forms in language (morphology), sentence structure (syntax), meaning systems (semantics) and how language is used in social contexts (pragmatics, discourse analysis, sociolinguistics) (YULE 1998).

Applied Linguistics

As far as we are aware, the term dates back to the year 1946 when the English Language Institute was founded at the University of Michigan by FRIES and LADO. This went along with the publication of a new journal called *Language Learning*, subtitled, *Journal of Applied Linguistics*. Despite various attempts to arrive at a clear definition of what the discipline is about, applied linguistics is *"an amorphous and heterogeneous field drawing on and interfacing with a range of other academic disciplines"* (CARTER/NUNAN 2001: 1). On a very general level one can say that applied linguistics seeks to establish the relevance of theoretical studies of language to everyday problems of language use in different contexts of practice, e. g. language learning, speech therapy or stylistics (COOK 2003).

Second language acquisition research investigates how second or foreign languages are learned. Researchers approach the question from different perspectives but they agree that language learning is a dynamic and multidimensional process. Two main approaches may be distinguished: those which claim that learning foreign languages is based on inborn principles and structures, and those which focus on language learning as a result of social interaction that emphasize the role of different contexts of acquisition (for a survey see LIGHTBOWN/SPADA 1999) .

Second Language Acquisition

Philosophy of Education discusses the general principles and purposes of human education of which the learning of foreign languages are a part. One of these principles, for example, is learner autonomy which has been characterized as the motivation to take charge of one's own learning. To do so, learners need to be able and willing to act independently and in cooperation with others (DAM 1994).

Philosophy of Education

This discipline describes how and why people learn. For example it investigates the cognitive differences in the ways individuals learn (= learning styles), and highlights the need for teaching to take account of these. It focuses on the relationship between language learning and the age of acquisition or factors affecting the motivation to learn (for a survey see CAMERON 2001).

Learning Theory and Psychology

This area discusses the nature of literary texts as one form of communication. It explores the factors that constitute this communication, such as the author, the written text and the reader (NÜNNING/NÜNNING 2001).

Literary Studies

This discipline analyses different cultural phenomena and the way they represent cultural meaning. It looks at how representations of cultures are defined by issues of race, gender, and class and incorporates a historical perspective in the analysis. It also considers the process of relating different cultures (intercultural learning) (SOMMER 2003).

Cultural Studies

3 The process of foreign language teacher education: How do people learn to teach?

In this chapter we would like to present a rationale for good teacher education practice: How is professional expertise best acquired in foreign language teaching? Whenever you ask experienced teachers or student teachers they will complain about the gap between theory and practice, so obviously this seems to be a crucial issue when we discuss models of professional education. Following WALLACE (1991) there are three major models of profes-

Good practice

sional education which will be described in the order in which they appeared historically.

a) Three models of teacher education

The craft model: Learning as imitation of a 'master teacher'

In the craft model the student teacher learns by imitating the techniques of an experienced professional practitioner and by following his or her instructions and advice. Professional competence is seen as the passing on of expertise in the craft from generation to generation. This model may be represented as follows:

Study with ‚master' practitioner: demonstration/instruction	→	Practice	→	Professional competence

Model 1.1: The craft model

Teachers as positive role models

The drawbacks of this model are obvious: it does not capture developments in dynamic societies where change is a basic feature. On the other hand the relevance of teachers as models cannot be dismissed completely. From various learning to teach studies we know that student teachers begin their education with images of teaching that they have acquired during their own learning experiences as students. These imprints are often very resistant to change unless student teachers encounter situations of practice where they observe teachers offering alternative practices. Change does not come about if they just read about alternative practices: these are often not credible as student teachers can't see how they can be put to practice: *"The main reason for the failure of teacher programmes is that they are based on extremely vague conceptions. Having an ideology is not the same as having conceptions and ideas of what should be done and how it should be done"* (Fullan 1993: 109). Student teachers need to see 'how it can be done' to be able to develop alternative and more appropriate images of teaching. Therefore teacher educators need to be positive role models from which students gradually learn by appropriating the mutually agreed on purposes and corresponding practices. However, this concept of 'teacher as model' must not be confused with the mechanical imitation of behavior, which characterized behaviorist-based teaching. Instead it is understood in the Vygotskyan sense of learning as relational imitation which he expressed in his concept of 'the zone of proximal development' (Vygotsky 1978).

The applied science model: Learning as application of knowledge

The applied science model is probably still the most prevalent model underlying most teacher education programmes. The idea is that practical knowledge may be developed by the application of scientific knowledge which is conveyed or transmitted to student teachers (in lectures, for example) by those who are experts in the relevant areas. It is up to the recipients of this knowledge to apply scientific findings by putting it into practice.

Scientific knowledge	→	Transmitted by experts (lectures, relevant readings)	→	Application of knowledge in practice	→	Professional competence

Model 1.2: The applied science model

Teachers reduced to applying what has been developed elsewhere

This classical Research-Development-Dissemination (RDD) model of innovation assumes that there are general solutions to practical problems, that these solutions may be developed outside practical situations (at universities, for example) and that solutions can be translated into teachers' actions by means of publications, training, administrative orders etc. (SCHÖN 1983). This model is not adequate for various reasons: There is an almost complete separation between research and practice, between those who think and those who do. By this division of labour a clear hierarchy of kinds of knowledge has been established, which expresses a genuine mistrust of practitioners who are reduced to merely applying what has been predefined in the academic and administrative power-structure above them.

Students' pre-knowledge is not integrated

In initial teacher education this model ignores the knowledge that student teachers have acquired during their many years as language learners which, as we know from many learning to teach studies, considerably determines what they learn: *"By the time prospective teachers enter college, their beliefs are well formed and tend to be extremely resistant to change. [...D]espite course work and field experiences, preservice teachers' beliefs about teachers and teaching remain largely unchanged"* (JOHNSON 1994: 440).

The reflective model: 'Reflected practice' to develop appropriate practical knowledge

To understand how we may bring about change in teacher education we need an adequate description of complex professional action. SCHÖN (1983) has analyzed different types of action in practice in a number of professions and has formulated the relationships between professional knowledge and professional action. For initial teacher education the model of reflected practice is particularly relevant as most student teachers will not be able to draw on accumulated practical knowledge that would allow them to act smoothly, routinely and adequately in a classroom. SCHÖN has described this type of routine knowledge as tacit knowledge in action: Thinking and acting are not separate activities but they go together, often without being planned or prepared. This is why practitioners are frequently unable to describe their 'practical knowledge'.

Coping with the complexities of classroom needs: Routines

The most important example of practical knowledge is routines which have been built up through frequent repetition and are executed largely unconsciously. They are essential to be able to cope with the complex demands of classroom interaction which would be impossible to do on the basis of a conscious application of principles alone (as implied by the previous model): *"One striking feature of classrooms is the sheer complexity, quantity and rapidity of classroom interaction. As many as 1,000 interpersonal exchanges each day have been observed, and the multiplicity of decisions which have to be made, and the volume of information relevant to each decision are such that for the teacher logical consideration and decision making would seem to be impossible"* (MAC LEOD/MCINTYRE 1977: 266, in: WALLACE 1991: 13). This is why coping with contexts of practice is so hard for student teachers as many of their actions will have to be consciously planned beforehand or while they are actually teaching. It is therefore not sufficient if student teachers read about the relevant areas but they need to develop experiential knowledge by actually improving their 'practical theories' and competences through action and reflection:

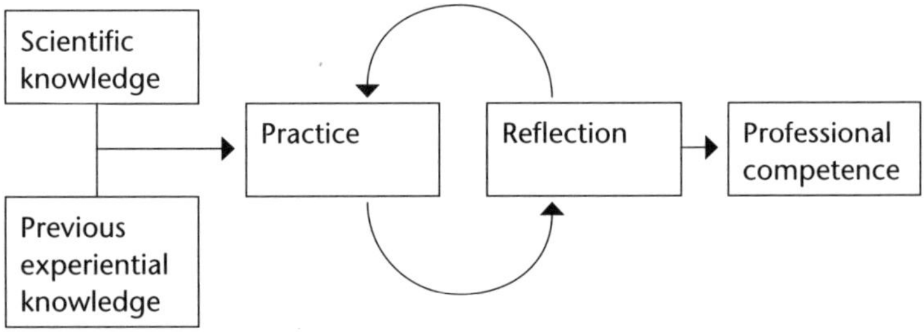

Model 1.3: The reflective model

b) Consequences for organizing teacher learning: Offering a multiperspective view on EFL classrooms

Coping with complex demands and becoming change agents

Teacher education programmes have come under growing criticism in recent years. It is argued that they often fail to provide the relevant knowledge base that would enable student teachers to cope with the complex demands of the school setting and, more importantly, to become part of the social change process (FULLAN 1993). To this day, very little is known about the effectiveness of teacher education programmes. What we do know, however, supports personal anecdotal observation: the dominant teaching formats at universities are transmission-oriented and therefore contradict current ideas of student-centredness and communicative methodology (LEGUTKE/THOMAS 1993). Programme components lack a coherent curriculum framework within which the practicum, if provided at all, often remains an alien element among university courses (GABEL 1997). Only recently have some learning-to-teach studies been published which investigate teacher learning in authentic contexts (SCHOCKER-V. DITFURTH 2001, CASPARI 2003). Research on the nature of teaching and findings from these studies suggest that teacher learning is organised following the three principles below.

Principle 1:

Develop a research approach to learning and a multi-perspective view on the EFL classroom

Integrating relevant perspectives on language learning

Student teachers learn to develop a research approach to EFL learning to understand the complex dynamics that determine language learning in EFL classrooms (see SCHOCKER-V. DITFURTH 2001). To do so, they learn to integrate the relevant perspectives on learning and teaching. These include three domains of knowledge:

- relevant published knowledge;
- student teachers' own perspectives on language learning: according to numerous learning-to-teach studies these affect their awareness and images of learning in classrooms and how they are likely to behave, regardless of whatever cognitive knowledge they may have encountered during teacher education;
- the perspective of practice as represented by the experiences of teachers and their students. It is up to them to judge if an innovation is actually relevant to their needs. Following STENHOUSE (1975: 143), we believe that *"the uniqueness of each classroom setting implies that any proposal* [...] *needs to be tested and verified and adapted by each teacher in his* [sic] *classroom"* (see chap. 2.5).

Principle 2: **Use experiential learning to develop action-oriented models for EFL classrooms**

Organize experiences of reflected learning

Seminars are organized in a way which allow student teachers to experience themselves the learning processes that they are supposed to organize with their EFL students. They work on projects, for example. They decide which topic they wish to choose to work on within their team, they use English as their language of communication, they evaluate selected aspects of the process and the product of their co-operation against mutually negotiated criteria and in doing this, they experience the highlights and the drawbacks involved in co-operative learning. This way, seminars follow an approach to learning which is based on reflected experience: they integrate the experiences of students in classrooms and the experiences of student teachers at university.

New teacher role

In both learning environments a teacher's role may no longer be adequately defined as a transmitter of knowledge to passive recipients. Instead, teachers need to offer expert guidance and support for students to be able to cope with the multiple skills this learning environment involves. Course organizers need to be positive role models from which students gradually learn by appropriating the mutually agreed purposes (see chap. 2.2).

Principle 3: **Build school development competences through co-operation in cross-institutional projects**

Develop dynamic qualifi-cations

The ability to develop a research approach to language classrooms implies that we overcome the traditional separation of the different institutions school and university. Teachers need what has come to be called 'dynamic qualifications', that is, competences and attitudes which are the basis for any innovation to be successful. These include an appreciation of problems that one has identified during the process, an experiment attitude to practice, and the ability to cope with controlled risks (see KRAINER/POSCH 1996: 25). This is why we ask student teachers to co-operate in teams to develop materials for EFL classrooms, for example, a process which involves intensive negotiation.

4 Perspectives and Developments

In order to do justice to the complexity of factors involved in language learning, we need to foster a multiperspective view on teacher education (see above), which is currently not mainstream teacher education practice.

Foster a multiperspective view

We also need to think of ways of individualizing learning in teacher education to take account of differing degrees of experience and commitment with student teachers, to document their learning process and to promote learner reflection. Some universities have started to introduce portfolios, that is written reflections of students' learning processes (see chap. 4.4). There are initiatives by MÜLLER-HARTMANN at the University of Education Heidelberg and QUETZ and BURWITZ-MELZER at the universities of Frankfurt and Gießen.

Individualize learning

2 CHAPTER

Language Teaching and Learning in the Classroom: Discussing Purposes, Participants, Practices

2.1 The Purpose: Developing Intercultural Communicative Competence

1 Introduction

The main goal of language learning

The *Common European Framework (CEF, see chap. 2.5)* describes intercultural communicative competence (ICC) as the main goal of foreign language learning. When someone is learning a second or a foreign language he or she is already *"competent in his or her mother tongue and the associated culture"*. In the process the learner does not lose this competence, but *"becomes plurilingual and develops interculturality. The linguistic and cultural competences in respect of each language are modified by knowledge of the other and contribute to intercultural awareness, skills and know-how. They enable the individual to develop an enriched, more complex personality and an enhanced capacity for further language learning and greater openness to new cultural experiences"* (Council of Europe 2001: 43). This is a complex goal to pursue. What are the various parameters that teachers have to keep in mind in the process?

Language learning contexts

Languages are learned in natural as well as institutional contexts. As teachers we will generally work in the latter, the foreign language classroom, which brings with it a number of advantages and disadvantages. On the positive side, we can concentrate on structured and intensive language work with a group of learners. In terms of constraints we have to deal with issues such as simulating a foreign language environment, handling a restrictive time frame of usually 45 minute periods, and we have to deal with the institutional necessity of giving grades. Our learners will move in and out of the classroom, experiencing language use in both contexts, meeting native speakers or other learners of English outside the classroom, as well as communicating in English with their co-learners in the classroom. At the same time learners bring their various identities and mother tongues to the classroom. As Breen (1985: 142) points out, the language classroom thus forms a culture in itself. *"A language class* [...] *is an arena of subjective and intersubjective realities which are worked out, changed, and maintained. And these realities are not trivial background to the tasks of the teaching and learning a language. They locate and define the new language itself as if it never existed before, and they continually specify and mould the activities of teaching and learning. In essence, the metaphor of classrooms as coral gardens insists that we perceive the language class as a genuine culture and worth investigating as such."* The teacher sets meaningful tasks and tries to create a rich learning environment (see chap. 2.4). The learners communicate by using the foreign language, negotiating the tasks. But how does a learner become an *"intercultural speaker"* in the process (BYRAM 1997: 31–32)?

An example of language use

To better understand the demands involved in developing ICC, an example from an e-mail project between an American and a German class (both 11th grade) will serve as a basis. We use an e-mail example because this new hybrid form of discourse combines oral and written language production (see chap. 4.3), and it connects the classroom with the outside world, i. e. native speakers or other learners of English. The German partners have already sent their first letter, introducing themselves and at the same time formulating a task for their American partners which asked them to list the stereotypes that exist in the U.S. about Germans. The following (shortened) exchange represents the answer to that task from an American girl and her German partner's reaction:

Hello, my name is Jennifer Brendon. I am very intrigued that your class is interested in our culture. I am a fifteen-year-old-girl [...]. *My height measures out to five feet and six inches, which I am very proud of. Some stereotypes of the German race include drinking a lot of beer, eating sauerkraut and brats (YUCK), didn't like the Jewish race, and big, burly women who don't shave. I hope I have not offended any of you. I think conversing with students from different countries is a really great idea.*
Jennifer (American student, e-mail 1)

Hi Jennifer,
How are you? I hope you are fine. My name is Thorsten Selters. [...]. *I were impressed about your dislikes and likes, but your thoughts about typical Germans are wrong. Maybe in south of Germany are a few people, who eat sauerkraut and drink a lot of beer, but here in Hessen, the most people hate sauerkraut and doesn't drink much beer and the most girls are not big and burly. The most are smaller than you are and they shave themselves. I hope I doesn't offend you with my aggressive opinion ...*
Yours Thorsten (German student, e-mail 2)

We will refer to these two examples below to illustrate the five competences of ICC.

2 From communicative competence to ICC

From a grammar translation method to communicative competence

Language learning and teaching has gone through a number of phases. The grammar-translation method of the late 19th century presented the instructed language through rules in the learners' L1 and then practised these rules by translating sentences. It did not to teach learners how to use the language, but how to translate the classics. It was replaced by the audio-lingual method which was developed by American structural linguists during World War II. Based on the psychological theory of behaviourism language learning was seen as *"a process of habit formation"* (ZIMMERMANN 1997: 5, 10–11), and not as a creative process. Communication in a foreign language was seen as learning the four discrete skills of listening, speaking, reading, and writing. That changed in the 1960s and early 1970s, when communicative language teaching (CLT) called for an integrated skills approach (see chap. 3), which stressed the interactive nature of communication: When people communicate they interpret each other's utterances and they collaborate to make or to negotiate meaning, as can be seen in the e-mail example above. The two learners relate to each other trying to negotiate the stereotypes that exist about Germans.

CLT

Communicative language teaching focuses on the meaning potential of language, i. e. on language use, and it stresses the social aspects of that context. Social democratic concerns in Germany in the 1970s called for the empowerment of the individual (cf. HABERMAS). This led to the creation of language material that encouraged learner choice and exploited social meaning in language structures (e. g. PIEPHO, BREDELLA, and CANDLIN, see SAVIGNON 2001: 15). Around the same time the American applied linguist HYMES rejected CHOMSKY's notion of the ideal native speaker to describe language competence since CHOMSKY disregarded the social factors in his linguistic theory, and *"proposed instead the term communicative competence to represent the use of language in social context, or the observance of sociolinguistic norms of appropriacy"* (SAVIGNON 2001: 16). Appropriate language use in e-mail 2 would be Thorsten's attempt at the end of the letter to downplay his criticism of his partner's thoughts on stereotyping when he writes: *"I hope I doesn't offend you with my aggressive opinion"*, attempting to come to a positive conclusion of the e-mail letter. While this last sentence is formally incorrect since he uses the structure *"I doesn't"* it is socially appropriate, since he tries to relate to the feelings of his partners and consequently tries to establish the basis of a positive relationship. HYMES thus laid the foundation for today's focus on ICC in the early 1970s by giving *"greater emphasis to the sociolinguistic and pragmatic factors governing effective language use"* (ZIMMERMANN 1997: 12). As a consequence the Council of Europe developed functional-notional inventories for language teaching in the 1970s that listed and described the speech acts learners needed to perform in a language (VAN EK 1975). Functions enable the learner to express the purpose of an utterance, such as giving advice ('Why don't you take that course? It'll help you.') or persuading somebody ('I really would like to see the other movie. It is so much better'). Notions, on the other hand are concepts of time, quantity or space, for example, if a learner wants to express the process or duration of an action (i.e. time) s/he would use a continuous form, such as 'she is writing an e-mail.' Levels of language ability were described for a number of European languages, setting out what learners should be able to do in the language. This formed the basis for the six competence levels in today's *CEF* (from A1= breakthrough up to C2 = mastery).

The four competences

'Communicative competence' comprises four competences, grammatical, discourse, sociocultural and strategic competence. As SAVIGNON (2001: 17) points out in her model, *"it shows how, through practice and experience in an increasingly wide range of communicative contexts and events, learners gradually expand their communicative competence."*

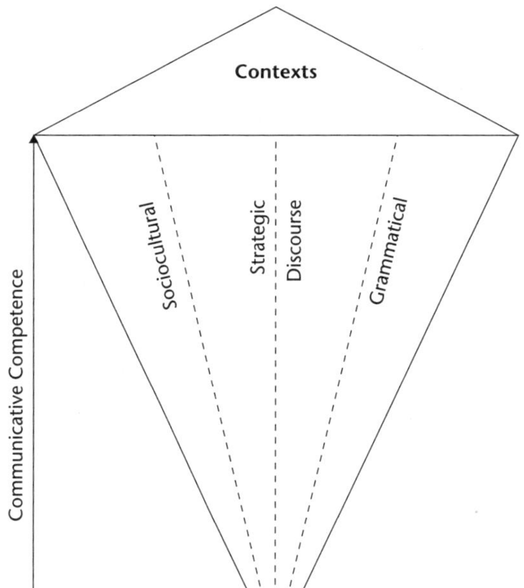

Model 2.1: Components of communicative competence
(SAVIGNON 2001: 17)

- 'Grammatical competence' comprises the sentence level grammar forms, such as lexical, morphological, syntactical, and phonological features of language. Since we are considering language use, this competence does not include the ability of the learner to state the rules for using grammatical forms. In our example above, Thorsten (e-mail 2) still has problems on this level when he writes *"the most people* [...] *doesn't drink much beer."*
- 'Discourse competence' concerns the ability to connect a number of utterances to form a meaningful oral or written text. In our example, both Jennifer and Thorsten are capable of doing this since they formulate quite well-structured and meaningful e-mail texts.
- 'Sociocultural competence' deals with the social rules of language use, i. e. the cultural meaning of language and cultural conventions, such as turn-taking (this is clearly established in an e-mail exchange, the partner class generally waits for their partners' mails and then reacts), appropriate content (is it really a good idea to talk about stereotypes of a culture in the first two exchanges of a cross-cultural e-mail project?), politeness conventions or nonverbal features of language use (something that is missing in an e-mail exchange and can only be integrated through smileys ☺ or other symbols).
- 'Strategic competence' deals with coping strategies, for example when a learner does not know a word and therefore has to find her way around this by being able to paraphrase.

The socio-cultural approach

Before we move on to ICC we will need to look at a development in the field of learning theories to help us understand this concept. The sociocultural approach to teaching and learning is based on the work of the Russian developmental psychologist VYGOTSKY (1978). He asserts that parents and other people in a child's environment are important for his or her mental development. Since for him language is one of the major tools to facilitate this development, his idea of a zone of proximal development (ZPD) helps understand the relationship between a language learner and those who help him in the process, i. e. the teacher and other students. He describes this zone as *"the distance between the actual development level (of the learner) as determined by independent problem solving and the level of potential development as determined through problem solving under adult guidance or in collaboration with more capable peers"* (VYGOTSKY 1978: 86).

This relationship between novices and experts which the teacher organizes through tasks is characterized by a fifth competence, that of mediation. Just as parents do this with their children in the home *"bringing objects and ideas to their attention, talking while playing* [...] *reading stories, asking questions"* (CAMERON 2001: 6) teachers and co-learners do the same in the language classroom. They mediate the content of learning by asking questions, explaining words, telling stories, or by working together in pair or group work tasks. In this process they mediate cultural meanings to the learners, supporting them in understanding the social conventions and rules of a language and a culture. This also works cross-culturally as in Thorsten's case (see our e-mail example 2) when he tries to mediate German regionalism and its respective stereotypes to Jennifer, unfortunately creating new stereotypes in the process *("Maybe in south of Germany are a few people, who eat sauerkraut and drink a lot of beer")*. To function as an intercultural speaker, though, Thorsten has to integrate the competences outlined above.

Mediation

3 A model of teaching ICC

BYRAM (1997) uses the five basic communicative competences and develops them into a complex model of ICC which again comprises five competences or *savoirs*. But in his model they specifically help learners to negotiate meaning among two or more cultures involved in the communicative situation, relating the home and foreign cultures or identities to each other in a process of intercultural learning. The basis for this process is a wide range of oral and written texts which learners produce inside and outside of the language classroom. We will present the different competences individually, but the intercultural speaker obviously has to integrate them.

Byram's model of ICC

	Skills interpret and relate *(savoir comprendre)*	
Knowledge of self and other; of interaction: individual and societal *(savoirs)*	**Education** political education critical cultural awareness *(savoir s'engager)*	**Attitudes** relativising self valuing other *(savoir être)*
	Skills discover and/or interact *(savoir apprendre/ faire)*	

Model 2.2: Factors in intercultural communication (BYRAM 1997: 34)

Affective level

Jennifer and Thorsten in our e-mail example show the necessary openness towards the other culture. They express curiosity and they relate to the partner in their mails. This forms the basis for tackling possible misunderstandings, such as the discussion of stereotypes. At the same time this level asks the learner to decentre from his or her own position and to possibly change perspectives. Jennifer succeeds in doing just that since she realizes how difficult the listing of stereotypes is for her German partner. As pointed out above, Thorsten here only partially succeeds in mediating German regionalism, creating a new stereotype in the process. In the English language classroom the following approaches facilitate the creation of openness and curiosity in relation to the other culture (see also chap. 4.2 & 4.3):

- using brainstorming, visual or other aids when working with texts to create curiosity and interest;
- using texts written by or about learners from other cultures which tell about their lives. This includes the whole field of children's and young adult literature which allows identification with the other culture;
- authentic texts which learners themselves bring to the classroom (e.g. songs, interviews);
- encounter projects such as the one described above. Here the initial getting-to-know-phase is important during which learners meet on a personal level and hopefully open up towards the partners and thus lay an emotional basis for further negotiation;

- face-to-face encounters abroad on field trips or school exchanges. Observation tasks and icebreaker games would offer here a first emotional access to the other culture.

During this initial phase cultural similarities, not differences should be in the forefront. Tasks like the one above, where stereotypes are evoked in the very first encounter, are dangerous since there is as yet no real common basis to negotiate possible misunderstandings.

Cognitive level

This level comprises traditional *Landeskunde* knowledge (see chap. 4.1), auto-stereotypes (positive/negative stereotypes a person has about his or her own culture) and hetero-stereotypes (positive/negative stereotypes somebody has about other cultures), as well as knowledge about social interaction. As pointed out above, Jennifer and Thorsten know about the appropriate forms of interaction in e-mails, but Thorsten still has difficulties with his auto-stereotypes since he presents Hessen in a very positive way in opposition to Bavaria.

Skills of interpreting and relating

This is the level where learners relate oral and written texts to each other and try to interpret each in the light of the other. This involves the skill of mediation. Thorsten's answer shows that he has mis-interpreted Jennifer's mail since it is not she personally who has the *"dislikes and likes."* She just solves the given task by listing general stereotypes that exist in the U.S. about Germans. Learners therefore need tasks which allow them to read texts carefully, analyse and interpret them, and thus by relating texts achieve a change of perspective:

- creative tasks when dealing with literary texts, which, for example, look at the action from different perspectives (e.g. of minor characters), where new scenes or a different ending is written (see chap. 4.2);
- project forms or simulations where learners experience a situation from a different cultural point of view (e.g. how does an American school work, what is important, what is a typical day/week like in such a school?);
- games that provoke a change of perspective, such as role plays.

Skills of discovery and interaction

By comparing the e-mails they have received from their American partners with their own, learners will be able to realize that for American teenagers height, for example, is an important aspect of their identity – something German teens do not necessarily mention when they describe themselves. That way they discover important phenomena of the other culture as well as their specific meanings and connotations. During study visits, for example, ethnographic observation tasks (looking out for sounds, smells, images, colours, structures of a new place) help learners to discover new aspects about a culture. At the same time this skill covers communication in real time which is easier to handle in an e-mail exchange since there is a time-lag before a mail is being answered during which the learner can consider his/her response. In a chat or a face-to-face encounter this is much more difficult. Learners need to be able to deal with all kinds of communication problems that arise in social interaction, such as different concepts of time and space (e.g. notions, see above), the negotiation of cultural misunderstandings as well as assuming the role of a mediator between representatives of different cultures. Role plays and simulations in the classroom facilitate this kind of foreign language interaction. Especially face-to-face and virtual encounter projects (e-mail, chat) promote this kind of experience. Since the latter 'conversations' are stored electronically, analyses of linguistic and cultural features are possible at the end of the project, allowing learners to gauge and evaluate their ICC.

Critical cultural awareness

Dealing with speakers from another culture always involves the evaluation of that culture. This might quickly lead to an exchange of stereotypes as in the e-mail example above. If we aim for a critical evaluation of another culture we need to develop competences in all the levels of ICC mentioned above. This includes the development of a critical perspective on one's own culture. The analysis of his e-mail can enable Thorsten to critically review his opinions about German culture and its regional aspects. Tasks will help learners to question existing views in their own or the other culture:

- dealing critically with positions in a text, for example, the question which kinds of ideological scripts lie below the surface of Disney films (see chap. 4.1);
- critical comparisons, for example, of how German and Australian society deal with immigration;
- engaging in project forms that support peace initiatives (see e-mail projects at I*EARN http://www.iearn.org/ 15.12.03).

ICC thus develops through the process of intercultural learning which eventually might also facilitate attitudes of empathy and tolerance. In the process of learning a new language and culture, learners will create a new identity between the cultures or identities they are involved with. KRAMSCH (1993) has called this identity a *"third space"*. By developing this space learners slowly evolve into intercultural speakers who integrate their newly developed competences with those they have already brought to the English language classroom at the outset of the learning process.

The intercultural speaker and the "third space"

2.2 The Teacher

1 The context

Effective language learning in the dynamic social context of classrooms depends on a number of factors. The multiplicity of identities, roles, relations and purposes of its members – teacher and learners – constitute a particular community of practice which determines the quality of language learning: "How learners interact with each other and other speakers, what they do when they are learning a language, what effect their attitudes, beliefs and feelings have on language learning, what kinds of personal investment they are prepared to make, how far they can draw on the support of others, what effects teaching have on learning, and to what extent the social conditions and priorities of the social world outside the classroom, and the learners' places in that world, affect what learners do in classrooms and how effectively they can learn" (CANDLIN/MERCER 2000: 3–4, in: CANDLIN 2003). The socio-cultural context and its participants constitute or create the conditions of language learning which may therefore either support or constrain the process of language acquisition. This view is in contrast to psycholinguistic approaches to language acquisition which reduce learners to individual input processing devices. In this chapter we will look at the consequences this view of classroom has for teachers' roles. Four aspects will be dealt with in turn:

Classroom as community of practice

- Teacher as language teacher.
- Teacher as expert in learning.
- Teacher as classroom manager.
- Teacher as researcher and learner.

2 Teacher as language teacher

Target language proficiency

How teachers and students use language to communicate in the foreign language classroom determines the quality of language learning. This is why foreign language teachers at all levels need a solid target language competence. The reasons are various:

- Teachers are the central means of language input. Exposure to comprehensible input and the quality of classroom interaction determine what language learning opportunities learners get so that they may learn from them (ALLWRIGHT 1985).
- Teachers are models. They need to feel comfortable using the target language as a natural means of communication and not treat it like a body of knowledge – a system of grammar – to be mastered. This way they may communicate something of the enthusiasm involved in being able to express oneself in a foreign language, which in turn will motivate their learners. Learners may experience plurilingualism as a personal asset which allows them to communicate with people of different cultures world-wide.
- There is another aspect of teacher as model: there is research evidence which seems to prove that children reproduce the language types used by their teachers (CAMERON 2001: 16).
- Teachers need to be able to use the target language spontaneously. They cannot assume that their learners will talk, act, or interact in predictable ways.
- Teachers need to be able to present language as naturalistic examples of the target language, to expose learners to examples of language currently in use, with features which are characteristic of authentic discourse in the target language.

Quality of teacher talk

To sum this up: The quality of teacher talk is crucial to support learners in their language acquisition process by helping them to understand and to communicate. KLIPPEL (2003: 57) distinguishes between two aspects of teacher talk, the teacher as instructor (when the teacher is presenting new language or providing practice opportunities, for example) and the teacher as a partner in communication (when teacher and learners exchange information or opinions, for example). Teachers can provide useful language learning support in both roles. Let's first turn our attention to what research into teacher talk has found out about language learning opportunities in the context of the classroom.

Features of classroom discourse

"Understanding the dynamics of classroom communication is essential since how students talk and act in classrooms greatly influences what they learn" (JOHNSON 1995: 5). The institutionalised nature of classrooms with their unequally distributed power and authority account for its particular uses of language and kinds of interaction

(Candlin 2003: 42). As a result of this unique context of communication, there are patterns of communication which seem to be typical in foreign language classrooms. Generally speaking, patterns of communicative behaviour are highly regulated: teachers, by virtue of the status they hold in their classrooms, play a dominant role in determining the structure of classroom communication: *"Teachers tend to control the topic of discussion, what counts as relevant to the topic, and who may participate and when. Students tend to respond to teacher-directed questions, direct their talk to teachers, and wait their turn before speaking. Teachers can ignore students who talk off-topic, or listen patiently and then direct them back on-topic. They can allow students to call out during a lesson, or insist that they wait to be called on before speaking. Teachers can place their students in small groups so they have more opportunities to control their own talk, to select which topics to talk about, and to direct their talk to whomever they wish. At any point, however, teachers retain the right to regain control over the structure of classroom communication"* (Johnson 1995: 4).

IRE pattern: initiation, response, evaluation

The underlying structure of much of classroom language has been described as following a pattern of different acts (Sinclair/Coulthard 1975): an act initiated by the teacher (usually a question), a response act by one of the students (usually the answer to a question), and an act of evaluation by the teacher (on the quality of the response, very often focussing on the form and not on the meaning of a message). This interactive pattern both impedes the quality of language input (which language acquisition research has identified to be one factor to contribute to successful language acquisition) and restricts learners' opportunities for language production and conversational interaction which again play an important part for second language acquisition. (For a summary of research into the effects of interactive patterns in language classrooms on language acquisition see Lightbown/Spada 1999: chaps. 2 & 5). Teachers need to recognize in what ways the patterns of communication are established and maintained in foreign language classrooms, the effect these patterns have on how students participate in activities, and how their participation shapes the ways in which they provide opportunities for language acquisition. (For excellent ideas on how teachers can become aware of this see Johnson 1995).

3 Teacher as expert in learning

Focus on the learner

The communicative classroom has been described as a site where learning arises from learners' experiences and minds. Therefore, valuing the multiple identities of learners is central in that teachers need to make learners aware of their own capacity. They will need to be able to support individual learning processes so that learners will become more autonomous as a result, for example, when attempting to communicate independently from the teacher with a world-wide peer audience, and to choose and produce texts of their own liking.

Focus on social relationships

Social relationships in the classroom orchestrate what is made available to be learned for learners, how learning is done, and what they may achieve. Learners navigate the discourse in two constantly interweaving ways: for learning purposes and for social purposes (BREEN 1998). STEVICK (1996) has described the conditions in a classroom that contribute to successful learning. Classrooms which expose students to negative evaluations by the teacher or by peers may promote anxiety which may in turn affect achievement. He therefore distinguishes between two kinds of learning, defensive learning and receptive learning. Teachers may promote states of receptive learning only if they achieve to reduce threats to our students' egos and this way exclude their defence mechanisms. STEVICK's idea is built around MASLOW's hierarchy of life motivations and human needs according to which it is difficult to be motivated by needs on a higher level until one's needs on the level before it have been tolerably met: *"Most fundamental* [...] *is the need for security, and a fundamental component of security is predictability.*[...] *The second level* [...] *is social: 'Am I accepted as a member of a social group that I can depend on to support me?'* [...] *A third level of need* [...] *is for ability to do those things that will maintain and improve one's standing in the group"* (STEVICK 1996: 8–9).

Focus on atmosphere: 'affective filter'

Related to this is the following aspect. Research has shown that the more relaxed and comfortable students feel, the better language acquisition proceeds. This is basically what KRASHEN's 'affective filter hypothesis' is about: *"The 'affective filter' is an imaginary barrier which prevents learners from acquiring language from the available input. 'Affect' refers to such things as motives, needs, attitudes, and emotional states. A learner who is tense, angry, anxious, or bored may 'filter out' input, making it unavailable for acquisition. Thus, depending on the learner's state of mind or disposition, the filter limits what is noticed and what is acquired"* (LIGHTBOWN/SPADA 1999: 39).

Focus on tasks

A teacher's role in the language classroom is central: Teachers need to be able to set tasks which allow learners to use language for a genuine purpose, which provide interactive opportunities. An example is when they organise processes of intercultural learning in computer-mediated e-mail projects where their learners use English as a means of co-operation to negotiate meaning with people from different cultures (see MÜLLER-HARTMANN 2000c). In addition, teachers need to motivate learners to engage in the learning process by designing tasks which are intellectually challenging enough to maintain students' interest.

Managing the interaction

What has been said will affect teachers' professional ideas of self: Interaction between participants in classrooms will be increased, will be more individualised and become less predictable as a result. This puts additional demands on teacher's flexibility. Their changing role has been described as having to step aside from the sage on the stage to the guide on the side. A term used to describe teachers' new role is that of a 'facilitator', "[who] *manages the interaction, usually in the background, by relating individual comments, by suggesting a different interpretation of an idea, or by clarifying a position and so forth"* (AHERN 1998: 230). BREEN's (1998) plea for a 'negotiated curriculum' between teacher and learners will become more and more relevant. All in all, teachers are faced with a multitude of new tasks for which most of them have probably not been prepared by their own language learning experiences (for a discussion of what this involves see chap. 2.4 on tasks).

Focus on mediation

In chapter 2.1 we discussed VYGOTSKY´S sociocultural approach to learning according to which language development is social development. In other words, the relationship between the language learner and the persons with whom s/he interacts influences language acquisition. It is assumed that if learners interact with more experienced peers – teachers, for example – they are able to advance beyond their present level of language development to a higher one. This idea has immediate implications for teachers' language use: What is it that they can do while interacting with their learners in conversation to support their language acquisition processes? This question has been researched by interactionists, that is researchers who explain language acquisition by investigating appropriate mediating strategies in conversations. They have identified various interactive strategies teachers may use to support their learners' language production. These 'interactional modifications' in conversations are for example confirmation checks to make sure that what you have understood is what a learner meant ('You mean ..., don't you?') or clarification requests to ask to explain or rephrase something that hasn't been understood ('Could you say that again, please? What do you mean?'). The assumption is that learners need to produce comprehensible output to develop in their language acquisition. To achieve this they need to be pushed to use alternative means of expression when communication breaks down. The following exchange is taken from an EFL lesson in a German *Realschule*, where a teacher supports a learner trying to describe a person. This person is Asian and the learner is trying to say that usually

Asian people are smaller than Europeans. It takes interactional modifications from the teacher and several turns for the learner to get his message across (example from SCHOCKER-V. DITFURTH 2001: 286):

T: *OK. What else do you find typical? Yes, please …*
L: *Their high is too little.*
T: *Sorry, their …?*
L: *High …*
T: *Tie?*
L: *How big they are …*
T: *Ah, you mean the height?*
L: *Yes.*

By giving learners the opportunity to interact teachers may lead them to adapt what they are saying until they have succeeded. Learners need to be pushed to negotiate meaning so that they will become actively involved in thinking about the meaning of what they are trying to say.

4 Teacher as classroom manager

Process competence

From what has been said it has become clear that teachers need to be able to organise, to create, to manage, and to evaluate co-operative process learning environments. The teacher maintains her or his managerial and instructional role but must make sure that it is not in conflict with learner autonomy. *"Aspects of classroom management involve teacher pre-course preparation, creating and managing an atmosphere in which the learner is encouraged to get involved, providing language resources and monitoring language use, and providing technical expertise and presentation skills, for example"* (see LEGUTKE/THOMAS 1993: 289 ff.).

5 Teacher as researcher and learner

Research classroom processes

The range of factors contributing to the quality of language learning in foreign language classrooms results in a multitude of teacher and learner roles. Teachers need to be able to explore the quality of the interactions by researching the ways in which they contribute to a successful communicative language learning classroom (CANDLIN 2003: 43). The more complex and autonomous learning becomes, the more important it is to understand the dynamic processes and to work out how these can contribute to improvement in learning. This is why teachers will have to step back from teaching and monitor the processes of learning and teaching as a participant observer (BREEN/CANDLIN 1980: 99). There is not the space to go into this in detail here. But there is an ample literature which supports teachers in initiating their own classroom research projects with their learners on various aspects of learning (see ALTRICHTER/POSCH 1994 and SCHOCKER-V. DITFURTH 2002).

2.3 The Learner

1 Introduction

The learner as social agent

The *Common European Framework* (COUNCIL OF EUROPE 2001: 9) views *"users and learners of a language primarily as 'social agents', i. e. members of society who have tasks (not exclusively language-related) to accomplish in a given set of circumstances, in a specific environment and within a particular field of action. While acts of speech occur within language activities, these activities form part of a wider social context, which alone is able to give them their full meaning."* As we have pointed out in the previous chapter, in the classroom teachers and learners constitute such a specific sociocultural community of practice. Here the teacher has the task of facilitating learning, i. e. he or she has to provide opportunities to the learners for interaction through meaningful language tasks (see chap. 2.4). This is not always easy, since no two classes are the same and some learners learn much more easily than others. Learners bring diverse knowledge and skills, different motivations, as well as varied personalities to the classroom (for a survey see LIGHTBOWN/SPADA 1999, chap. 3). Each learner also brings his or her own cultural identity along when he or she embarks on the process of becoming an intercultural speaker. The language learning process is not an even, linear one, thus making it difficult for the teacher at times to gauge learner needs correctly in different phases of a language course. It is therefore imperative that learners are supported in developing strategies that help them in the process of becoming good language learners and consequently autonomous learners. Since we differentiate among different learner types, the sooner the learner knows how to best learn a language, the sooner she will be able to voice her language learning needs, signalling to the teacher where she is, what kinds of problems she is encountering, and where she wants to go to, thus participating in the negotiation of the curriculum (BREEN 1998). In opposition to the image of the learner as agent, some view learners as passive language processing devices, who do not control their own learning process. Instead we consider learners as active agents who contribute *"to the process of making meaning"* and who are problem-solvers, testing hypotheses about how language works and using strategies *"as a means for solving problems, either of communication or learning"* (ELLIS 2001: 74–75). This view of the learner also *"acknowledges learner differences both with regard to what particular problems individual learners choose to focus on and how they set about solving them"* (ELLIS 2001: 76). What has research identified to be characteristics of a good language learner?

2 The good language learner

Self-directed learning or learner autonomy

Teachers have a clear view of what a good language learner should be able to do. According to a study by HEDGE (2000: 76) the learner should have *"an ability to define one's own objectives; awareness of how to use language materials effectively; careful organization of time for learning, and active development of learning strategies."* These criteria define a learner who takes responsibility for his/her own learning, and thus becomes a self-directed or autonomous learner. While this is the teacher's view of a competent language learner, learners bring different capacities for language learning to the classroom. In part this depends on their age (see chap. 4.6). Here we will focus on the role of intelligence, aptitude, personality, motivation, and learner preferences (based on LIGHTBOWN/SPADA 1999, chap. 3).

Intelligence

Research supports the view that a higher IQ score is related to certain language learning abilities, such as language analysis (focus on form) and the learning of rules, but that it is not that important in terms of communication and interaction skills. Intelligence is a very complex concept, but experience has shown that *"many students whose academic performance has been weak have experienced considerable success in second language learning"* (LIGHTBOWN/SPADA 1999: 53).

Aptitude

Some learners appear to have a special aptitude for language learning, i. e. they learn very quickly and efficiently. The Modern Language Aptitude Test (MLAT), for example, looks at learners' ability to identify and memorize new sounds, to understand the function of words in a sentence, to figure out grammar rules, and to memorize new words. While these abilities were mainly tested in relation to grammar translation and audiolingual teaching (see chap. 2.1), they do play a role in communicative language teaching as well so that more research in this area is warranted (e. g. how important is a skill of identifying new sounds in a communicative classroom?).

Personality

The two traits that seem to influence language learning are extroversion and inhibition. Some learners seem to benefit from the fact that they are assertive and outgoing and therefore engage more easily in language production, but this cannot be generalized. Inhibition on the other hand has been found to discourage risk-taking, such as using newly learned words, which is important for language use. Learners, especially teenagers and adults, often feel self-conscious when using a foreign language. Even though research is not conclusive, other personality traits, such as empathy or responsiveness probably play an important role in language learning.

Motivation

Learners' motivation and their attitude(s) towards the target language and culture are often decisive for successful language learning (see DÖRNYEI 2001a, 2001b). Positive attitudes towards the language and its speakers will certainly increase motivation since learners want to learn how to communicate. The attitude towards a language is often influenced by the social standing of a language, e.g. how powerful the language is in relation to other languages. In Germany many parents want their children to learn English in primary school instead of French because they perceive it as more relevant for their children's career. We talk about integrative motivation, when somebody learns a language for reasons of personal growth and cultural enrichment, and instrumental motivation, when a learner does it for immediate and practical goals (e.g. preparing for a job). In the classroom context, learners show motivation when they *"participate actively in class, express interest in the subject matter, and study a great deal"* (LIGHTBOWN/SPADA 1999: 57). As LIGHTBOWN and SPADA (1999: 57) further point out, teachers can increase learners' motivation by making the classroom a place *"where students enjoy coming because the content is interesting and relevant to their age and level of ability, where the learning goals are challenging yet manageable and clear, and where the atmosphere is supportive and non-threatening."*

Learner preferences

Motivation is also related to learner preferences. Apart from motivation and attitudes learners bring certain learning preferences to the classroom. Learners often have a specific learning style or a combination of styles, i.e. a *"natural, habitual, and preferred way of absorbing, processing, and retaining new information and skills"* (REID 1995, in: LIGHTBOWN/SPADA 1999: 58). We differentiate between visual learners (they need to see a new word written down to remember it, for example), aural learners (they learn by listening to new language items a couple of times), and kinaesthetic learners (they need to combine new language with some kind of physical action to remember it, such as miming the actions to go with a new word or writing words down). Apart from their perceptual differences, learners also bring certain beliefs or subjective theories of what teaching and learning should be like into the classroom. If a learner has been taught by the grammar-translation method, he or she will usually expect this instructional approach in another learning context as well, and might find it difficult if the teacher opts for a communicative approach. These beliefs often correlate very strongly with instructional traditions in a culture, and may lead to frustration when they are not met. For example, learners in a language course at an American University which was based on an e-mail exchange with native speakers of the language, gave the instructor bad evaluations because they had expected a more grammar-oriented way of teaching and not an interactive approach based on communication (MÜLLER-HARTMANN 2002, personal correspondence). There are also other ways of classifying different learner types, i.e. NUNAN's (1999: 57) who distinguishes between concrete, analytical, communicative, and authority-oriented learners.

'Concrete' learners	'Analytical' learners	'Communicative' learners	'Authority-oriented' learners
tend to like games, pictures, films, videos, using cassettes, talking in pairs, and practising English outside class.	like studying grammar, studying English books and reading newspapers, studying alone, finding their own mistakes, and working on problems set by the teacher.	learn by watching, listening to native speakers, talking to friends in English and watching TV in English, using English out of class in stores, trains, and so on, learning new words by hearing them, and learning by conversations.	prefer the teacher to explain everything. They like to have their own textbook, to write something in a notebook, to study grammar, learn by reading, and learn new words by seeing them.

3 How to become a good language learner

Learning strategies

Learner preferences will especially influence the strategies learners use to learn a new language. RUBIN (1987: 19) defines learning strategies as *"any set of operations, steps, plans, routines used by the learner to facilitate the obtaining, storage, retrieval and use of informa-*

tion [...] that is what learners 'do' to learn and 'do to regulate' their learning." The organization of new words that make up a semantic field in form of a mindmap, for example, would be a typical learning strategy to store words (see also chap. 3.2). Since we do not see the learner as an input processing device, but as a person with social and emotional resources, we may distinguish the following strategies (based on HEDGE 2000: 77–79, and OXFORD 2001: 2002):

1. Affective strategies: These strategies help to reduce inhibition and anxiety when using a new language, such as positive self-talk (I can do this!) or praising oneself for a performance. Writing about one's emotions in a diary or journal when learning a language can also be helpful.
2. Social strategies: These strategies are especially important for the development of ICC since learners use them to understand the other culture and language, i. e. being able to ask questions for clarification, asking for help, working and studying together as well as inquiring about social or cultural norms and values.
3. Cognitive strategies: These involve learners' thought processes that help them establish connections between new information and information they already know, as well as deal with tasks and materials. They include memorizing (with the help of visual clues, for example, drawing pictures of words that need to be learned) taking notes and structuring them, analyzing, and inferencing (guessing words from the context).
4. Metacognitive strategies: These involve organizing tasks or learning by finding resources (for example, literary texts that are attuned to one's language level, such as easy readers), establishing a time schedule, and general goals for language learning. They also include ways of finding out about one's own interests, needs and learning styles as a language learner.
5. Compensatory or communication strategies: They include guessing the meaning of unfamiliar words from the context when listening or reading (see chap. 3.1). When speaking and writing these involve the use of circumlocution (e.g. paraphrases to express a difficult term in a different way). Learners also use gestures and mime to support communication.

Depending on how learners use strategies they will become more or less successful language learners. As OXFORD (2001: 169) points out, *"more successful learners typically understand which strategies fitted the particular language tasks they were attempting. Moreover, more effective learners are better at combining strategies as needed."*

How to support strategy use

Teachers need to help learners find out about learning strategies which support their respective learning preferences. Unlike a learner-centred approach which puts the learner at the centre with his or her wishes and choices, strategy use forms an important part of a learning-centred approach where the teacher helps learners organize their own learning. OXFORD (2002: 128–29) makes a number of suggestions for supporting learners' effective strategy use:

1. To find out about learners' strategies one can employ diaries, surveys, and informal discussions about strategies learners use.
2. Consider all strategies, not just cognitive and metacognitive ones, but also affective and social ones, and help learners combine strategies. *"For example, begin with a metacognitive strategy (such as planning for the task), then unite a cognitive with a social strategy (analyzing or practicing expressions in cooperation with other students), and finally combine a metacognitive and an affective strategy (such as self-evaluating progress self-rewarding for good performance)"* (OXFORD 2002: 129)
3. Look closely at learners to find out which aspects of the good language learner they are lacking. Then identify appropriate learning strategies.
4. Study the effectiveness of strategies with your learners, i.e. which strategies are most useful for certain kinds of tasks.
5. Teach strategies explicitly and integrate them into your tasks regularly.
6. Assess learners' strategy use and learning styles and show them how their learning styles influence their strategy use.

4 Outlook

Learning styles

Even though learning strategies and different learning styles have been considered an essential feature of a good language learner, we know relatively little about *"the interaction between different learning styles and success in second language acquisition"* (LIGHTBOWN/SPADA 1999: 58). More qualitative research, such as learner interviews and classroom observation data is needed in this respect (see also NUNAN 1999: 63).

Classroom interaction

Another important aspect is to look below the surface of learner participation in classroom interaction. Learners are constantly *"shaping the social practices they regard as appropriate to the situation"* (BREEN 2001a: 136). For example, they will talk to their neighbour to enliven a boring lesson. How are these interactions in the classroom generated and sustained and what kind of meaning does the individual learner attribute to certain interactions? This is part and parcel of the hidden curriculum, i.e. *"the learning which goes on in covert ways beneath the surface of what the teacher sets out to teach"* (HEDGE 2000: 83). Socio-political aspects, such as the importance of a language in international communication, or the social position of learners in a society (for example, as immigrants), form part of this hidden curriculum and might have an impact on what happens in the classroom. In terms of the role of the learner, future research therefore needs to consider three aspects (based on BREEN 2001a):

1. Studies over time (longitudinal) in the same classroom, to see how language routines and procedures are negotiated between teacher and learners.
2. An attempt to get as close as possible to the learner's interpretation of what happens in terms of interaction in the classroom. How does the learner experience a certain way of teaching vocabulary or his/her role when communicating with other learners?
3. And a close look at *"what learners 'actually' acquire from having participated in interaction,"* since there is evidence that *"learners do retain different things from even the same shared interaction"* (BREEN 2001a: 137–38). Only then can we draw conclusions as to what kind of interaction will affect language learning.

2.4 The Process: The Task-based Approach

1 Introduction: Task-based language learning (TBLL)

Interaction in the classroom

Having looked at the roles of teacher and learners in the language classroom, we now turn to the interaction among them, and look at how the processes of language learning and teaching are organized. As RICHARDS and RODGERS (2001) have shown, the task-based approach is part and parcel of the underlying learning theory of the communicative approach to language learning. Many teachers still seem to believe in an approach that views language learning as a linear process where discrete language items are successively put together as building blocks of the new language. The task-based approach to syllabus and curriculum design is different in that it organizes *"activities in which language is used for carrying out meaningful tasks to promote learning"* (RICHARDS/RODGERS 2001: 161). Tasks provide a methodological tool to organize interaction in the target language by allowing the teacher to select and sequence activities in the social context of the classroom.

Example: The Airport Project

An example of this is the various tasks that make up the Airport Project (Legutke/Thiel 1983) which has been copied in various ways and in a number of countries since its original design. In this project learners of a 6th grade class go to the airport in Frankfurt to interview people. They then bring the collected language data back to the classroom and present their findings. To be able to move about the airport and carry out their interviews learners need to prepare themselves both in terms of content and language since they will meet proficient speakers of English at the airport. In the following we will use this example to highlight the characteristics of TBLL.

ICC and learning-centredness

The focus on negotiation of content that is meaningful to learners (i. e. asking interview questions to find out about the passengers' lives) makes TBLL especially valuable for developing intercultural communicative competence. Apart from supporting a learning-centred approach, it also favours learner-centeredness since learners have a means of designing their own contributions in the classroom to a much larger extent, thereby disrupting the IRE sequence (see chap. 2.2) and becoming more autonomous in the process.

2 Characteristics of TBLL

Developments

In the late 1980s Prabhu (1987) and others developed task-based process syllabuses which saw language development not as a result of focussing on form, but as an outcome of natural processes of interaction in which learners used language to produce meaningful content. In a next step Breen and Candlin (in Candlin/Murphy 1987) designated a curriculum negotiated between teacher and learners in which learners have the opportunity to develop their own learning plan which will be the basis of choice of classroom activities. In contrast to this development, second language acquisition research looked at procedures of task selection and sequencing from the point of acquisition in the early 1990s, demanding a clear focus on linguistic form (Crookes/Gass 1993). But it seems that in recent years TBLL has become an important approach which allows psycho-linguistic and sociocultural approaches to language learning to find common ground. The *Common European Framework* (Council of Europe 2001: 159), for example, supports the combination of focus on meaning and form in TBLL: "[...] *a changing balance needs to be established between attention to meaning and form, fluency and accuracy, in the overall selection and sequencing of tasks so that both task performance and language learning progress can be facilitated* [...]" Thus, while learners must be able to pose linguistically correct questions at the airport in order to be understood they also need to be able to negotiate meaning if passengers engage in a longer conversation.

Definition of task

NUNAN (1989: 10) defines task as *"a piece of classroom work which involves learners in comprehending, manipulating, producing or interacting in the target language while their attention is principally focused on meaning rather than on form."* WILLIS (1996: 23) emphasizes the role of activities which *"achieve an outcome"* for learners as a result of using the foreign language (L2) for a communicative purpose. During the simulated interviews in the classroom and the real interviews at the airport learners communicate in a meaningful way with other speakers of English, trying to achieve an outcome by finding out interesting facts about their interview partners. In this respect a task may be distinguished from an exercise which focuses on having the learners produce correct linguistic forms, such as asking them to fill in blanks with correct grammatical forms to complete sentences. The purpose in the interview example is communicative and learners produce discourse that might occur like this in other natural language production contexts (for an overview of task and exercise characteristics see SKEHAN 1998). Learners gain confidence by trying out the language they know, they learn how to interact spontaneously and thus negotiate turns, try out communication strategies and in general produce natural language, not just restrictive *"one-off sentences"* (WILLIS 1996: 35–36).

Real-world and pedagogic tasks

There is also another classification of tasks, between real-world tasks and pedagogic tasks. 'Real-world tasks', such as simulating an interview situation, are those that *"require learners to approximate, in class, the sorts of behaviours required of them in the world beyond the classroom"* (NUNAN 1989: 40). In contrast to this, answering true or false statements about a text would be 'a pedagogic task' since a task like this will probably just occur in the classroom. While it is sometimes not easy to differentiate between the two, one can say that pedagogic tasks are more geared towards practising linguistic skills as a prerequisite for communication (see COUNCIL OF EUROPE 2001: 157–58), whereas real-world tasks take the sociocultural background of participants and the social contexts in general into consideration, developing linguistic competence in the process of doing tasks (see ELLIS 2000: 195–97). In the Airport Project other teachers or speakers of English (older students) are invited to the classroom for the learners to practise their interview skills. Even though this is still a simulation learners have to consider the social context of speaking to a real person who brings her way of behaviour and language choice to the interview situation.

PPP versus TBLL

The above distinction is related to two different approaches to learning language, the 'presentation', 'practice', and 'production' approach (PPP) and TBLL. In the PPP approach (see also chap. 3.2) the presentation of linguistic material is followed by practice activities to help learners to quickly produce the discrete language items. In the production stage learners are offered opportunities to freely use the language. But, as HEDGE (2000: 61–62) points out, *"it has been the experience of many teachers that it is very difficult to control the language which can occur naturally in such activities (esp. the last phase). Students will use whatever language resources they have at their command* [...] *Directing their attention to the form in efforts to persuade them to practise it while they are focused on the messages they are trying to communicate to their peers is distracting and counter-productive in terms of fluency."* Thus PPP will probably not lead to fluency because it focuses on the production of discrete linguistic items. TBLL on the other hand focuses on meaningful language use, seeing *"the learning process as one of learning through doing – it is primarily engaging in meaning that the learner's system is encouraged to develop"* (SKEHAN 1996: 20). In TBLL, learners may choose whatever language they have available and they learn to take risks by using language creatively. Another disadvantage of the PPP approach is that teachers often expect learners to be able to produce language that they just have presented more or less immediately. It may raise unrealistic expectations of what learners can achieve. But a learner's internal grammar does not change instantly. It takes constant revision of new language items in varying contexts until learners will eventually be able to confidently reproduce new language in spontaneous speech. TOMLINSON (1998: 16) stresses this when he says: *"I am sure most of you are familiar with the situation in which learners get a new feature correct in the lesson in which it is taught but then get it wrong the following week. This is partly because they have not yet had enough time, instruction and exposure for learning to have taken place."*

Framework of communicative tasks

With respect to a sociocultural view of language learning we therefore rely on NUNAN's definition of TBLL, which includes all the parameters that define the social context of the language classroom.

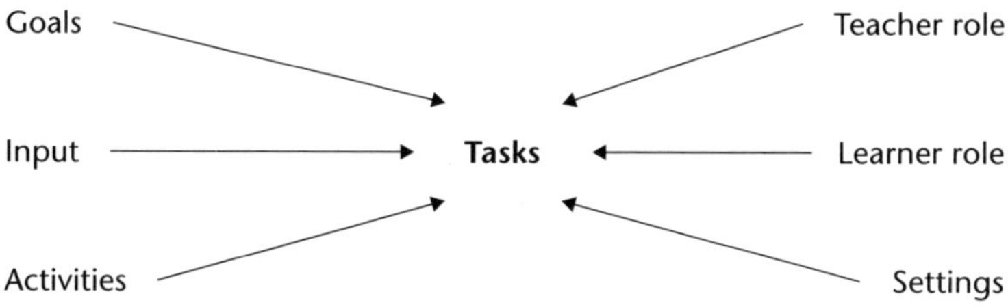

Model 2.3: A framework for analysing communicative tasks
(NUNAN 1989: 11)

Goals, Input, Activities

'Goals' comprise all the aspects that lead to intercultural communicative competence, such as knowledge of the world, sociocultural knowledge, mediating skills, learning skills and basic practical skills. The airport situation requires learners to consider their knowledge of what airports look like and function, and it requires them to use their sociocultural and mediating skills to gain information from speakers of English who might be very difficult to understand because of their accent (e.g. How do you approach a person? Do you pose open or closed questions? etc.). 'Input' involves the language data in oral or written form learners need to work on. While textbooks often only provide specifically written materials for the classroom, teachers need to look out for authentic materials (for a list and the differences between the two kinds of material see NUNAN 1989: 53–55). The 'activities' describe what learners actually do with the material, practising their language skills in an integrated way (asking questions, listening to the interviewee's answers, writing down the results. See also chap. 3.1). If the tasks are real-world tasks, the activities will be authentic as well since they represent meaningful language use.

Teacher and learner roles

The three factors above will be heavily influenced by 'learner' and 'teacher' roles (see chap. 2.2 and 2.3) as well as the 'setting'. As CANDLIN (2003: 42) has pointed out, classrooms are *"places where particular kinds of interaction occur and are situated, and where participants enact a range of mutually involving roles and work towards achieving particular personal and group purposes."* While the teacher designs the task in form of a 'task-as-workplan' (i.e. the lesson plan the teacher prepares before the lesson), learners will interpret tasks in relation to their own sociocultural backgrounds and the specific settings or teaching/learning situations of the classrooms they are working in. Consequently they (re)create the 'task-in-process' leading to what BREEN (1987: 25–26) has called a negotiated curriculum: Both teachers and learners bring their own views and ideas to the task process. To achieve a balance of power in the classroom, to break through the IRE sequence, and to ensure that task goals are reached, a negotiated curriculum between teacher and learners is necessary. This involves learners in the choice of material (Which book are we going to read?), the procedures (How much time do we need to complete this task? Who is going to work with whom?), and the kind of product the task aims for (Will we produce a collage, a reader, or give a presentation?).

Setting

The setting will play an important part in task design as well. Usually the task will take place in the classroom, but it could also be done outside of the classroom, e. g. when learners are interviewing people. This will necessitate specific activities, such as simulating face-to-face encounters. Scaffolding during the activities and the question of social forms play a decisive role in this. For example, for an interview the teacher needs to help learners frame the right kind of question (open) to get as much information as possible and learners have to consider aspects of politeness (How to start an interview? How to end it?). At the same time learners usually profit more from doing tasks in pairs or small groups since they negotiate the language data, helping each other.

3 Issues: How to design tasks

Designing tasks

Tasks are one of the most important methodological tools for teachers who try to provide a rich learning environment for their learners. But designing tasks is also very demanding. LEGUTKE and THOMAS (1993: 49–64) have presented a number of criteria that need to be considered (for an example see below): (1) 'Topic relevance' is paramount to ensure learner-centeredness. The content area chosen by the teacher has to be linked to the target culture to give learners' processes of self-discovery a direction. At the airport learners encounter all kinds of Englishes. By freely choosing their interview partners they engage in a process of discovery concerning different English cultures. (2) 'Creating awareness' on the part of the learners to help them to broaden their *"understanding of self, the group, and the external world"* (1993: 50–51). Learners will be able to find out through the airport experience how far they can function in an authentic situation. They will have to work in a team to reach their goal. And the learners will increase their knowledge about the airport world where speakers of English meet and communicate in the language they are learning. (3) 'Learners' prior knowledge' needs to be taken into account. Their knowledge about the airport and the fact that you will meet people from all over the world will prepare for the diversity of their language encounters. (4) 'Self-determination' of learners in interpreting the task and contributing to its outcome. Having made their interviews, learners will be able to choose those facts they find especially interesting for a final presentation. (5) Learners' 'motivation' to learn about themselves as well as their resistance to open up to others in public has to be taken into consideration. Thus an atmosphere of mutual trust is decisive for communicative tasks. Meeting new people is not easy, thus the simulation of interviews in the classroom and the teacher's support helps learners get used to the situation. (6) Learners' 'language needs' and the task's actual discourse outcome might show a discrepancy to the teacher's expectation so that he/she has to facilitate the learning process in many ways. Understanding the signs at the airport, carrying out interviews with strangers and dealing with different accents and personalities necessitates intensive preparation to cover the possible language needs (see example below). (7) 'Process relevance' of tasks in the overall frame of learning the language is important, i.e. what does the teacher want to achieve with the task? In the Airport Project, posing questions, engaging in a short conversation, understanding different English accents and presenting results all form part of the general aim of learning the target language. On the level of organizing tasks, SKEHAN (1996: 30) has listed a number of things teachers need to be able to do in the process:

- *an ability to select and sequence tasks for supplementary activities*
- *the competence to organize, appropriately, pre- and post-task activities*
- *a willingness to adapt task difficulty during the actual task phase*
- *a sensitivity to individual differences and the capacity to adapt tasks to take account of differences in learner orientation.*

Research to support task design

SLA and sociocultural research has presented findings (based on ELLIS 2000; WILLIS/WILLIS 2001: 175–6; COUNCIL OF EUROPE 2001: 157–167) concerning task performance which may support teachers' decision-making:

- Time to plan a task: If learners have more planning time before embarking on the task and if teachers give sufficient guidance in that respect (for example, well-structured and clear instructions), learners produce longer and richer discourse. Learners also engage better with the task. The same is true if a task type or theme is repeated since the cognitive load of processing the task is reduced.
- Tasks seem to produce more negotiation of meaning if there is an information exchange between partners and if it flows both ways (two-way instead of one-way tasks), i.e. both contribute to the outcome of the task, such as comparing two pictures and finding similarities and differences. The same is true when you compare tasks with closed outcomes (convergent task) with tasks with open ones (divergent task): when learners, for example, have to decide on the three most important characteristics of a literary character and rank these in terms of importance.

- Unfamiliarity with the task, a human or ethical type of problem to be solved, and presentation of the task in a narrative mode (see storyline below) also facilitate negotiation of meaning.
- While researchers differ in judging how the amount of focus on linguistic form affect task performance, they all agree that only meaningful use of the targeted forms will help learners to acquire new language items, that is, integrate them into their grammar.
- If learners have the opportunity to scaffold each other, i. e. construct a task collaboratively through dialogue, then they are able to independently produce certain linguistic features.

These findings are helpful in understanding what may facilitate language learning. But how should teachers actually proceed?

4 How to work with tasks – different frameworks

Tasks types

When designing tasks, the basic question is *"who does what with whom, on what content, with what resources, when, how, and why?"* (Breen 1987: 30) There are different ways of organizing tasks. Apart from comparing open and closed tasks in terms of their general structure and the degree of goal specificity, Willis (1996: 26–28, 149–54) lists six types of tasks (for a different list see Legutke/Thomas 1993: 71–150):

- Listing (a list learners put together or a mindmap)
- Ordering and sorting (sequencing items according to some logical or chronological order; ranking items according to value; categorising items in groups; classifying items)
- Comparing (finding similarities or differences, e. g. by comparing pictures)
- Problem solving (from short puzzles to real-life problems)
- Sharing personal experiences (e. g. likes and dislikes)
- Creative tasks (here: more complex tasks that could involve task forms 1–5)

Task cycle

The general task structure would involve the stages preparation, core activity, and follow-up language work. Willis (1996) has elaborated on this by developing the following framework (for an example see below).

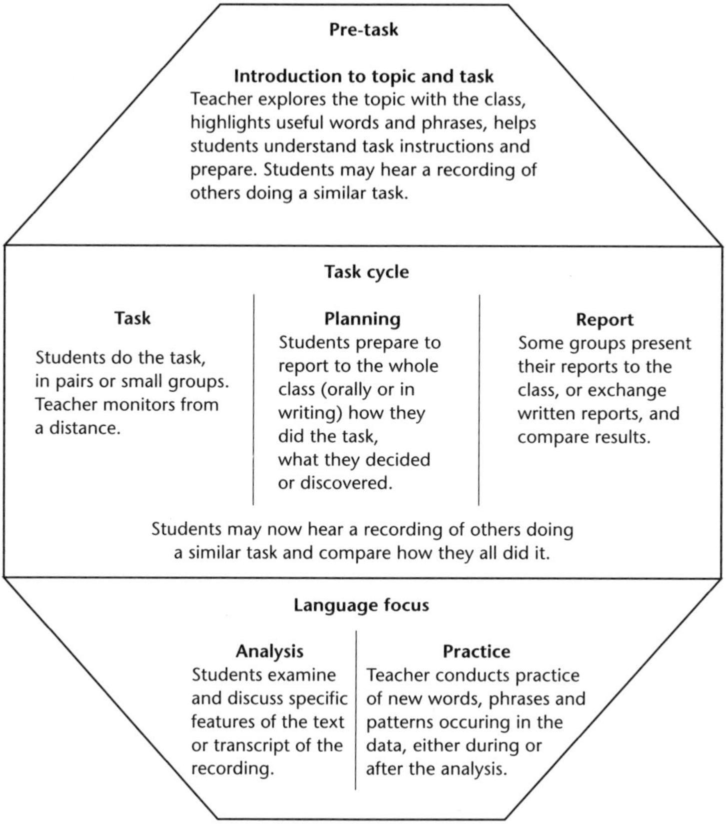

Model 2.4: Components of the TBLL framework (WILLIS 1996: 38)

For a similarly practical approach to TBLL see ESTAIRE and ZANÓN (1994). Apart from shorter tasks such as pre-, while, and post-listening or -viewing activities when listening to a song or viewing a film (see chap. 4.1 and 4.2), there are also more complex task cycles.

Project work

Project work is an example of an extensive task cycle. Project work *"is a theme and task-centred mode of teaching and learning which results from a joint process of negotiation between all participants"* (LEGUTKE/THOMAS 1993: 160). Teacher and learners decide together on a project idea, such as the visit to the airport, and then they negotiate a project plan which defines goals and procedures to implement the idea. Based on this plan learners work individually or in small groups to reach the goal. The goal is usually some kind of product, such as the presentation of findings from their interviews at the airport. At the same time project work focuses on the process of realizing the project plan, since it constantly asks learners to make decisions concerning the meaningful use of the target language (Which questions should we ask the visitors at the airport? How do you pose such questions?). The process thus is experiential (learners simulate the interviews in the classroom, which includes such questions as: How do you involve the whole project group in the interview, i. e. who holds the tape-recorder, who takes the picture of the interviewee? before they do the interview at the airport) and it is *"holistic"* since it combines *"body and mind, theory and practice"* (LEGUTKE/THOMAS 1993: 160).

Project types

Projects can take many different forms, they can be of short duration, but they can also stretch over a few weeks or a whole term. They might be linked to real-world issues, simulated real-world issues or *"students' interest with or without real-world significance"* (see STOLLER 2002: 110). In terms of data collection techniques and information sources, STOLLER (2002: 111 based on HAINES 1989 and LEGUTKE/THOMAS 1993) differentiates between research projects (learners engage in library and/or internet research), text projects (learners encounter various text genres), correspondence projects (learners communicate with other people via letter, e-mail, chat), survey projects (learners design survey instruments or collect and analyze information from people), and encounter projects (learners meet people face-to-face inside or outside the classroom). For still another way of organizing project types and examples for each type see EYRING (2001: 338–40).

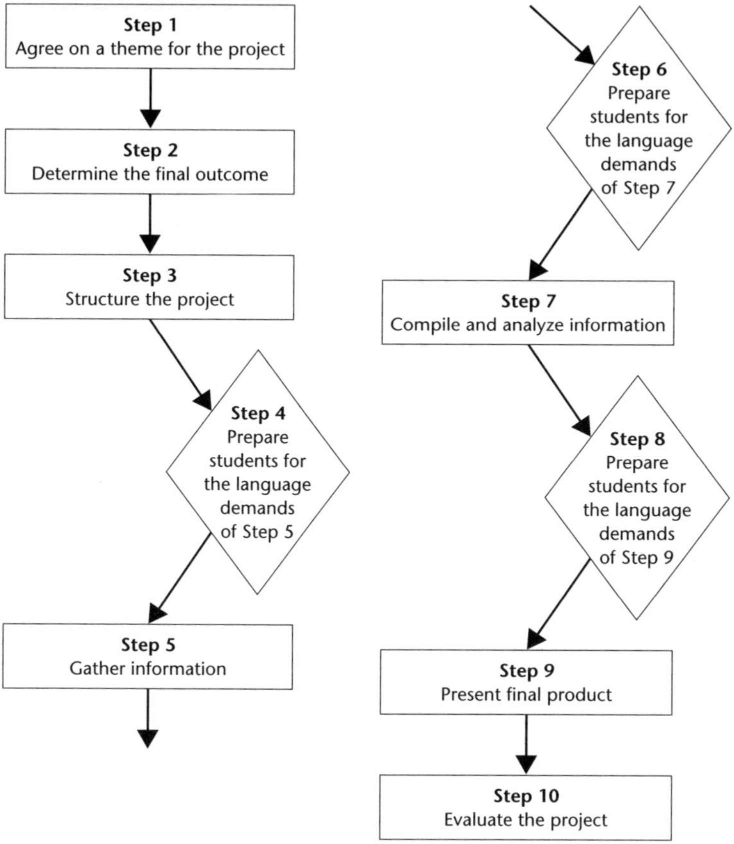

Model 2.5: Developing a project in a language classroom
(STOLLER 2002: 112)

Project steps

The Airport Project is a typical encounter project. Learners need to prepare themselves in terms of content as well as language since they will meet proficient speakers of English at the airport. It is therefore a good example of the integration of a focus on form into the general project plan. Following STOLLER's 10-step procedure (see above) the individual sub-tasks, such as collecting information about the airport or practising interviews in class form a coherent part of the target task of interviewing people at the airport and presenting the collected data to others back home. After having decided on the topic airport (step 1), the teacher helps learners to open a field of awareness by brainstorming all the things one can do at airports. In the process, learners themselves decide on interviewing travellers (step 2). After having formed groups, the next larger sub-task (step 3) is to structure the project

(What do we need to do? Collect information about the airport as a place to visit, design questions for interviews and practise interviews). Having decided on this task-as-workplan, the first focus on language is due (step 4), since learners have to learn how to form closed and open questions and they practise the interview with other teachers who are invited to the classroom, i.e. simulating the real-world situation in their classroom first. After having actually visited the airport and collected the language data (step 5), they again have to focus on language, since now careful listening (step 6) is necessary to transcribe the interviews and to prepare them for presentation (step 7). For the presentation further language work is necessary since students have to develop captions for pictures or write short informative texts about the people they have met (step 8). The presentation (step 9) in front of other classes and parents is the final product or outcome of the project. As a last step learners and teacher evaluate the project (step 10) to decide what they would like to do differently next time and in how far they profited from doing the project. This focus on process learning also involves formative assessment procedures, such as a portfolio (see chap. 4.4).

Storyline approach

There are also other specific forms of task-based language learning in a project format, such as the storyline concept. It was developed in Scottish primary schools to promote interdisciplinary work in content-based learning (BELL 1995). This has been adapted to the foreign language classroom (see KOCHER 1999). In the storyline approach, the teacher provides a narrative structure, for example, a detective story, which involves the reading and writing of various text genres, as well as language production through communication with other learners and native speakers outside the classroom and the presentation of results. While the storyline approach is a specific project form, it allows for the clear sequencing of tasks based on its narrative structure and allows learners to negotiate tasks-in-progress collaboratively.

Szenariendidaktik

Still another approach is PIEPHO's (2003) *Szenariendidaktik* which is similar to the storyline approach. Learners work individually or collaboratively on a number of text impulses (such as different text genres on the topic friends), the results of which they present to the class. This offers the opportunity to receive feedback in terms of content and language. In a last step, learners present their revised products to other classes or people from outside the classroom.

5 Future developments

Classroom-based research

While task-based language learning seems to offer a bridge between opposing views on learning languages, there is an obvious need for more classroom-based research since much of the psycholinguistic research has been produced under lab-like conditions which ignores the influence of the setting. But learning in classrooms is influenced by a number of variables: *"The 'same' task might be done quite differently according to where it comes in the teaching cycle, the role taken by the teacher, the learners' interpretations of what is expected, the learners' previous experience of the task type and the topic or content matter and other implementation variables, such as time limit, group size and participant roles"* (WILLIS/WILLIS 2001: 176). This includes knowledge about how *"participants co-construct the 'activity' they engage in, in accordance with their own socio-history and locally determined goals"* (ELLIS 2000: 193). More research findings as to these variables would be helpful so that future language teachers can have a more informed basis on which to design their classroom activities and thus facilitate language learning. At the same time, language teachers need to know how to carry out their own site-specific research to find out more about the quality of language learning in their own classrooms (see chap. 2.2).

2.5: The Context: Language Policy, Curriculum, Classroom

1 Introduction

Language policy and classrooms

State and national governments supervise and influence what is taught and learned in schools. They define the standards, purposes, contents, procedures and forms of evaluation which find their way into schools by way of curricula, guidelines, syllabuses, and recommendations. In many countries textbooks, for example, have to be approved by the Ministry of Education before they are allowed to be used in classrooms. This is of advantage because it guarantees continuity and stability, but it narrows down the options schools have. For example, some languages are privileged (in most states English is the first foreign language) while others are not represented at schools at all. It is pre-defined how many lessons are provided in the time-table for the teaching of a language or if its mark is relevant for moving to higher classes. In this chapter we will look at some of the relevant instruments language policy uses to regulate the teaching and learning of foreign languages in Germany. We will then focus on how the participants in the EFL classroom may use and create classrooms successfully to make the most of their learning potential.

2 Language policy: Global and national issues, regulations and developments

Global issues and regulations

Linguistic diversity vs. linguistic imperialism

We are living in a globalized world where nation states and their economies and cultures are becoming increasingly interconnected, in part due to technological developments. Discussions about globalization influence approaches to language teaching and issues of everyday practice. To give an example: Until recently the spread of English was seen as linguistic imperialism threatening linguistic and cultural diversity. Such diversity is seen as a good thing in itself. *"Each language has its own way of seeing the world and is the product of its own particular history. All languages have their individual identity and value, and all are equally adequate as modes of expression for the people who use them"* (EUROPEAN COUNCIL OF CULTURAL CO-OPERATION 2001: 1).

EIL to cope with *lingua franca* situations

However, in recent years, other ways of looking at the spread of English have resulted in a more reflective approach to language teaching (for a survey see BLOCK 2004). Given the fact that, in the not-too-distant future, the number of L2 speakers of English will surpass the number of native speakers (GRADDOL 1999, in: MCKAY 2003: 1) it is argued that English as an international language (EIL) is becoming de-nationalized, which will have consequences for the way it is taught: *"(T)he entire notion that learners of EIL need to learn the culture of native speakers of English must be challenged. (…T)he purpose of teaching an international language is to facilitate the communication of learners' ideas and culture in an English medium (as) there is no necessity for L2 speakers to internalize the cultural norms of native speakers of that language"* (MCKAY 2003: 1).

***English Only* is not an option**

English learned as a medium to cope with *lingua franca* situations may understandably be seen as a threat to plurilingualism and cultural diversity. This is why the COUNCIL OF EUROPE (1996) suggested that every European citizen should learn two more European languages apart from his or her mother language, one of which should be English. European language policy promotes a trilingual language profile which recognizes the fact that the establishment of a *lingua franca* alone does not promote understanding and communication. Everybody accepts the important role of English but at the same time no one considers *English only* to be appropriate. But what is?

In the Year of Languages 2001, the Council of Europe published a document which has become one of the most widely discussed and used publications in Europe, The *Common European Framework of Reference for Languages: Learning, Teaching, Assessment* (short: *CEF*). It is probably the most powerful political paper to inform language teaching and learning in Europe. Its general purposes are defined as follows: *"[T]he Council is concerned to improve the quality of communication among Europeans of different languages and cultural backgrounds. This is because better communication leads to freer mobility and more direct contact, which in turn leads to better understanding and closer co-operation. The Council also supports methods of learning and teaching which help [...] learners to build up the attitudes, knowledge and skills they need to become more independent in thought and action, and also more responsible and co-operative in relation to other people. In this way the work contributes to the promotion of democratic citizenship"* (COUNCIL OF EUROPE 2001: xi-xii). To do so, it defines different competence levels in communicative activities, so called 'can-do-statements', which describe what people can do at six different levels from beginners to highly-skilled. These activities are based on the traditional distinction of the four skills, with the exception that speaking is split into interaction and production (see chap. 3.1). For a report of different ways in which the CEF is being used, see MORROW (2004). For a critical evaluation, see BAUSCH et al (2003).

The Common European Framework of Reference for Languages

National Issues and Regulations

Apart from these global or European considerations and recommendations, national governments regulate foreign language teaching through various instruments.

National regulations

Richtlinien (sometimes referred to as *Rahmenrichtlinien*) describe general government-approved orientations for an overall concept of school learning. They contain detailed subject-specific regulations. *Rahmenrichtlinien Englisch Hessen* (1996), for example, provide information on the purposes of teaching English, methodological considerations, topics, skills and sub-skills, or assessment procedures.

Guidelines

Curriculum and *Lehrplan* (syllabus) are plans of what is to be achieved through teaching and learning. In Germany it is formally documented by the state governments and defines the aims, content, methodology, and evaluation of language teaching and learning for particular groups of learners (primary, secondary levels). These documents are particularly relevant for textbook writers who have to base their choices of topics and activities on these documents to be admitted in classrooms. The difference between the two concepts cannot easily be described: The term *curriculum*

Curricula and syllabuses

was introduced in Germany in the 60s to reform education on a scientific basis because until then purposes, contents and procedures in *Lehrpläne* were influenced by the subjective pedagogic ideas of their respective authors. But meanwhile the two concepts are often used synonymously (QUETZ 2003: 122), with *Lehrplan* referring particularly to the time frames in which contents are to be taught.

Different types of curricula (or syllabuses)

BREEN (2001b) distinguishes between four different types of syllabuses currently used in language teaching. Their main characteristics reveal the development of syllabus design over the last two decades.

Formal, functional, process

Before the advent of communicative language teaching, syllabuses focused on the formal development of linguistic knowledge. It was not until the 1970s when a growing dissatisfaction with learners' failure to use linguistic knowledge outside the classroom and research in the social use of language initiated a change which focused on language use and how particular purposes could be expressed linguistically (COUNCIL OF EUROPE 1971). Soon, the teaching of a general repertoire of speech functions was considered to be limiting learners' potential and individual purposes of language use to certain fixed communicative situations and roles. There was a growing awareness that language learning should mirror language use in a multitude of social situations which could not be predicted and therefore its linguistic means could not be pre-defined. Therefore new directions for syllabus design were based on accounts of how language learning is actually undertaken by the learner. This led to the development of task-based and process syllabus types (see chap. 2.4).

Progression

In Germany, language knowledge and competencies are still sequenced following the traditional grammatical/structural progression which is combined with listing the communicative functions that may be expressed with them. To illustrate this we use an example from the table of contents of a textbook published by Cornelsen for *Realschule (English G 2000, B3)*:

Main themes/speech functions	**Structures**
Ein Kriminalfall im Fernsehstudio Vermutungen anstellen; Vorhersagen machen; Über Absichten sprechen; Auskünfte geben und einholen; Angebote machen	Das Futur mit *going to* (Vorhersagen) Das *simple present* (futuristische Bedeutung) Das *will-future* (Angebote etc.)

This sequencing of language learning has been aptly criticized for the unnatural language input that results from it as large numbers of illustrating examples of the respective structure to be practiced are found in an activity or text. As most of school language-teaching is based on textbooks, learner-oriented task- or scenario-based approaches to language teaching and learning will therefore only find their way into mainstream EFL teaching through a new generation of textbooks which are beginning to be used in schools.

3 The classroom: A neglected dimension of foreign language teaching

On the potential of classrooms

No matter how political decisions and their manifestations in textbooks influence who we are and what we do as teachers, they are but one side of the story. If we look at the potential classrooms offer it may sharpen our awareness of both the significance of the room which defines participants' space for action and of how these participants use and create the potential of classrooms through their interaction.

Features of 'good pedagogy'

Legutke (1998, 2003) has repeatedly challenged our notion of the classroom and its language learning potential. Our understanding of its potential defines our roles as educators and foreign language teachers (see chap. 2.2). Following individual accounts of different case studies of 'classrooms in action' whose successes depended on the specific contexts and the personalities of teachers and learners involved, he delineated classroom-based examples of 'good pedagogy' and has initiated discussions on what is locally feasible.

Design features

Legutke (1998) identified seven salient features which describe good language learning pedagogy:

1. Situated practice: learners have opportunities to interact in the target language and negotiate meanings
2. Audience: learners interact with an authentic audience
3. Task orientation: learners are involved in meaningful tasks
4. Learner texts: learners are encouraged to produce a variety of texts and engage in creative language use
5. Resources: students have access to a variety of resources and are encouraged to construct the learning environment
6. Evaluation: learners are induced to become aware of the learning process and take responsibility for outcome
7. Cooperative learning: learners work in small, self-directed groups and act as peer teachers.

Metaphors for the classroom

In an attempt to describe the foreign language classrooms he found in these case studies, he came up with a diversity of different metaphors: 'workshop' (large selection of materials, free access to different media, various work zones), 'training ground' (for the present and future use of language), 'observatory' (aspects of foreign language and culture are brought into focus), 'studio' (places of constant design and creation), 'communication center' and – 'classroom' (a place of learning and instruction as we all know it). 'Classrooms' are no longer confined to the physical space provided by the room in which language learning takes place but learners' space for action may be expanded beyond that – through e-mail projects, field trips, www research projects, challenging real-life tasks, for example.

3 CHAPTER Language Learning and Language Use: Developing Skills and Subskills

Different frameworks of classification

In chapter 2.1 we defined the purpose of language teaching and learning as developing intercultural communicative competence (ICC). This complex competence comprises several components. In the literature various frameworks are put forward which organize them in different ways.

The four language skills

Traditional methodologies, such as HEDGE (2000) and UR (1996) classify the language skills in what UR calls *"the so-called 'four skills'"* (1996: 109), that is reading, writing, listening, and speaking. These categories are the 'classical' ones used to describe the 'what' of language teaching (for a discussion of the 'subskills' of grammar and vocabulary see chap. 3.2). The term skill emphasizes the fact that language learning *"is not only concerned with acquiring knowledge (about grammar and pronunciation systems, for example) – it is not just something we learn about. Rather, it is a skill, or a set of skills – something we learn to do, like riding a bike. So, students need meaningful, interactive practice in the skills in order to learn to use the language"* (GOWER et al 1995: 85). The four skills may be further classified into receptive skills (listening, reading) and productive skills (speaking, writing). Publishers usually produce a series of 'skills books' which offer activities to practise the individual skills for various language learning levels (see for example SCHOCKER-V. DITFURTH (1997): *Learning to Listen*). Textbooks and exams also follow these categories.

Critique of the skills approach

The skills-based approach has been criticised for two main reasons: it aims at developing language skills by continuous practice, ignoring learners' mental processes and backgrounds; and it is based on an inappropriate view on language learning: *"Fertigkeitenorientierter Fremdsprachenunterricht in der Tradition der audiolingualen Methode sieht sein Ziel in der Beherrschung der Summe der einzelnen Fertigkeiten, die im Unterricht nacheinander und systematisch erlernt und dann in Realsituationen übertragen werden sollen. Sprachunterricht wird damit in eine manipulative und eine kommunikative, eine Anwendungsphase getrennt, was dann das Problem des Transfers aufwirft. Auch wer die einzelnen Fertigkeiten beherrscht, scheitert eventuell in komplexen Realsituationen"* (KRUMM 2003: 117–8). This is why DUXA (2003: 306) is right when she argues that *"ein vornehmlich auf die sprachliche Dimension ausgerichtetes Einüben von Redemitteln ist nicht ausreichend, wenn nicht zugleich die Bereitschaft und Fähigkeit der Lerner unterstützt wird, diese Redemittel anzuwenden und sich dabei […] auf den Kommunikationspartner und die Kommunikationssituation einzustellen."*

Integrated skills

Most situations of language use involve a mixture of skills which are interrelated: for example, someone is listening to a radio broadcast, while doing so, she is writing down some notes on bits of information she would like to talk to her friend about later. In language learning situations, too, skills may be developed in an integrated way, that is, not in isolation and independently from each other. For example, a listening activity may be introduced by a note-making activity to tap into students' experiences, and may be followed by a role-play in which some of the information students have taken from listening to a text is used in oral production (for examples see SCHOCKER-V. DITFURTH 1997, 1999). The objections in principle to a skills-based approach remain, and this is why completely different ways of categorizing dimensions of language use have been developed. These take into account the learner and the social contexts in which language learning takes place.

Competence-based approaches

A different classification is offered by the COUNCIL OF EUROPE'S *Common European Framework of Reference for Languages* (*CEF*) (COUNCIL OF EUROPE 2001). Here language use and learning are described in an action-oriented way. It views *"users and learners of a language* […] *as 'social agents', i.e. members of society who have tasks (not exclusively language-related) to accomplish* […] *within a particular field of action.* […A]*ctions are performed by one or more individuals strategically using their own specific competences to achieve a given result. The action-based approach therefore also takes into account the cognitive, emotional and volitional resources and the full range of abilities specific to and applied by the individual as a social agent"* (COUNCIL OF EUROPE 2001: 9). This is why the *CEF* talks of *competences* as the more comprehensive term which includes certain skills but which stresses the fact that language learning and language use consist of more than just language-related skills: *"Competences are the sum of knowledge, skills and characteristics that allow a person to perform actions"* (COUNCIL OF EUROPE 2001: 9). To illustrate the approach adopted, here are some examples from the *CEF*: 'knowledge' may be related to day-to-day living (i.e. organisation of the day) or it may be knowledge of the shared values and beliefs held by social groups in other countries (i.e. religious beliefs or taboos). 'Skills' refer to the ability to carry out activities (see COUNCIL OF EUROPE 2001, chap. 4.4) which may be 'productive' (i.e. to describe one's family background spontaneously in a private conversation), 'receptive' (i.e. to understand a radio broadcast), 'interactive' (i.e. to participate in a discussion with friends) or 'mediating' (i.e. informal oral interpreting for foreign visitors in one's own country).

A discussion of the traditional skills and subskills in terms of activities is also the approach taken in the *Handbuch Fremdsprachenunterricht* (BAUSCH/CHRIST/KRUMM 2003). There are no chapters on skills (or competences) at all, instead you find different articles on *Aufgaben* and *Übungen* for pronunciation, vocabulary, grammar, reading comprehension, writing, listening comprehension, listening-viewing comprehension, communication, interaction, creativity, intercultural communication and mediation under the heading 'methodological aspects of the teaching and learning of foreign languages' (see chap. E3 *Übungen* in BAUSCH/CHRIST/KRUMM 2003).

Activity-based approaches

A third classification is presented in CAMERON's book on *Teaching Languages to Young Learners* (2001). She distinguishes between learning the spoken language (speaking and listening) and learning 'literacy skills.' The term literacy focuses on the purpose of learning to read and write which is to express and share meanings between people. *"Literacy in this sense is both social and cognitive. Socially, literacy provides people with opportunities to share meanings across space and time. Cognitively, literacy requires that individuals use specific skills and knowledge about how the written language operates in processing text"* (CAMERON 2001: 123). She then proceeds to identify the skills needed to be literate in English, i.e. being able to read and write different sorts of texts for different purposes in English.

Literacy-based approaches

We will retain the traditional language skills classification in this chapter. This is for practical reasons. To this day, textbooks and exams follow the 'skills'-structure when they classify language-related teaching aims. At the same time we will integrate the reference levels for describing learner proficiency *(Niveaustufenbeschreibungen)* which the Council of Europe has defined. They have developed a set of descriptive categories to map out communicative language competence (see rationale in COUNCIL OF EUROPE 2001, 2.2 and examples in chap. 4 & 5). We will refer to examples for these 'can-do-statements' which allow teachers and learners to evaluate language performance against the defined aims.

Approach adopted here: integrate skills and competences

3.1 Language Skills

3.1.1 Speaking and Mediating

1 Background

Speaking – a recent focus in EFL

Speaking has only in the last two decades begun to become a relevant aspect of teaching foreign languages. BYGATE (2001: 14) identifies three reasons for this: the huge influence of grammar-translation approaches on language teaching (to this day) has marginalized the teaching of communication skills. Until the mid-70s with the advent of tape-recording technology it was difficult to study teacher or learner talk (for features of oral discourse, for problems EFL learners face and the skills they need to overcome them to communicate). Most approaches to language teaching 'exploited' oral production to practise correct pronunciation, and pronunciation had to be correct 'before' coherent production of text was encouraged.

Features of speech production

According to information-processing models, speech production is a very complex process and involves the following major elements which need to be automated to be successful (see SCOVEL 1998):

Conceptualisation
= planning the message content and drawing on various knowledge sources while doing so (background, topic, speech situation, discourse patterns);

↓

Formulation
= finding the words and phrases to express the meanings, sequencing them, and preparing the sound patterns of the words and phrases to be used;

↓

Articulation
= controlling the articulatory organs (such as lips, tongue, teeth);

↓

Self-monitoring
= identifying and self-correcting mistakes during oral production.

Model 3.1: Model of speech production

What makes speaking a complex skill to develop is that it is usually reciprocal (often there are simultaneous and immediate contributions of interlocutors in communication); it is also less predictable than written interaction, and there is often time pressure to produce language with no time to plan it.

2 Developing speaking in the EFL classroom

The context: Promoting speaking is a challenge

Promoting oral production in the target language in a classroom seems something of a challenge. KURTZ (2001: 14–5) suggests that the increase in methodological 'know-how' has not resulted in a corresponding 'do-how' in language classrooms when it comes to developing speaking. *"Die alltagsunterrichtliche Versteinerung der Sprachhandlungsprozesse* [...] *lässt das freie, selbstgesteuerte und selbständige Sprechen in der Zielsprache kaum zur Entfaltung kommen. Das fremdsprachenunterrichtliche Sprechhandeln erstarrt vielmehr in einer gleichförmigen, an der Schriftsprache der jeweiligen Textvorlage orientierten, mehr oder minder mühsam aufrecht erhaltenen Mündlichkeit, der es an Unmittelbarkeit, Lebendigkeit, Emotionalität und vor allem auch an Erlebnisqualität mangelt* [... weshalb] *die curricularen Vorgaben im Bereich der fremdsprachlichen Sprachhandlungsfähigkeit nicht erreicht werden"* (KURTZ 2001: 14). Student teachers of EFL confirm this when asked about their own foreign language learning biography (SCHOCKER-V. DITFURTH 2001).

Effects of the context on oral production

There are a number of reasons why this is so: classrooms are institutionalised contexts and this affects the quality of teaching and learning. The notion of 'hidden curriculum' refers to the sociocultural norms and values emphasized by schools which influence considerably what teachers accept as 'normal' in their classrooms. There is, for example, an established power relationship within which teachers are expected to use control to maintain discipline, where they have to mark students' achievements, and have to teach along the lines of a course book which defines the contents and the often repetitious activities which learners perceive as monotonous and demotivating. These context features may have a negative effect on the general language learning atmosphere which does not encourage students to experiment freely and easily with the target language to express their personal meanings. There is evidence that it is students' main concern to produce language which is formally accurate. Personal response or initiation of topic is not usually asked for: "[...] *the learners never choose what to say, they simply work out how to say what they are told to say"* (THOMPSON 1996: 13). *"Fenced in by syllabus commands, often represented by the dominance of a textbook, learners do not find room to speak as themselves, to use language in communicative encounters, to create text, to stimulate responses from fellow learners, to find solutions to relevant problems"* (LEGUTKE 1993: 310).

Teachers as non-native speakers of English

MEDGYES identifies another reason for the controlled approach of non-native teachers of English in our EFL learning context: "[N]*on-native teachers of English are usually preoccupied with accuracy* [...]. *Many lack fluency* [...]. *It is only logical to deduce then that they place the emphasis on those aspects of the language that they have a better grasp of.* [...] *If they are engrossed in fighting their own language difficulties, they cannot afford to loosen their grip over the class* [...]. *As groupwork and pairwork often create unpredictable situations full of linguistic traps, non-native English teachers favour more secure forms of classwork* [...]. *On a general plane, the same motives encourage the non-native English teachers' more controlled and cautious pedagogic approach"* (MEDGYES 1994: 57–60). What can we do to promote spontaneous speech under the restrictions of institutionalised language learning in an EFL context? To answer this question, we will first classify different kinds of oral production which we will have to prepare our learners for, and then suggest some ways of supporting speaking. Finally we will survey some types of activities that promote oral production.

3 Classifications of oral production

The Council of Europe

The Council of Europe distinguishes between three types of activities (2001: 58–90):

- 'Oral production (speaking)', that is producing an oral text for one or more listeners, for example giving information to an audience in a public address. This may involve reading a written text aloud, speaking from notes, acting out a rehearsed role, speaking spontaneously, improvising (see ideas in KURTZ 2001) or singing a song.
- 'Spoken interaction', that is *"the language user acts alternately as speaker and listener with one or more interlocutors so as to construct conjointly, through the negotiation of meaning* [...] *conversational discourse. Reception and production strategies are employed constantly during interaction. There are also* [...] *discourse strategies and co-operation strategies concerned with managing co-operation and interaction such as turntaking and turngiving,* [...] *proposing and evaluating solutions, recapping and summarising the point reached, and mediating in a conflict"* (COUNCIL OF EUROPE 2001: 73). Examples of interactive activities include conversation, discussion, debate, interview or negotiation.
- 'Oral mediation', that is the language user does not express his or her own meanings but *"acts as an intermediary between inter-*

locutors who are unable to understand each other directly – normally [...] *speakers of different languages"* (COUNCIL OF EUROPE 2001: 87). Examples of mediating activities include spoken interpretation or summarising and paraphrasing texts. Contexts include simultaneous or consecutive interpretation at conferences or meetings, informal interpreting for foreign visitors, for friends, family clients etc.

If we wish to prepare our learners to use the target language to accomplish certain tasks in society, we will have to develop these competences even though the classroom seems a rather unfavourable language learning context, as we have seen. To help with this, the following section lists some ideas on how teachers can support learners' oral skill development.

4 How to encourage and support speaking

Implications for teaching

Teachers need to be aware of these context factors and have to find ways to create a relaxed, supportive, low stress atmosphere where students are not afraid to speak but are instead encouraged to take risks and produce language to express personal meanings and ideas. The basic requirement is that teachers establish a comfortable target-language atmosphere where English is used as the 'natural' means of communication, that is, English is used for classroom discourse and management and students get as much exposure to the target language as is possible. Students need models of language use to listen to. The role of the teacher as model is crucial in that s/he uses the target language flexibly and as naturally as s/he possibly can. Teachers may organise pair- and group work activities to provide a safe, less public environment for students to practise production without worrying about errors to become more self-confident about speaking to the class. They have to allow for some preparation time for oral production by doing pre-tasks that activate students' ideas and target language resources to make them available for production (see example below). Teachers may offer language production support by developing ideas on how to express what they wish to say together with their students (see speech bubbles in example below). They encourage student participation and response by offering motivating topics and tasks which give students choice in what to say and which allow learners to talk about their personal backgrounds and experiences (see chap. 2.4): "[...I]*f children are to talk meaningfully in foreign language classrooms, they must have something they want to say* [... and] *the teacher must take on the responsibility for adjusting tasks and topics so that they relate to pupils' interests.* [...] *Sharing with the pupils the expected outcomes of the task will usually help pupils. It helps too if a task has a clear goal or purpose,* [... that is] *a communicative or interpersonal purpose"* (CAMERON 2001: 58).

Example of task to promote oral production

The following example task was designed by SCHOCKER-V. DITFURTH for a 7th form *Realschule*. She changed the activity as it was suggested in the course book which she used then. It had asked students to answer questions on a text about an old woman who lives in a street in London to check if students could reproduce its content. The text spread over two pages. The purpose of the task she set instead was to share ideas with her students about what life in our streets is like. They could then compare differences between their streets and the life of an elderly woman living in London. The task illustrates the principles which support language production and interaction as outlined above (i.e. purpose, choice, language production support, focus on personal meaning, expected outcome).

Talking about life in our streets

This is to find out and talk to each other about what life in our streets is like.

You may wish to say something about
- your home and other peoples' homes
- the people who live in your street
- any special events you celebrate
- any difficulties there are, things you don't like very much
- anything else you think is interesting / strange / funny etc.

These phrases may help you:

There is / there are ...
I think it's good, that ...
I think it's bad, that ...
What gets on my nerves ...

HOMEWORK to prepare your ideas
Take notes on your ideas or write a text. You will use your notes / tests tomorrow to talk about your street to your group. If you don't know how to say things, find a way round it, talk to your group or use your dictionaries.

BACK IN CLASS
Talk to each other about what life in your street is like.
In your group you may
- ask each other questions about things you don't understand
- wish to talk about what is different or what is the same or what is particulary interesting / funny / strange etc.

Report back to your class what you have learned about your group partners' street. First agree on what you think is particularly interesting to report back to your class.

Research on features of task that affect development of oral skills is ongoing and there are quite a few issues that still need to be explored in more detail. Following BYGATE (2001) it seems as if attention to one of the aspects of speech (fluency, accuracy, complexity of speech) limits one's capacity to develop others. This implies that learners need tasks to promote oral production which focus either on opportunities to use language to communicate meanings, or on accuracy. The problem then is how to bring together fluency and accuracy. It has been suggested that task repetition may shift learners' attention from the process of conceptualisation towards formulation, which is why task recycling seems to be a way to allow learners to integrate fluency, accuracy and complexity (see for example ideas in WILLIS 1996).

Research on oral production in the L2

5 Types of speaking activities

You find different classifications/typologies for speaking activities but generally authors distinguish between accuracy-based and fluency-based activities:

Accuracy- and fluency-based activities

1. Fluency-based activities are free discussions, role-plays, and so-called 'gap'-activities which require learners to negotiate meaning. These activities try *"to create the 'gap' of information or opinion which exists between speakers in the real world, and which creates the unpredictability of normal discourse"* (HEDGE 2000: 58). Examples of gap-activities which promote the negotiation of meaning are

- Information-gap activities which involve a transfer of given information from one person to another.
- Opinion-gap activities which involve identifying and articulating a personal preference, feeling, or attitude in response to a given situation (for examples see KLIPPEL 1984).

2. Accuracy-based or form-focused activities are controlled in that they focus on the development of one aspect of language and there is a high degree of control over student input. The focus may be on a number of language features, i.e. on a grammatical structure, a communicative function, or the time sequencers when telling a story (HEDGE 2000: 273).

Activities may be either authentic, that is, language production is directed towards an authentic audience (as for example in an e-mail exchange project) or they may be simulated.

Authentic or simulated activities

6 Developments and issues

Language – a means of social interaction

Language is used as a medium for social interaction. Therefore interactive activities need to be developed that work in large classes and that make use of 'the here and now' of the classroom for oral production which is personally relevant. *"Ein vornehmlich auf die sprachliche Dimension ausgerichtetes Einüben von Redemitteln ist nicht ausreichend, wenn nicht zugleich die Bereitschaft und Fähigkeit der Lerner unterstützt wird, diese Redemittel anzuwenden und sich dabei emotional und rational auf den Kommunikationspartner und die Kommunikationssituation einzustellen"* (Duxa 2003: 306). These skills need to involve negotiation of meaning and the use of discourse strategies that learners will have to acquire to prepare them appropriately for situations of language use within and outside classroom doors (see chap. 2.2).

Promote use of formulaic language

In many language classrooms there is a strict divide between grammar practice activities and vocabulary practice activities. But the *"heavy mental demands of speaking are believed to be one of the causes of the phenomenon of formulaic use of language (*Wray *1999). [...S]peakers seem to rely on such 'chunks' of language that come ready made and can be brought into use with less effort than constructing a fresh phrase or sentence.* [... Chunks] *can be useful in talk by providing a basic pattern* [...] *with 'slots' that can be filled by different nouns or adjectives"* (Cameron 2001: 50). Teachers may offer conversational phrases as units of language to support production as was illustrated in the task example above.

Assessment to include oral production

Oral production and interaction will have to be part of the assessment of language competence. We will have to develop descriptors of aspects of language production and criteria for rating scales (e.g. accuracy, appropriacy, range, flexibility, size; see examples in Council of Europe 2001).

Research demand

It is not clear if tasks can be designed so as to lead learners to work with particular kinds of language features. While some methodologists deny this (Willis 1996), there are empirical studies that show how the language used in tasks can be traced back to features of the input or task design (see summary in Bygate 2001: 19). This needs to be explored further.

3.1.2 Writing

Writing: a full-scale skill

For a long time writing in the EFL classroom has not received much attention as a skill to be developed in its own right, that is, as part of students' communicative competence and literacy. Instead, it has been used as a 'support skill': *"Much* [...] *writing in language classrooms happens in support of other aspects of language learning, such as writing down vocabulary to remember it or reinforcing new grammar patterns"* (CAMERON 2001: 155). Only recently has the development of writing as a skill begun to focus on the process of writing itself (i. e. on the audience, the purpose and the topic one wishes to write about), drawing on insights from mother and target language composition theory and pedagogy. Various developments have contributed to this.

1 Developments: Establishing writing as a skill

Composition theory: Writing as a complex cognitive process

Research interest in the study of process composition strategies and techniques began during the 1980s. The 'creative' or 'expressive approach' views writing as a process of self-discovery. It entered EFL classrooms a decade later as the 'process writing movement' which focuses on three aspects:

1. it emphasizes the composition process of writers (such as planning, drafting, and revising) and recognizes the fact that writing is a complex, cognitive process which involves various recursive non-linear procedures, that is procedures of re-writing which may be repeated a number of times (WHITE/ARNDT 1991, in: NUNAN 1999: 273–4);
2. writing is writing for learning and not writing for display, that is, one seeks to improve students' writing skills through developing their use of effective composing processes (RAIMES, in: NUNAN 1999: 273);
3. while product-oriented approaches focus on the final product (a coherent, error-free text) and often emphasize imitation of different kinds of models, process-oriented approaches focus on the steps involved in drafting and redrafting a piece of work (even though there is no dichotomy between process and product).

Second language acquisition research

Research into features of learners' developing foreign language *(interlanguage)* has resulted in a different attitude towards the role of errors in language teaching and learning. Errors are seen as a natural and inevitable product of a learner's developing target language competence, and they have been studied to discover the processes learners make use of in language production. This has resulted in developing the skill of writing through a process of repeated re-drafting where learners edit their writing and become aware of their language development. *"[R]esearchers have demonstrated that error should not be stigmatising; rather, it is often systematic and reasonable"* (REID 2001: 31). Progress in language acquisition research has also resulted in a general shift in EFL pedagogy from the so-called PPP approach to language learning (see chap. 3.2) to a task-based approach which takes account of the view that language learning is a process of creative experimentation in which students use whatever resources they have available to get their meanings across.

Language policy and CMC

The growing need for intercultural understanding and learning in a multicultural European society has resulted in a view of learners and users of a language that sees them primarily as members of a multilingual society who have various (communicative) tasks to accomplish (see COUNCIL OF EUROPE 2001). Along with this, the development of computer-mediated e-mail communication has lead to a growing importance of purposeful interactive writing with a real audience. As a result, traditional distinctions between speech and writing can no longer be maintained and writing has become a collaborative process (KREEFT PEYTON 1999).

Purposes of education

Last but not least: developing writing skills is seen as part of developing students' literacy of which learner autonomy is a part.

2 Purposes of real-life writing

Different classifications

As with speaking, there are different classifications of writing. The Council of Europe distinguishes between written interaction, production and mediation (COUNCIL OF EUROPE 2001: 61–2, 82–4, 87):

- 'Written interaction' includes activities like passing and exchanging notes or memos, correspondence, or participating in computer-mediated discourse, for example.
- 'Written production' includes activities like completing forms or questionnaires, writing articles or reports, producing posters, making notes, creative writing, or writing letters.
- 'Written mediation' we find in translations of contracts, for example, or when summarising the gist of newspaper articles.

3 Research into writing and consequences for EFL writing in the classroom

A model of the writing process

Research into writing has studied the mental processes of writers when writing in their mother language for about twenty years. In the 1980s two teams of researchers developed cognitive models of the writing process which were based on results of their experimental research on the writing process, FLOWER and HAYES, and BEREITER and SCARDAMALIA. They based their research on protocol analysis of students talking aloud while they were writing. The following figure shows the FLOWER and HAYES model as represented in GRABE and KAPLAN (1996: 92):

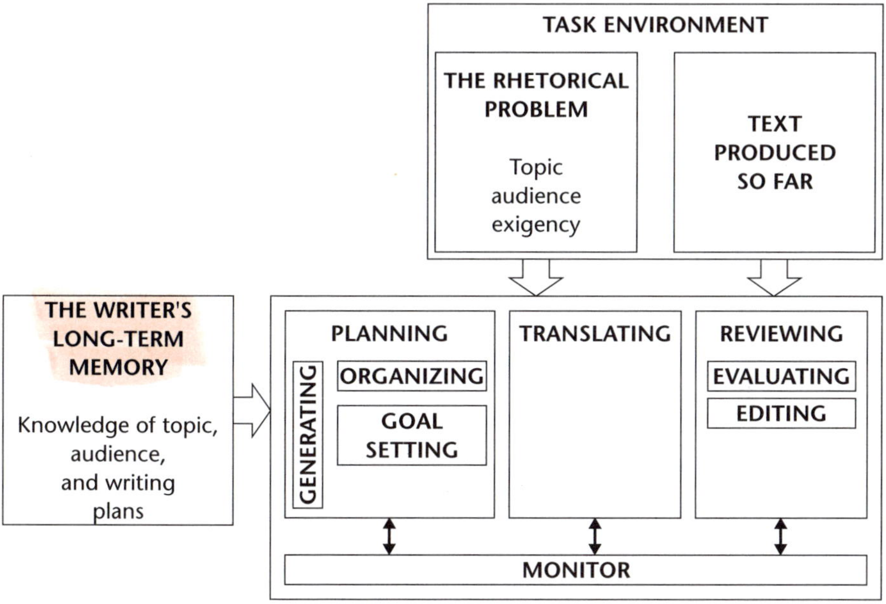

Model 3.2: The FLOWER *and* HAYES *writing process model*
(GRABE/KAPLAN 1996: 92)

It divides the composing processes of a writer into three major components: 'the composing processor' (three processes generate the written text: 'planning, translating, reviewing'; these processes are managed by a control called monitor); 'the task environment', and 'the writer's long-term memory.' As a result writing has been described as a complex cognitive skill and multi-draft process: *"The process of writing sees it as thinking, as discovery. Writing is the result of employing strategies to manage the composing process, which is one of gradually developing a text. It involves a number of activities: setting goals, generating ideas, organizing information, selecting appropriate language, making a draft, reading and reviewing it, then revising and editing. It is a complex process which is neither easy nor spontaneous for many second language writers"* (HEDGE 2000: 302). Different authors have tried to depict this complex process using slightly different foci in their models. KEH (1996), for example, defines writing as a process which consists of *"generating ideas (pre-writing); writing a first draft with an emphasis on content (to 'discover' meaning/author's ideas); second and third (and possibly more) drafts to revise ideas and the communication of those ideas. Reader feedback on the various drafts is what pushes the writer through the writing process on to the eventual end-product"* (KEH 1996: 294; for more alternative models see COUNCIL OF EUROPE: 63–4: Production strategies). Further research findings relate to the following aspects:

Choice of topic

Students write more in their target language when they are writing about information which they are familiar with (FRIEDLANDER 1990, in: GRABE/KAPLAN 1996: 205).

The social context

The social context of learning (the classroom, the other students, the interactions among the teacher and the students) has a profound impact on the development of writing ability (HEATH 1993, JOHNS 1990, RAIMES 1991, in: GRABE/KAPLAN 1997: 239).

Support and teacher role

Students value student-teacher conferences where the teacher is able to ask for clarification, check comprehension of oral comments made, help the writer sort through problems, assist the student in decision-making. This has not only had a beneficial effect on writing, but also helped to build up the students' confidence in oral work (KEH 1996: 300). "[T]*eachers need to show a positive attitude, believing that students are capable of doing the work* [...]. *Teachers need to provide students with a wide range of opportunities for writing* [... and] *to develop among students a sense of community and sharing so that writing can become a collaborative and cooperative endeavour.* [...] *They need to be aware* [... that] *writing takes time to develop,* [... that] *writing can sometimes be difficult and frustrating, and students need positive feedback and enough success to maintain a willingness to work;* [...] *students should be encouraged, at times, to take risks, to innovate, and to rethink assignments in more complex ways"* (GRABE/KAPLAN 1996: 254–255). The central role of the teacher has been supported by socio-cognitive approaches to writing development which have evolved out of VYGOTSKY's theories of language and literacy development (see chap. 2.1).

Instruction

Another insight into research on writing derives from studies which have tested how effective different instructional techniques are. Some of the factors that are important are multiple drafting, time for planning, and drafting and revising. There is also evidence that writing tasks produce poor results not because the process is too demanding for learners but because they get bored by all the drafting, editing, and polishing of their texts (GRABE/KAPLAN 1996: 243–244).

Feedback: Content or form?

Studies have shown that a focus on form during feedback is no less effective than a focus on content. But feedback ought to focus on both content and form to contribute to improvement in revisions (GRABE/KAPLAN 1996: 238). CAMERON suggests a good example for classroom procedure: when students are editing their drafts and checking work with others *"it may be helpful to focus on one or two features only at each stage. An initial draft might be read aloud to a group for comments on how well others will understand its overall idea. A later draft might be checked in pairs for verb endings or use of the definite and indefinite articles"* (CAMERON 2001: 156).

4 Writing in the EFL classroom

A neglected skill

Few teachers feel adequately prepared to teach writing because writing composition pedagogy has only recently received attention in teacher education. Therefore it may come as not much of a surprise when student teachers report that they have received little if any process writing instruction during their EFL lessons at school.

Features of EFL-writing

Research into EFL composition has been substantially influenced by mother language writing research. Similar patterns have been identified but there are also some differences. Writing problems that are typical of composition in the mother language, such as planning, structuring, choice of content, for example, are aggravated due to the fact that writing is in a foreign language. ESSER (2003: 292) mentions orthographic ('How do I spell ...?'), grammatical ('Do I need the definite article here?'), lexical ('What is ... in English?') and text type – related problems (Which address form is appropriate?). They interrupt the flow of L2 text production, which is why the text production process is slower, and not as automatized as in students' mother language, and therefore needs more support and time to develop.

Types of writing

Writing may focus on students expressing their feelings and ideas in a climate of encouragement – creative writing. Or it may focus on different types of discourse organisation in written texts (= 'genres' or 'text types') – genre writing: *"As children develop as readers and writers, and cope with longer texts, they will begin to notice and use the patterns of organisation in different text types. Teachers can support this by using texts from a range of genres and by making explicit the structure of typical information texts or story texts, and showing children how the parts are put together"* (CAMERON 2001: 156).

Activities

Activities suggested in methodology books follow the chronology of the writing process in that they structure activities which help to prepare writing, to produce texts and to revise texts (ESSER 2003: 293–94). HEDGE (2000: 308–16) follows a similar structure and gives examples for activities which help students to generate ideas, to provide practice in planning, to develop a sense of audience and to encourage revision strategies.

5 Perspectives

Assessment

Assessment of process writing products is extremely time-consuming. One appropriate way of assessing process writing is portfolio evaluation, *"in which several representative, drafted samples of student writing are considered in an overall evaluation. Despite the advantages* [...] *the design of evaluation criteria [is] extremely complex, and results do not seem to differ substantially from more traditional writing assessment formats (Hamp-Lyons 1996)"* (Reid 2001: 31).

CMC writing

Encourage computer-mediated writing in EFL classrooms with authentic audiences so that students experience the real-life purposes of writing and develop the skills needed to do so. This is best done in collaborative action research projects where teachers integrate their students' perspectives to identify efficient classroom procedures.

3.1.3 Listening

Dimensions of listening

The development of listening skills is essential for various reasons. Understanding input gained from listening triggers language acquisition and is therefore a primary vehicle for language learning; listening is not only important as a receptive skill (in 'non-participatory listening' situations, when we listen to a radio broadcast, for example), but is an integral part of an individual's communicative competence (it is essential to the development of speaking as part of interaction in 'participatory listening', as in face-to-face conversations, for example). It is a challenge for learners to understand authentic language as native speakers actually use it; and learners may attend to new forms in the language that is being presented to them while they listen (Rost 1994: 141–2). Listening is also the most widely used language skill in everyday life: of the time an individual is engaged in communication, approximately 45 per cent is devoted to listening – and only approximately 9 per cent to writing, 16 per cent to reading, and 30 per cent to speaking (Hedge 2000: 228).

The current situation

Listening is a very complex process, but it has been well researched and therefore there are quite a lot of useful suggestions about how teachers can support learners to become good listeners. However, teaching methodology in the mainstream has not yet caught up with theory and has taken insufficient account of what we know about the processes applied by learners while they listen. We will therefore begin by describing the process of listening and we will use this information to set out classroom procedures that actually help learners to develop the ability to listen. As you will see, much of what we say about how the process of listening works relates to reading as well.

1 What do we know about the listening process?

Different types of knowledge: bottom-up and top-down skills

Listening comprehension is a very complex process in which different types of both linguistic and non-linguistic knowledge are involved. On a very general level it can be described as an active process of constructing meaning which is carried out by applying knowledge to the incoming sound (BUCK 2001: 31). There has been much debate about how this knowledge is applied, and there are two views that refer to the order in which the different types of knowledge are applied during the comprehension process: the bottom-up view and the top down view (i. e. BUCK 2001: 2).

Bottom-up: The input to the listener: Applying knowledge of the language

In the bottom-up part of the listening process we use our knowledge of the language (phonology, lexis, syntax, semantics, discourse) to make sense of the sounds we hear. The information we use is contained in the speech itself. We segment speech into sounds which we structure in terms of words, phrases, sentences. The acoustic input is often indistinct (speakers modify the sounds, there are elisions and weak forms, for example), but there are several clues we can use to infer meaning from the developing speech. Types of knowledge we use when we try to understand spoken language involve the following:

1. In English, the prosodic features of the language, stress and intonation, carry a great deal of communicative information and are therefore closely related to meaning. Speakers stress what they consider important, they use pauses to mark the boundary of 'sense' groups or idea units; intonation marks questions or indicates when it is appropriate for the listener to respond. Songs are particularly suitable for practising recognition of word divisions in that learners use the context to help them choose the correct form (for example, did she say 'I scream or ice-cream?'). You can raise awareness of this (and add some fun to your work!) if you make 'mondegreens', that is the mishearing of popular song lyrics, the topic of some of your listening lessons (see SMITH 2003). Funny examples include the mishearing of 'Excuse me, while I kiss this guy' *(Excuse me, while I kiss the sky, J. Hendrix)*, 'Dead ants are my friends, they're blowing in the wind' *(The answer my friend, is blowing in the wind, B. Dylan)*, 'Doughnuts make your brown eyes blue' *(Don't it make your brown eyes blue, E. John)* or 'Partially saved was Mary and Tom' *(Parsley, sage, rosemary and thyme, Simon* and *Garfunkel)*. Enter 'mondegreen' in one of the search engines and you will be surprised how much fun difficult listening input can be.

2. There are quite a number of other linguistic features apart from stress, intonation and recognition of word division listeners use to process incoming speech. WHITE (1998: 8) provides the following checklist of sub-skills involved in bottom-up listening which shows the wide range of possible skills:

Perception skills

- *recognizing individual sounds*
- *discriminating between sounds*
- *identifying reduced forms in fast speech (for example, elision and assimilation)*
- *identifying stressed syllables*
- *identifying stressed words in utterances*
- *recognizing intonation patterns.*

Language skills

- *identifying individual words and groups and building up possible meanings for them*
- *identifying discourse markers which organize what is being said, for example then, as I was saying, as a matter of fact, to start with.*

3. Listeners also *use their lexical and syntactical knowledge* to help them make sense of what they hear. HEDGE (2000: 230) uses the following example to illustrate this point: On picking out a sequence of known words from a news broadcast: 'hurricane … coast … Florida … damaged property … families homeless' we are able to assign the semantic roles of agent to the hurricane, the coast of Florida as the location, the damage to the property as the action and homelessness as the outcome. Or we may use 'connectors' (such as however, therefore, despite this) as clues to mark what is going to be the next part of the discourse.

Top-down: Using world knowledge

In contrast to bottom-up comprehension strategies which use the information that is available within the text itself, top-down strategies refer to the knowledge a listener brings to a text. This is therefore sometimes also referred to as 'inside the head' information. Processing texts presupposes a great deal of non-linguistic general knowledge about the world we live in which BUCK (2001: 18) classifies into two categories:

- knowledge of the context which may support or restrict understanding and
- knowledge of specific facts or of how things usually happen that can be used to fill in details that are not explicitly stated in the text.

We apply our knowledge of the world by means of 'inferencing' (for different types of inferences see BUCK 2001: 18–9) which is based on shared background knowledge. It is assumed that this background knowledge, our world knowledge, is stored in memory and used when comprehension of texts is asked for. A number of theories have been developed to understand the way in which our knowledge is stored, two of the most commonly used are 'script theory' and 'schemata'.

Script theory

The idea of script theory (SCHANK/ABELSON 1977 in BUCK 2001: 20) is *"that an utterance sets up expectations, in the form of a script, about what normally happens in that context. The script is a mental structure which describes stylised, everyday situations"*. Typical scripts, for example, are the routines performed at an airport check-in desk, at a restaurant, or when buying a ticket. The knowledge of a familiar sequence of events about an often experienced situation which listener and speaker share, makes many listening situations quite predictable. From this it follows that scripts tend to be culture bound as they may vary from one culture to the next.

Schemata

Schemata (RUMELHART/ORTONY 1997, in: BUCK 2001: 20) describe the structure which explains the organization of a text or discourse. The schema underlying many stories, for example, is that there is a formulaic introduction ('Once upon a time'), that it consists of a setting where time, place, and characters are identified, where different episodes lead to an outcome which is possibly followed by a moral comment.

Context

The social situation in which communication takes place considerably influences interpretation. Aspects of context include visual non-verbal information which may either supplement or contradict the verbal message, or they may include a shared knowledge of sociocultural norms and how they may be interpreted appropriately.

Summary

It would be wrong to assume that the two models of language comprehension – bottom up and top down – oppose each other. *"It is now generally accepted that both function simultaneously and are mutually dependent. The current model of listening is therefore an interactive one in which linguistic information, contextual clues, and prior knowledge interact to enable comprehension"* (HEDGE 2000: 234–5). Processing of the different types of knowledge does not occur in a fixed sequence. Rather, different types of processing may occur simultaneously, or in any order. This is why the process of listening is also sometimes referred to as an interactive process (BUCK 2001: 2–3) or as parallel processing (ROST 2001: 7), where representations at one level creates activation at other levels: *"To summarise the process, the listener takes the incoming data, the acoustic signal, and interprets that, using a wide variety of information and knowledge, for a particular communicative purpose; it is an inferential process, an ongoing process of constructing and modifying an interpretation of what the text is about, based on whatever information seems relevant at the time"* (BUCK 2001: 29). Before we look at the ways in which these research results can be used to develop effective listening procedures in the classroom, we will first take a brief look at what types of text and what purposes for listening we find in real-life listening, as they will determine the range of listening purposes relevant to our students' lives outside the classroom. We will have to take account of these when we develop listening comprehension in our classrooms.

2 Purposes for listening

The *Common European Framework* lists the following listening activities (2001: 65; for a review of different lists of purposes as provided by different authors see HEDGE 2000: 243):

- *listening to public announcements (information, instructions, warnings etc.);*
- *listening to media (radio, TV, recordings, cinema);*
- *listening as a member of a live audience (theatre, public meetings, public lectures, entertainments, etc.);*
- *listening to overheard conversations etc.*

In each case the user may be listening:

- *for gist*
- *for specific information*
- *for detailed understanding*
- *for implications etc.*

Text selection for the classroom may range from 'scripted' talks to 'unscripted' natural spontaneous conversation. Texts may also fall into a third category which has been termed 'semi-authentic' texts which GEDDES and WHITE define as follows: *"language produced for a pedagogical purpose but exhibiting features which have a high probability of occurrence in genuine acts of communication"* (GEDDES/WHITE 1978: 137, in: HEDGE 2000: 246).

3 What makes listening easy or difficult?

Uncertainties for learners

Listening has various features which make it a very challenging skill to develop. In contrast to written language, speech is encoded in the form of sounds, takes place in real time with no chance of review, and is linguistically different from written language (BUCK 2001: 4; for a detailed survey of research results see BUCK 2001, chap. 1 and 2). Some linguistic features that are typical of spontaneous speech include repetitions, pauses, fillers, restructurings in complex sentences, self-corrections, false starts, incomplete utterances, contracted forms, a random order of information, speakers speaking at the same time or interrupting each other, and a higher proportion of colloquial language with a variety of accents. Teachers need to know about these difficulties so that they can help learners build confidence in dealing with 'difficult' texts. HEDGE refers to a useful framework provided by a communications researcher who categorized *"the major areas of uncertainty"* in foreign language listening. Among these are uncertainties in speech sounds and patterns, in language and syntax, in content, and uncertainties caused by environmental noise and disturbance which create gaps in the message (CHERRY 1957, in: HEDGE 2000: 236). We will draw on this work in the following section.

Purpose

Often learners have unrealistic ideas about what is expected of them when they are listening. In some classrooms learners believe that successful listening is about trying to understand each word of a listening text and they immediately give up and lose confidence if they come across a word they do not understand. But listening is not about training parrots and learners are not tape recorders (both metaphors used by ANDERSON/LYNCH 1988); they do not need to be able to reproduce a message word-by-word but rather need to learn to be able to interpret and use the information to complete a particular task for a particular purpose. In real-life situations we listen for a number of different purposes which will determine what we need to understand. Therefore, learners need to be clear just about why they are listening so that they can focus their listening on the content relevant to complete the task (see above for a survey of purposes and see task example below for how you can give a purpose for listening).

Activating context and prior knowledge

Consider the following text (SCHOCKER-V. DITFURTH 1997: 34). What is it about? What do you think you would remember about it after you have listened to it ? *"First of all you need the motivation. It takes a lot of time and commitment on your part and discipline, too. A good motivation is travelling, I found. And I find what helped me a lot was – um – listening to tapes, trying to pick up books: first, children's books, very easy reading, where you can go ... it's not too difficult. One thing you should try and always do is read. Read as ... read, read, read, as often as you can. Don't try and read a book that's too complicated, that's very discouraging. But if you have a fairly easy text, don't be shy to pick up a children's book. That's how everybody starts. And that way it's fun, it's interesting ... all the time. And what I do is I keep a journal and I just have to keep going over and over it. I also make – er – little show cards ... I play with them, really, you know. And I would rent videos. I would go and find videos of fairy-tales and – er – these are fairy-tales we grow up with as children so you know the story already."* While most learners in their fifth year of English at *Realschule* would have little trouble in comprehending the words and phrases in this message (the example is taken from authentic listening materials that have been compiled for this group of learners), they would probably find it difficult to demonstrate comprehension by giving a precise verbal recall of the text. If you provide the context of the text, however, then the task becomes relatively simple: If listeners are told that the text is about a young woman who is talking about how she learns foreign languages, then the individual constituents of the text are much more readily interpretable. The task becomes easier still, when teachers

- support listeners to activate their own knowledge resources before they listen; they will support understanding by raising expectations and asking them to make predictions about what they might hear and
- give the reason why learners are to listen to a text.

In the example above you may ask learners first to think about and discuss their own language learning strategies, maybe ask them to agree on five strategies they all favour ('pre-listening task'). While listening they could then tick the strategies the young woman favours and add any new strategies she is talking about ('while-listening purpose'). This helps learners to focus their listening on content relevant to doing the task.

Features of texts and tasks

One element in the listening process that makes listening easy or difficult obviously is the kind of text you present. Apart from the text features that are typical of speech and distinguish spoken language from the language of written texts (see above), the degree of difficulty will depend on a number of other factors:

- the amount of information that needs to be processed (but mind you: short texts may be more difficult than longer texts if the information they provide is very dense and if there is not much redundancy, that is, repeated information re-stated in different ways);
- the number of speakers involved;
- the pace of delivery (do they speak slowly or rather fast);
- the speaker's accent;
- the environmental background noises (which may be distracting);
- if speakers can be seen on video so that visual clues can support understanding (the use of audio cassettes unnecessarily restricts understanding);
- on the familiarity of topic for learners and if they are interested in what they will hear.

To build learners' confidence they will have to get used to dealing with authentic speech. Different types of listening texts and careful grading of text selection is therefore important. Regardless of the inherent difficulty of text, the task and the kind of preparation learners get will have an influence on text difficulty. It makes an enormous difference if, for example, you present learners a text where different people discuss the quality of the local public transport system at a bus-stop and ask them to find out if people generally approve or do not approve ('listening for general understanding') or if they have to find out the pros and cons that every individual speaker comes up with and take notes on these to demonstrate what they have understood ('listening for details').

Interactive strategies

Developing listening skills, as we have seen, is just as important as developing speaking skills as we cannot communicate face-to-face unless the two skills are developed in tandem. Under many circumstances, listening is a reciprocal skill where there is the opportunity for speaker and listener to exchange roles. This is in contrast to how learners experience listening skills development in the classroom: *"Too often in the classroom, students are listening to disembodied and unfamiliar voices on a tape recorder which they cannot stop, interrogate, or interact with in any way.* [... But] *listeners play a very important and active role in keeping conversations going, by showing interest and sympathy, and by causing speakers to modify or repeat things. (...) Good listeners make good speakers, and vice-versa"* (WHITE 1998: 6). This is why strategy training to compensate for uncertainties in understanding is important as this prepares learners to take an active role in real-life communication. This way they may build up confidence and autonomy: they need to learn how to signal that they need clarification if part of a message has not been understood. And, vice versa, they need to be able to indicate to the speaker that he or she is still holding our interest. Some examples for conversational modification strategies that learners need to be familiar with are (see LIGHTBOWN/SPADA 1999: 43):

- comprehension checks to ensure that the message has been understood ('Do you see what I mean? Do you understand'?)
- clarification requests or queries to get the speaker to clarify something that has not been understood or to confirm that it has been understood correctly ('Sorry, I didn't get this. Could you repeat that, please? Are you saying that ...'?)
- self-repetition or paraphrase to repeat the message partially or entirely using different words to do so ('We went to the movies, to the cinema, to see a film, a film about ...')

For an example of how you can practise this strategy with your learners see SCHOCKER-V. DITFURTH (1996: 56). For excellent suggestions of ways of teaching listening that will help learners resolve comprehension problems see LYNCH (1996). Let us now use the points and issues raised above and see how they translate into a methodology for the teaching of listening in classrooms that supports learners to develop their listening abilities.

4 An effective methodology for the teaching of listening

Task example

There is now wide-spread uniformity of approach to listening which allows teachers to follow a relatively comfortable routine procedure for dealing with listening texts (WHITE 1998: 3). We would therefore like to illustrate a typical procedure of pre-, while-, and post-listening stages by giving you an example task first and then discussing the rationale behind it, and by offering more examples of activity types you can use at each of the three stages. You find the example in SCHOCKER-V. DITFURTH 1999 (11, 36, 38–40). In the text example different students are talking about their ideas of friendship.

Pre-listening

As we have already said, the teacher will have to tell learners why they are going to listen to the text, what it is they should find out ('listening purpose') so that they can focus their attention on the relevant aspects of the text. Learners will need to 'tune in' to the topic and the context of the text. To help them to do this, you can use tasks that 'activate what they already know' and that 'raise their expectations' of what they might hear. You may also ask your learners to explicitly 'predict' what they may hear. In the example above this is achieved by asking learners to write a text about their own ideas of friendship and to share ideas in their group. The network they produce as a result of this ('product') is used to prepare the while-listening stage, during which they will be asked 'to confirm their expectations' while they are listening. It also helps learners to understand if you inform them about the 'context' of the text (who is talking to whom, what is their relationship to each other, why are they talking to each other, where are they). In the example above you might say: 'You are going to listen to five students who are talking about their ideas of friendship. They are from different countries: Senta, Dietmar and Karl-Heinz are from Germany, Helen is from England, and Matt is from the United States'. Whatever it is you do to prepare listening, make sure that the kind of activity you offer reflects what you would normally do with a listening text in a real-life communicative situation. Some of the pre-listening activity types you can use are looking at pictures and talking about them, looking at lists of items or making lists, reading a text, reading or generating questions to be answered while listening, labelling, completing a chart, predicting/ speculating, pre-viewing language or a class discussion (UNDERWOOD 1989).

While-listening

While-listening *"needs to link in relevant ways to the pre-listening work"* (HEDGE 2000: 252). In the example above this is achieved by asking learners 'to compare their thoughts and ideas' on friendship to the views they get from the students they are asked to listen to. Another principle is to design tasks that allow learners 'to focus on listening' and not add to the processing load by asking them to write or read lengthy texts. Activities that are useful in this respect include marking or checking items in pictures, matching pictures with what is heard, putting pictures in order, completing or drawing pictures, carrying out actions, making models, following a route, completing grids, forms, charts, labelling, using lists, true/false statements or multiple choice questions, text completion (filling gaps), or spotting mistakes (UNDERWOOD 1989). It is also important 'to progress from easy to more difficult tasks' within the comprehension of one text. To do so, you may 'progress from global understanding to listening for detail' (like in the example above, where people discuss the quality of public transport and learners are first asked to find out for each person if he or she approves or disapproves of public transport and while listening to the text a second time they are asked to take notes on the reasons why they approve or disapprove). Finally, it helps to build confidence in learners if you ask them to do the listening tasks in pairs if they are not used to working on this skill. In this way they can discuss together what they think they have understood first before they give their feedback.

Post-listening

There are basically two purposes you can think of when you ask learners to get more intensively involved in the topic that they have dealt with in the listening text. You may either focus on activities that lead to a 'consolidation of the language' presented in the text or on ones that offer 'extension of content': You either use additional texts to do with the topic or you 'integrate' listening comprehension with developing the other skills – reading, speaking, writing activities – to develop the topic further. Here are some examples for each focus of post-listening work:

- consolidation of language: you may practise phrases to express a certain speech function that learners have heard in a dialogue they listened to or you may practise connectors that learners have heard in a story to write their own stories
- extension of content by integrating skills: activities include the completion of forms or charts, extending lists, matching what you have heard with a reading text, extending notes into written responses, summarising, using information for problem-solving and decision-making activities, role-play and simulation (UNDERWOOD 1989).

For more examples of how to stage the listening process using authentic texts for secondary school learners (including songs) see SCHOCKER-V. DITFURTH (1997, 1999).

5 Issues and perspectives

Teacher talk

Developing listening skills is not just about asking learners to listen to cassettes or watching videos with authentic recordings of language. Following HEDGE we are convinced that probably the most vital element in learning to listen effectively is confidence, which comes with practice from an early stage (HEDGE 2000: 255). This can only be achieved if the teacher is a positive role model, that is, if he or she is able to manage classroom discourse in the target language and to establish routines with learners to enable them to participate in the classroom discourse in the target language. This way listening and interacting in the target language becomes an established routine of classroom work.

Classroom research

WHITE (1998: 5–6) draws our attention to the fact that one of the things that we perhaps do not spend enough time on is looking at how students are failing to hear: *"If enough students do not get the right answer, my typical reaction is to play that section of the tape once more, and hope that hearing it again will magically help the students to get the answer next time. I do not look at what might be causing the problem. This goes with a tendency for me as the teacher to focus on the product of listening (did the students get the right answers?) rather than the processes that are going on while they are actually listening."* Studying individual learners' listening processes with regard to how much a learner understands (product), the strategies a learner uses to gain understanding (process) and how the learner views or experiences his or her own difficulties and progress (learner perception) can be made the content of classroom research projects (ROST 2001: 12). LYNCH (1996) provides some interesting studies for these three aspects of listening that teachers may use as models to create their own listening research projects.

Students as active participants

Many authors of books about teaching listening express their dissatisfaction with the situation of classroom listening where learners are often reduced to the role of passive 'overhearers' as teachers take the responsibility for building up an understanding of the listening text in students, not developing individual responsibility. WHITE (1998) offers a multitude of ideas on ways in which learners can be given a bigger role in the choice of materials and types of activity and a greater control of the listening process by making the listening more personal to them.

3.1.4 Reading

Importance of reading

Reading in second language settings has become increasingly important: *"The overwhelming majority of societies* [...] *around the world are multilingual, and educated citizens are expected to function well in more than one language. L2 reading ability, particularly with English as the L2, is already in great demand as English continues to spread, not only as a global language but also as the language of science, technology and advanced research"* (GRABE/STOLLER 2002: 2).

Insufficient research

As reading teachers we face the difficult task of having to prepare our learners without the support of a generally agreed on body of research knowledge. And the number of variables involved makes it hard to generalise from the research literature to a specific classroom context: *"We actually know very little about how people become good L2 readers* [... T]*here are too many diverse types of L2 learners to generalise from the few existing studies that have been done well"* (ibid). On the other hand, much of what has been learnt about L2 reading in the past few years has not made its influence felt in the classroom (WALTER 2003: 314). In our current understandings of how children learn to read much remains unknown which is why CAMERON (2001: 123) concludes that *"in the absence of relevant research findings, we will often need to rely on clear thinking and carefully monitored practice as guides in the classroom."* We will first illustrate some aspects of the nature of reading with an example from our secondary EFL context.

1 What is reading?

A task example

Just as with listening, we are concerned here with a highly complex skill which is made up of a number of sub-skills. Take the following example: The text has been used with a 5th form *Realschule* (1st year of learning English) as part of a mini-unit on pets by SCHOCKER – V. DITFURTH. Groups of learners chose an internet text about a pet of their liking (www.petoftheday.com) and tried to guess the meaning of the underlined words which were unfamiliar to them. We asked them to identify the clues that helped them find out. Which kinds of knowledge, do you think they used to work out the meanings? The text we chose as an example is about a pot-bellied pig called Madeline who lives with a family in New York.

Pet of the Day

October 5, 2001

- Today's Pet
- Nominate Your Pet
- Previous Pets
- Pet Talk
- Pet Poll
- Search
- Links
- Mailing Lists
- Viewing Tips
- Why
- About Us

Name: Madeline **Age:** Three months old
Gender: Female **Kind:** Pot-Bellied Pig
Home: New York, USA

Madeline is about three months old, and is a beautiful pet to have. We adopted her when she was about one month old. She is the boss in our household and she can do a ton of tricks, and is very clever, and she loves to eat. Her favorite meals are corn, tomatoes, and apples. One of her best tricks is to "pirouette", which she can easily do... [she goes around in a circle, like a ballerina]. She can also hop. She likes to snuggle with me in the evening on the sofa. She loves to be with people and she is a wonderful new addition to our family.

Types of knowledge involved

Learners were struggling to make sense of the meaning of words by using the following types of knowledge:

- Morphological knowledge: Learners were familiar with the word 'add' and therefore they recognized the derivation by affixing the bound morpheme '-ition' to mark nouns. This is why they had no difficulty in identifying the word meaning of 'addition'.
- Syntactic knowledge: 'hop' follows the modal 'can' which makes it likely that 'hop' is a main verb, something that the little pig 'can do'. Combined with learners' L1 knowledge most learners were able to guess the meaning correctly.
- Semantic knowledge / knowledge of co-text: in the text the statement 'she is very clever' is followed by an example of why Madeline is clever: 'she can do a ton of tricks'. Combined with learner's L1 knowledge they found it easy to identify the meaning of 'a ton of tricks'.
- Knowledge of word meaning inferred from L1: many of the unknown words in the text can be inferred by making analogies between L1 words learners are familiar with as they resemble the words in the target language, for example 'adopt' (adoptieren), 'corn' (Popcorn), 'ballerina', 'tricks', 'household'. *"When we meet a new language, our brain / mind automatically tries to apply the first language experience by looking for familiar cues"* (CAMERON 2001: 136). But mind you: this may be problematic because despite their formal similarity learners need to be aware of 'false friends' and be prepared to develop new understandings that differ from those of their first language: "[T]*hey come with linguistic knowledge of their L1, even if most of it is tacit knowledge, and this knowledge can either support the transfer of reading skills or become a source of interference"* (GRABE/STOLLER 2002: 41).
- General world or topic knowledge: many learners guessed the meaning of 'snuggle' correctly because they knew from their own experience that this is what you may do with a pet in the evening on your sofa – 'snuggle up with it'.

So, as with listening comprehension, learners combine the information given within the text and other sources of information that are not inside the text but come from the reader's world, that readers bring to the text while reading to make sense. And just as with listening comprehension, different types of knowledge interact, and sometimes various types of knowledge interplay when a reader decodes the language of a text (see for example the decoding of the word 'hop'). For classroom methodology it follows that developing strategies for guessing word meanings from contextual clues and background knowledge is one major focus in helping students to build vocabulary for reading.

2 Models of reading comprehension

Models of reading

General models of reading which have been developed from reading research into L1 English interpret the many processes involved in reading comprehension in three ways: bottom-up models, top-down models, interactive models (GRABE/STOLLER 2002: 31). They are compatible with L2 reading research of the past decade (ibid: 37). As with listening comprehension these models may be described as follows:

Bottom-up: focus on text

In the bottom-up model, the reader creates a mental translation of the information in the text, from processing individual letters and words to processing sentences and the discourse organisation of a text. Skilled readers approach texts with expectations about how the texts will be organised. Take children, for example: From their early experience, they are likely to be familiar with narrative structure and their knowledge of the discourse organisation of stories help them *"know where important information will be found, and they can thus direct their attention efficiently, focusing in on key passages and skipping more lightly over passages with less important information"* (CAMERON 2001: 129). Text-focused research has shown strong links between phonemic awareness, the ability to process words automatically and rapidly and reading achievement (WALLACE 2001: 23). Genre theorists focus on texts as a whole. They emphasise the value for readers of an awareness of the distinctive features of different types of texts (particular discourse patterns and conventional ways of organisations of texts) and make them explicit to learners to support comprehension.

Top-down: focus on reader

This perspective on the reading comprehension process pays greater attention to the role of the reader. S/he has a number of expectations about the information s/he will find in the text. Expectations are based on the background knowledge (general knowledge of the world, topic knowledge) and values which the reader brings to the reading. Existing schemata allow a reader to relate new, text-based knowledge to existing knowledge (WALLACE 2001: 22). Inferencing and the reader's background knowledge are two prominent features of this model. While reading, expectations may be confirmed or rejected. Research is concerned with the strategies or resources which readers employ in reading. In this approach, reading is best seen *"as a process heavily mediated by the reader's ability to make informed predictions as he or she progresses through the text"* (WALLACE 2001: 24). This is why reading instruction may also focus on what the reader brings to reading: it attends to recovering existing knowledge before reading the text ('pre-reading activities') and making use of resources during text processing ('while-reading activities').

Interactive: focus on integration

In this model, bottom-up and top-down perspectives on the reading process are integrated: readers combine information from the text and the knowledge they bring with them to reading it: *"The 'construction' of meaning that occurs in reading is a combination of 'bottom-up' processes [decoding and understanding words, phrases and sentences in the text] and 'top-down' ones* [our expectations, previous knowledge constructs [schemata] of the text content and genre]. [...]*Thus, learners should be encouraged to combine top-down and bottom-up strategies in reading"* (UR 1996: 141). For more metaphors to explain the reading comprehension process see GRABE and STOLLER 2001, chap. 1.4. In second language classrooms readers will need help with both processes, bottom-up and top-down (HEDGE 2000: 190) and therefore reading methodology may pay attention to either the reader or the text, depending on the focus of the reading strategy training. *"No 'right' way of learning to read has been found, and when we consider the complexity of what has to be learnt, this should not be surprising"* (CAMERON 2001: 134).

3 On the relationship between L1 and L2 reading

L1 versus L2 reading

Much of what has been said above deals with first language reading (L1). The question is: How far does reading in a second language (L2) fit these orientations? There are two positions: either reading comprehension is perceived as a reading problem or it is seen as a language problem (WALLACE 2001: 22). In other words: Positions differ in that they emphasize the knowledge of the target language as a strong factor in reading comprehension or in that they emphasize general L1 reading ability for successful reading comprehension in the L2. Given a minimum level of L2 language competence, proficient L2 readers have been found to be good readers in their L1 (WALLACE 2001: 22). But transferability of knowledge across languages depends on how the two written languages work. As regards the relationship between English and German we can say that *"English is a complicated alphabetic written language, and almost always requires learners of it as a foreign language to develop new skills and knowledge, in addition to what can be transferred"* (CAMERON 2001: 136). L2 learners must broaden their linguistic knowledge, deal with transfer effects (see the text example on *pets* above), and learn to use L2 specific resources such as dictionaries (GRABE/STOLLER 2002: 41). For a detailed account of factors affecting learning to read in English as a foreign language see CAMERON 2001, chap. 6.3 and GRABE and STOLLER 2002, chap. 2.

4 Levels of involvement: Purposes and styles of reading

The level of involvement of the reader varies with the reason or purpose of reading. A variety of reading styles have been described where someone might read:

Varied involvement

'for gist (skimming)': readers wish to get a global impression of what the text is about – either about its main points or its global meaning; example: a reader is interested in the gist of a report about the probability of power cuts in the future. She wants to find out if it is an issue or not.

Skimming

'for specific information (scanning)': readers search rapidly through a text to find a specific point of information; example: a reader comes across an article on green energy but is only interested in solar energy and therefore scans the text for keywords to do with this aspect of the topic only.

Scanning

'for detailed understanding (intensive reading)': readers study a text carefully for all of the information it provides; example: a reader may analyse the use of the metaphors in a poem or study the conditions of a contract in detail. Intensive reading activities in the classroom often train students in the strategies needed for successful reading which is why texts are usually short.

Intensive

'for general understanding (extensive reading)': Extensive reading in the classroom has been characterized as follows: it is reading of large quantities of longer texts (short stories, novels, newspaper articles, for example), reading consistently over time on a frequent and regular basis, primarily for pleasure or interest, during class time but also engaging in individual independent reading at home, often of self-selected material (HEDGE 2000: 202). This is *"to give the child a sense of achievement and a taste of the pleasure to be derived from this accomplishment"* (HEDGE 2000: 200). Example: this effect can already be achieved in the primary EFL classroom when children are proud when they are able to understand an authentic picture story book in English. There are many ways of encouraging extensive reading. A very convincing suggestion which integrates the reading of young adult literature and writing has been recently put forward by HESSE (2002).

Extensive

Critical

Reading purposes may encourage a reader's critical engagement with a text. For this purpose, readers are encouraged to consider the underlying cultural contexts and purposes of texts and are guided to pay greater attention to social and ideological factors which mediate in readers' access to text (WALLACE 2001: 24 & 26; see chap. 4.1). The development of critical reading skills depends on an awareness on the part of the reader of how elements of language can be manipulated by writers. To help readers challenge the ideology of texts, quite a few procedures have been identified to help learners develop a critical perspective on what they read. CLARK (1993), for example, suggests the following pre-reading questions for students having to deal with academic texts. This activity may also be useful for learners of English in secondary school contexts:

Before reading the text
ask yourself the following questions:

- *Why am I reading this? What is my purpose? Why is it on my reading list?*
- *What do I know about the author, the publisher, the circumstances of publication and the type of text? How do these affect my attitude towards and expectations of what I am about to read?*
- *What are my own views of the event(s) or topic before I start reading this particular text?*
- *What other texts (written and spoken) on this or similar topics am I familiar with? What are my views about them?*
(CLARK 1993: 120, in: HEDGE 2000: 214).

Different purposes for reading determine different strategies in approaching texts. The next paragraph gives a brief overview of this.

5 The teaching of reading: Focus on strategy training

Pre-, while-, post-reading stages

Most methodological approaches use the three-phase procedure involving pre-, while-, post-reading stages. As similarities with listening comprehension are obvious, we have decided to depart from this standard staging, and structure tasks that help learners develop reading ability according to different strategies that may support reading comprehension. In L2 reading contexts not a lot of discussion is devoted to this topic, or so it seems. Strategy training seems to be a widely neglected area of teaching reading. In the following, we will refer to the reading activities to promote reading comprehension as provided by EHLERS (2003, chap. 4) and GRABE and STOLLER (2002, chap. 1.3).

Activities to promote development of lower-level skills: One of the most fundamental requirement for fluent reading comprehension is rapid and automatic word recognition or lexical access – the calling up of the meaning of a word as it is recognised. *"As amazing as it may seem, good readers can actually focus on a word and recognise it in less than a tenth of a second.* [...] *For good readers, lexical access is automatic. In addition to being very fast, it cannot be readily reflected on consciously, and it cannot be suppressed.* [...] *Both rapid processing and automaticity in word recognition* [...] *typically require thousands of hours of practice in reading"* (GRABE/STOLLER 2002: 21). As we already said above, learners need to be familiar with various strategies for identifying the meaning of unknown words, such as deriving word meaning from context, applying knowledge of word formation, or looking up the meaning of unfamiliar words in dictionaries. Fluent readers are also able to take in and store words together so that basic grammatical information can be extracted, a process known as syntactic parsing: *"The ability to recognise phrasal groupings, word ordering information, and subordinate and superordinate relations among clauses quickly is what allows good readers to clarify how words are supposed to be understood.* [...] *Syntactic parsing helps to disambiguate the meanings of words that have multiple meanings out of context"* (GRABE/STOLLER 2002: 22). Strategies to use syntactic knowledge are not developed by grammar instruction, but rather readers need countless hours of exposure to print, if they are to develop automaticity in using information from grammatical structures to assist them in reading (GRABE/STOLLER 2002: 23). A third basic process to build automaticity in reading comprehension that GRABE and STOLLER mention is semantic proposition formation: This is *"the process of combining word meanings and structural information into basic clause-level meaning units"* (ibid). As useful as activities to raise awareness of strategies at the level of syntax and semantics may be, we must not forget that intensive exposure to motivating texts in the target language is probably what promotes reading comprehension best.

Strategy training: lower level skills

Activities to promote development of higher-order skills: EHLERS (2003) gives examples of activities to help readers recognise connections that go beyond the level of sentences and which help readers to identify the internal structure of a text (discourse organisation, genre), or to identify the main ideas contained in a text. Higher-order skills are about reading for various purposes. *"Usually, a specific reading purpose will lead to greater or lesser emphases on different reading processes. So, reading to find simple information will emphasise word recognition abilities and some background knowledge anticipation of what items* [...] *to look for. Reading for general comprehension will use a balanced combination of text model compre-*

Strategy training: Higher-order skills

hension and situation model interpretation" (GRABE/STOLLER 2002: 29). GRABE and STOLLER emphasise that these processes do not operate efficiently when readers encounter texts that are too difficult for them – then successful reading comprehension is not likely to occur and learners may lose any motivation for reading. This may be a truism but it takes more than intensive strategy training to support reading comprehension.

6 Issues and perspectives

Internet

The age of technology growth is likely to make greater demands on people's reading abilities. At the same time, the availability of numerous texts from the internet makes it necessary for teachers and learners to be able to use indicators and criteria to evaluate the quality of internet resources. In other words, critical reading abilities become more and more important for learners. At the same time, being able to use online dictionaries to process texts with a certain number of unfamiliar words will be just as important (see survey on electronic learners' dictionaries by TRIBBLE 2003).

Classroom research projects

GRABE and STOLLER point to the fact that we actually know relatively little about how people become good L2 readers. *"It is also true that connections between research and reading instruction in L2 contexts are not well supported for a variety of reasons.* [...T]*here are too many diverse types of L2 learners to generalise from the few existing studies* [... or] *differing student L1s may limit general assertions from research* [... and] *great differences in L2 proficiency levels among student groups limit the generalisability of claims"* (GRABE/STOLLER 2002: 2). These difficulties reveal the need for teachers to develop their own investigative practices in their classrooms. GRABE and STOLLER hope to persuade teachers to carry out small-scale research projects on different aspects of reading in their classrooms so that by means of action research teachers may learn about their own teaching practices and improve student learning. They therefore outline a range of manageable action research projects in their book which is based on specific reading-related questions to help teachers add basic research enquiry to their expertise as teachers.

3.2 Subskills

3.2.1 Language as Discourse: Teaching Vocabulary and Grammar

1 Introduction

Lexis, grammar, and discourse

This chapter focuses on the teaching and learning of lexis and grammar, which are important aspects of linguistic competence (see chap. 2.1). The *Common European Framework* defines lexical competence as *"the knowledge of, and ability to use the vocabulary of a language"* which *"consists of lexical elements and grammatical elements"* (COUNCIL OF EUROPE 2001: 110). The grammar of a language is described by a *"set of principles governing the assembly of elements into meaningful labelled and bracketed strings (sentences),"* grammatical competence then is the ability to *"understand and express meaning by producing and recognising well-formed sentences in accordance with these principles"* (COUNCIL OF EUROPE 2001: 112–13). When you think back to your own school days, you will remember that grammar and vocabulary were generally taught separately as discrete items – as bilingual vocabulary lists and catalogues of grammar rules – which were rarely presented as being interrelated. But when we view language as a tool that you use to create meaning, then it is more appropriate to look at the different subsystems, such as words, grammar, and sounds as a coherent whole under the notion of discourse. Discourse has been defined as *"a general term for examples of language use, i.e. language which has been produced as a result of an act of communication. Whereas grammar refers to the rules a language uses to form grammatical units such as CLAUSE, PHRASE, and SENTENCE, discourse refers to larger units of language such as paragraphs, conversations, and interviews."* (RICHARDS et al 1992: 111). Instead of discrete building blocks that form sentences, discourse thus goes beyond the sentence level, covering all kinds of spoken and written texts.

Meaning, form, and function of language properties

This view of language has important pedagogical consequences for the teaching and learning of words, grammar, and sounds. We need to look afresh at what kind of language learners actually need to learn and how they most effectively make use of it in a communicative situation. The three language properties are characterized by the interrelated dimensions of form, meaning or function, and use. Words and sounds form the main building blocks of a language, providing basic units of meaning. While words may stand alone (e.g. Quiet!), they mostly take the form of language chunks which, *"when combined, produce continuous coherent text"* (LEWIS 1993: 7). If learners do not learn individual words but lexical units it is suggested that they will be stored as units or chunks in their mental lexicon and may therefore be recalled for production more easily. So, instead of learning the word 'bus' (which learners usually know), they might just as well learn 'get on the bus' or 'get off the bus', for example. Or, instead of just learning the work 'cake', they learn it in different contexts of use: 'Would you like to have a piece of cake?'; 'I like chocolate cake best'; 'This is a piece of cake'. Fluency is supported when a large pool of these *"fixed and semi-fixed prefabricated items,"* is available. On this basis a learner's grammatical competence allows *"the creative re-combination of lexis in novel and imaginative ways"* (LEWIS 1993: 15), and it allows meaning or function to be attached to his or her words, through a question ('Would you like to have a piece of cake?'), by a comment ('I like the chocolate cake best'.), or by using a fixed expression or metaphor ('This is a piece of cake', meaning: This is really easy.) An important part of this process is the emerging focus on the grammatical form by the learner. Supported by the teacher, who helps the learner notice the new grammatical forms, the learner begins to understand the rules that govern the language, and develops language awareness in the process.

Intercultural communicative competence

As we have seen, the main purpose of language learning is ICC (see chap. 2.1, also for a historical overview from a grammar-translation to a communicative approach). The meaning potential of lexis is crucial in this endeavour, since miscommunication is rarely *"caused by the interlocutors getting their linguistic facts wrong.* [The] *miscommunication occurs at the level of discourse. Communication breaks down because one person misinterprets the function of the other person's utterance"* (NUNAN 1999: 129). When participants in a conversation have different cultural codes the potential for miscommunication is increased since discourse functions are culturally determined. When taking leave of somebody in the U.S., for example, the lexical chunk 'See you later' might be employed. But this does not signify, as it would in a German context *(Wir sehen uns nachher oder: Bis später)* that you are actually going to meet that person again soon. Consequently, to avoid misunderstandings, learners must be supported in understanding culturally specific meaning of words and grammatical functions. The increasing focus on ICC was accompanied by a rising research interest in the lexical properties of language. One of the central questions was how language chunks are stored to facilitate language use. Research into the structure and function of the mental lexicon thus went hand in hand with the conviction that grammar and vocabulary are very much interrelated in language learning.

2 The mental lexicon: From storage to language production

Size of the English language

While reports on the size of the English language range from 400,000 to over 2 million words, a more reliable count are the 54,000 word families that *Webster's Third New International Dictionary* (1963) comprises. A word family consists of the base word (e.g. stimulate), all of its inflections (stimulated, stimulating), and its common derivatives (stimulative, stimulation) (NATION/WARING 1997: 6–7; SCHMITT 2000: 2–3). Native speakers (university graduates) know about 20,000 word families. Apart from frequency, another helpful category for important word knowledge is range, i.e. the occurrence of a word across the different written and oral texts of a language. Words that are not limited to appearance in one text form (e.g. in a poem) should be given the priority.

Frequency of words

How many words then do language learners need to know to get by? Since not all words are equally useful, high-frequency words (*the*, for example, makes up 7% of the words in written and spoken texts) are more important for learners. The best known frequency list, WEST's General Service List (1953), covers 2,000 word families which ensure a comprehension of about 80% of any text. Successful guessing through context of the unknown words in a written text is possible, but only if learners already know at least 95% of a text's words. Thus learners would need to develop a vocabulary pool of about 3–5,000 word families to possess a sufficient basis for reading comprehension (NATION/WARING 2000). Modern dictionaries, such as the *Collins Cobuild English Dictionary*, are based on linguistic corpora (see below) and include frequency as one criterion of usage in their selection of words. While frequency is an important criterion for word selection, topic specificity, i.e. what learners actually want to learn, and words that are necessary for classroom management are other important criteria that need to be taken into consideration when selecting the words that are directly taught (SCHMITT 2000: 144).

The mental lexicon

But how is this vast amount of language stored in our brain? Storing takes place in the mental lexicon, *"the word-store in the human mind"* (AITCHINSON 1992: 59) which functions like an interface that allows the storage of sense impressions (sounds etc.) in mentally represented knowledge structures, as well as the production of language from these knowledge structures, i.e. language use. In the mental lexicon words are stored semantically by association, i.e. the stimulus of a certain word brings up other words. The stimulus word bicycle, for example, would bring up associations such as ride, fall off, sport, fun, exhaustion or transport, depending on one's personal and cultural knowledge. SCHMITT (2000: 39–40) distinguishes between three kinds of associations: (a) clang associations (which are not related semantically, but in terms of sound), such as reflect-effect; (b) paradigmatic associations, where words are related to other words of the same class such as synonyms (e.g. stream and brook) or antonyms (e.g. hot and cold) as well as derivations, such as prefixes and suffixes (e.g. im/possible or help/ful), and word combinations (e.g. blackboard; (c) syntagmatic associations that generally focus on different word classes such as adjective-noun pairs (e.g. broad shoulders) or verb-noun pairs (e.g. ride a bicycle) that often form larger units such as collocations (e.g. the line is busy) and idioms (e.g. to kick the bucket).

3 Lexicogrammar or the lexical approach

Lexico-grammar

The mental lexicon thus creates lexical cohesion among words, establishing *"a spiderweb of grammatical and semantic relationships between a large number of words"* (SCHMITT 2000: 106). Language then is organized more or less in form of lexical phrases, *"multi-word lexical phenomena that exist somewhere between the traditional poles of lexis and syntax."* They may be organized into three fields for teaching purposes which reflect the functional-notional approach to language learning: *"social interactions"* (how to communicate in a restaurant, i.e. asking for the bill etc.), *"necessary topics"* (e.g. talking about food), and *"discourse devices"* (e.g. avoiding repetition: expensive, costly) (NATTINGER/DECARRICO, in: LITTLE 1994: 115).

Chunks of language

As NATTINGER (1988: 75) further points out, *"vocabulary is stored redundantly, not only as individual morphemes, but also as parts or phrases, or even as longer memorized chunks of speech, and that it is oftentimes retrieved from memory as these preassembled chunks."* Words in the semantic field of pets will include names of pets, adjectives to describe them, and verbs as to what pets can do. But when learning about pets, learners do not just learn the discrete items (dog, rabbit), instead they also learn them in larger chunks to be able to use them in a meaningful context (e.g. 'I like/don't like dogs because …'; 'My pet has got black/… eyes'; 'Her favourite food is grass/…'; 'My dog is bigger/… than yours'.). This form of storing language supports learners in developing language fluency, since it relieves "[them] *of concentrating on each individual word as it is used by allowing them to focus attention on the larger structure of the discourse and on the social aspects of the interaction"* (NATTINGER 1988: 77). It also helps them to develop a more colloquial use of English. Learners who are used to learning and storing individual word lists tend to translate utterances following their L1 grammar patterns.

This knowledge has found expression in the so-called lexical approach (LEWIS 1993). LEWIS argues that *"language consists of grammaticalized lexis not lexicalised grammar"* (1993: 89). Words and sounds form the basis of language learning. Combining them in meaningful ways and learning them in chunks allows the learner to communicate without focusing on grammar right away. For the learner it is important to tell her classmate that her horse is faster (see above), but not to have the exact knowledge of how to form the comparative. This implies an emphasis *"on the main carrier of meaning, vocabulary. The concept of a large vocabulary is extended from words to lexis, but the essential idea is that fluency is based on the acquisition of a large store of fixed and semi-fixed prefabricated items* [...]. *Grammatical knowledge permits the creative re-combination of lexis in novel and imaginative ways,"* but only if *"the learner has a sufficiently large mental lexicon to which grammatical knowledge can be applied"* (LEWIS 1993: 15). Lexical knowledge and grammatical knowledge are interrelated in a kind of 'lexicogrammar'. At some point learners want to express notions of space (see chap. 2.1) by using prepositions. They will want to point out that the cookies are 'in' the cookie jar that it is 'on top of' the cupboard, 'next to' the cereals. The use of the last two prepositions is different to what a learner with German as his/her L1 is used to. Knowing the words is therefore not sufficient, learners need to understand their grammatical function as well. As BATSTONE (1994: 8) points out, *"grammar does not exist on its own. It is inter-dependent with lexis, and in many cases grammatical regularity and acceptability are constrained and conditioned by words."* Through vocabulary acquisition, grammatical knowledge is extended and it becomes more transparent since learners actually want to be able to tell the English-speaking friend where the cookies are (SCHMITT 2000: 143). In fact, it is possible to divide the lexical system of most languages into *"grammatical words,"* such as prepositions, articles, adverbs, and so on, which form the majority of the high-frequency words, and content words (e.g. food items etc). *"The 'grammaticality' of vocabulary also manifests itself in word morphology, that is, the grammatical particles that we attach to the beginning and ends of words in order to form new words"* (NUNAN 1999: 101; e.g. help, helping, helper, helpful, unhelpful).

The lexical approach

Recent research in the field of language corpora has supported this view of *"showing the lexical patterning in discourse"* (SCHMITT 2000: 58). Looking at the frequency and distribution (patterns) of words in actual English language usage, corpus linguistics has shown, for example, that the term 'handsome' mainly appears in combination with male persons (MUKHERJEE 2002: 42). Dictionaries, such as the *Collins Cobuild English Dictionary* or the *Collins Cobuild English Grammar* are based on corpus research. The latter,

Research into language corpora

for example, also covers language functions, such as the function of showing strong feelings by using emphasizing adjectives. Apart from listing the adjectives, it describes the lexico-grammatical realizations of this function (from MUKHERJEE 2002: 124–25): *"He made me feel like a complete idiot. Some of it was absolute rubbish."* You generally use an adjective of this kind when the noun indicates your opinion about something. Because they are used to show strong feelings, these adjectives are called 'emphasizing adjectives'. SCHMITT (2000: 59, 73, 96) further suggests that while collocations (words that typically go together, e.g. a galloping horse) play an important role at the interface between vocabulary and grammar, *"most words can be described in terms of the pattern or patterns in which they typically occur,"* and if they share patterns they also share meanings (e.g. a handsome man, a beautiful woman). And *"corpus evidence is beginning to show how choosing one word in discourse often affects the lexical choices for the surrounding text."* As a result lexical patterns become the major category in learning and teaching discourse.

Cultural meaning

The interrelatedness of vocabulary and grammar in the mental lexicon is further anchored in its cultural meaning(s) and the speaker's world knowledge. Language speakers of a German background, for example, expect a certain way of being treated in a restaurant. If you are being seated by the waitress in an American restaurant it is not what you expect as somebody of a German background. Or, consider the following situation:

Native speaker: See you later.
Non-native speaker: What time?
Native speaker: What do you mean? (NUNAN 1999: 129)

Based on her cultural background, the non-native speaker understands the phrase quite differently, expecting a new meeting soon. The communal meanings shared by members of a cultural group provide the context knowledge that influences the choice of words in specific communicative situations. Since words possess multiple meanings, there are different meanings for different contexts. Our knowledge of the world decides how we understand specific discourse features (as the leave-taking above by the native speaker). Thus miscommunication often does not take place at the level of grammar or vocabulary, but at the discourse level. SCHMITT (2000: 27) distinguishes between the core meaning of a word, such as the word bachelor, the core aspects of which *"might be defined as +human, +male, +adult, and –married"* and the encyclopaedic knowledge which *"consists of the other things one knows about bachelors: for example, they are often young, date women, and have exciting lifestyles."* All these meanings which we attach to words and lexical phrases are culturally specific. They are organized in frames or schemata and help us to make sense of discourse in a communicative situation. When we order a meal in a restaurant or buy a ticket at the train-station, we employ language in relation to a specific schema or framework we expect (asking for the menu, ordering drinks first, then the meal etc). As NUNAN (1999: 133) states, *"schema theory suggests that the knowledge we carry around in our heads is organized into interrelated patterns. These are constructed from all our previous experiences of a given aspect of the experiential world, and they enable us to make predictions about future experience."* In a multi-ethnic communicative situation where different registers and discourse varieties play an important role, the culturally defined schemata might help or hinder us in interpreting the discourse of our interlocutor(s) and thus in applying appropriate language use.

4 The process of learning discourse

Learner-centeredness and learning-centeredness

What does this interrelatedness of grammar and vocabulary in the mental lexicon mean for the learning of discourse? The learning of vocabulary and grammar should be learner-centred in the sense that it is the learners' language needs that are taken into consideration, and not necessarily the progression the textbook prescribes. For example, this is the case when the teaching of the past tense is postponed in the textbook and no past tense forms are allowed to appear in the texts even though learners need them for important language functions, such as in story-telling. At the same time the learning of discourse should be learning-centred. We have to ask what the role of the teacher is in the learning process. Basically language learning, and hence the learning of discourse, proceeds in three steps (see HEDGE 2000: 10–16):

Comprehensible input

1. Learning takes place if the learner is provided with 'comprehensible' language input either by the teacher and /or by her peers that is slightly above the learner's understanding at that point (see also chap. 2.1, VYGOTSKY's ZPD). When a learner has to describe a picture, for example, she might produce the following text: "[...] *it's a man and he walk street* [...] *it's a many car and* [...] *it's aeroplane fly sky* [...]" (example from BATSTONE 1994: 39). There is very little grammar in this description. She first of all tries to get her description across. In the beginning when learners produce language according to semantic and pragmatic decisions, these are based on the pre-fabricated chunks (e.g. it's a...) or lexical phrases that allow them to produce meaning-focussed language (e.g. to get a description across), and thus be more or less fluent language speakers. This is an elliptical approach to language use (see above: 'it's a many car' [plural 's' is missing]; 'it's aeroplane ...' [indefinite

article is missing]), since aspects that seem redundant, such as articles or endings are not verbalized (ROCHE 2001: 134). At the same time there is already grammar in that description in the use of 'it's a' which includes a determiner (it), a copula (is), and the article (a) (see BATSTONE 1994: 39–41). The learner though is not aware of those items being grammar, for her it is a lexical item.

Creative construction process

2. The second step is a 'creative construction process' in which the learner formulates 'hypotheses', such as how the past tense forms are built. She then produces the form, testing out its correctness. This often leads to over-generalization when, for example, 'speaked', is formed based on the general rule of regular past tense forms. In the process of learning, the learner thus needs to 'notice' the correct form to be able to use it more efficiently. She needs to turn it into 'intake' and incorporate it into her interlanguage (the language level she can perform at at that point in time). But she will only notice the new form, if it is important for her, i. e. when comprehension in a communicative situation depends on it, and not necessarily when it is presented to her in form of an abstract rule. Learners thus will not process all the language they receive, since *"some of what they hear or read may not be understood, and some parts of input will receive more attention, because* [...] *they seem more important or salient to the learner at a particular stage of development"* (HEDGE 2000: 12). HEDGE further points out that one should see *"vocabulary knowledge as a scale running from recognition of a word at one end to automatic production at the other, through intermediate stages of making greater sense of the word and how it might be used in different contexts. However, knowledge of some words will remain at the recognition end of the continuum and will be called on in reading and listening but might never become part of a learner's productive ability"* (HEDGE 2000: 116–17). These words and lexical phrases then will remain part of the learner's receptive knowledge and will not move into her productive knowledge. Since learners often will not notice new features because of reasons of motivation (they might not be interested in a text) or emotion (they are frustrated, bored or tired), the teacher cannot completely control the learning process.

Comprehensible output

3. Related to the concept of input is that of 'comprehensible output'. Learners must practise by producing language output which allows them to test their hypotheses about how English works through feedback from the teacher or other learners which then allows them to restructure their interlanguage. Consequently, once learners develop new communicative needs their language use becomes more complex and they need more specific grammatical forms. Vocabulary knowledge forms the basis, since *"knowing the words in a text or conversation permits learners to under-*

stand the meaning of the discourse, which in turn allows the grammatical patterning to become more transparent [...]. Learners can see for themselves how certain grammatical structures and sequences of words lead to certain meanings" (SCHMITT 2000: 143–44).

Process of language use

Children's first structures are essentially lexical and thematic in nature (e.g 'it's a man', 'it's a many car'), and they do not acquire functional categories. Psycholinguistic research shows that there is a priority on words at first and that syntactic rules cannot be elicited (see also chap. 4.6). As LITTLE puts it, *"learning a second language becomes a matter of establishing an L2 lexicon and a 'toolkit'"* (LITTLE 1994: 107). Eventually learners need to be able to access their language knowledge on the spot, in real-world communicative situations with all its time pressures and insecurities. Having developed a large mental lexicon and having constantly restructured their interlanguages through language use and corrective feedback, they now have a procedural knowledge of the language in question. They are now aware of culturally-specific meanings of lexical phrases. They know, for example, that when a native speaker says 'See you later', you answer 'See you later', as well, without necessarily expecting a new meeting soon. Realizing the meaning potential of words and structures gives learners the means to understand the social and cultural dimension of discourse by analysing the linguistic and cultural meaning of the new language features in relation to their own cultural background (for an example see chap. 4.3). At the same time learners' functional and pragmatic needs also depend on their age and social situation.

Focus on form

While research has shown that learners automatically focus on words and their meaning potential for communication, the institutional learning context of the foreign language classroom asks for teacher guidance to improve language awareness and language accuracy because exposure time to the target language is short. Research in recent years has called for a renewed focus on form (see LARSEN-FREEMAN 2001: 37 for an overview). CAMERON (2001: 101) describes this process as follows: *"Cognitive psychology suggests that our brains/minds work always with a limited amount of attentional capacity (or mental attention) that is available to concentrate on getting a task achieved. When that task is communicating an idea or message through the foreign language, then it seems that finding the right words takes up attention early on, but that, once those words or chunks are well known, using them takes up less capacity, and attention is freed for grammar. This will be a repeating process of moving from lexis to grammar, as language resources get gradually more extensive. As a counter-balance to that, social factors will influence the actual need for grammar to communicate. If you can get your message through without grammar, as when a very small knowledge of a language makes it possible to buy food in a foreign shop by naming the item and amount, then there may be little impulse to drive grammar learning. It seems increasingly likely that paying attention to grammatical features of a language is not something that happens automatically in communicating, and that therefore some artificial methods of pushing attention are needed, i.e. teaching!"* The teacher thus has to support the learner in noticing language features, such as overgeneralizations (e.g. 'speaked'). Learners at first avoid grammar since lexis carries sufficient meaning. On the basis of tasks the teacher can help learners choose grammar for respective social contexts, such as questions in a role-play situation, or the teacher may support revision processes of learner-produced texts based on certain grammar items (like checking correct usage of past tense forms in learners' stories, for example, where production precedes practice of correct tense forms; see chap: 3 on developing writing skills). Then there is a functional motivation for language production which allows learners to manipulate language in such a way that s/he actively has to structure grammar instead of *"working around the target grammar"* (BATSTONE 1994: 61). The teacher needs to make sure that in-depth processing of vocabulary as well as grammar takes place which means that the learners actively work on the words meanings (see examples above). How can this complex process of developing the learner's discourse competence be initiated in the foreign language classroom?

5 Teaching vocabulary and grammar

Major phases

Knowledge of the set-up of the mental lexicon and the processes of second language learning have consequences for the three major phases in the teaching of discourse. First of all we need to present the different language properties (sounds, words, grammar) in a way that different learner types are able to notice new lexical phrases. In a second phase teachers need to support learners in structuring the language material in a way that it is networked in the mental lexicon as intake and thus properly put into storage (in form of semantic fields, synonyms, antonyms, etc). To facilitate retrieval and sensible language use in the third phase the teacher has to design communicative situations that allow intensive language practice and restructuring of the learners' interlanguages to a point where they are enabled to speak fluently in the target language.

Direct versus indirect approaches

NATION (1997: 241) differentiates between direct and indirect approaches to vocabulary teaching. Direct approaches include *"word-building exercises, matching words with various types of defini-*

tions, studying vocabulary in context, semantic mapping [...] *There may also be regular vocabulary testing and possibly assigned rote learning* [learning by heart]." Using an indirect approach, the teacher can incorporate *"vocabulary learning into communicative activities like listening to stories, information gap activities, and group work* [...]" At the same time teachers need to be aware of the difference between receptive and productive language use. Since most forgetting happens right after the learning session, the teacher needs to set up a programme of recycling language to facilitate the shift of lexical phrases from the short-term to the long-term memory. This is especially important since the attrition process in productive language use is higher than in receptive language use. As RUSSELL says, *"one explicit memory schedule proposes reviews 5–10 minutes after the end of the study period, 24 hours later, 1 week later, 1 month later, and finally 6 months later"* (RUSSELL 1979. in: SCHMITT 2000: 130).

Teaching vocabulary

The following basic approaches should be taken into consideration when teaching vocabulary (see HEDGE 2000: 126–38):

- Using different techniques to present new words: physical demonstration, mine and gesture, verbal explanation, the use of synonyms or antonyms, pointing to objects, translation, visual support, such as pictures, realia or blackboard drawings, having learners check the dictionary.
- Helping learners in developing strategies for learning new words. Instead of the traditional unstructured bilingual lists students can set up notebooks that, while including the word in the L1 and L2 as well as an phonetic transcript and a phrase as an example, organize the words according to their frequency in their functional, notional, and situational relevance (PICKETT 1978, in: HEDGE 2000: 110). PICKETT also suggests the development of different vocabulary lists, a chronological one, an alphabetical one, and a third list that is organized according to grammar issues or situations where the learner can group for example word classes. Designing topic-based word-networks and word cards of multi-word items that help learners store lexical chunks (i.e. a card with the entry 'go by bus' instead of just 'bus') are still other strategies.
- Developing vocabulary though reading and training lexical inferencing (finding out words through the context).
- Teaching the effective use of dictionaries.
- Teaching learners didactic skills of demonstrating word meaning: Learners use different strategies when presenting topics they have researched in a group, for example, to make the meaning clear to their fellow learners (for example when doing a topic-based www research project).

Grammar teaching: PPP

While vocabulary teaching has already integrated many of these features for quite a while, grammar teaching has been more resistant to the research results presented above. Traditionally grammar teaching has been pursued on the basis of the presentation, practice, and production approach (PPP) (see KIEWEG 1996: 4–5). At first the new grammatical feature is 'presented' to the learners via semi-authentic or heavily constructed texts in textbooks that feature the grammatical phenomenon in an often unreal and not very motivating context. By way of a deductive (the teacher explains) or an inductive (the learners discover the phenomenon) approach, the grammatical feature is analyzed and rules are formulated and signal terms are designated (e. g. since for the use of the present perfect) which are supposed to help the learners 'practise' the new language structure. Second language acquisition research has shown though that this is not sufficient since learners need to have pre-formulated language concepts and signal words cannot replace these. Also, the rules are often not formulated according to the learners' language level. Language 'production' finally is divided into form-oriented drill and practice exercises, followed by pre-communicative exercises and communicative exercises which are meant to provide real-world communicative situations to allow automatic language use in a meaningful context. But as KIEWEG points out, often there is no clear communicative intention to be detected. Either the information gap is missing (one learner has important information for the completion of a task, such as the sequence to a picture story, the other one does not have) or the social relations of that situation as well as important notions, such as space and time, are not clear. HEDGE (2000: 61–62) also rejects the PPP approach because *"it has been the experience of many teachers that it is very difficult to control the language which can occur naturally in such activities (esp. the last phase). Students will use whatever language resources they have at their command and may* [...] *avoid using forms they are uncertain of. Directing their attention to the form in efforts to persuade them to practise it while they are focused on the messages they are trying to communicate to their peers is* [...] *counter-productive in terms of fluency."* In opposition to PPP, the task-based approach (see chap. 2.4) facilitates discourse use since it allows learners to engage in meaningful interaction.

Grammar teaching: TBLL

KIEWEG (1996: 6–11) suggests five important questions that need to be answered before we begin to teach grammar:

- Is it necessary to analyse a grammatical feature on the cognitive level? This can be avoided if the feature is very similar in the L1 and L2 (e. g. first if-clause), and if the structure can simply be learned as a lexical phrase (e. g.:' I want to help him').

- How can the students learn the structural elements of the grammatical feature? Students should be supported in discovering (inductive learning) the differences between L1 and L2, and the grammatical feature should be presented in different sentence forms (positive/negative statement, question forms: 'I want to go to the movies'. 'I don't want to go to the movies'. 'Do you want to go to the movies?') to signal different kinds of usages.
- Which functions of the grammatical feature need to be presented? Here frequency of a grammatical function and its importance for the learner (i. e. learner-centeredness) need to be analysed and it should be presented by way of a communicative problem. Grammar pictures, experiential tasks, games, songs, interactive tasks etc. are helpful in this regard (see KIEWEG 1996: 8–10).
- Do we have to analyse the differences between L1 and L2 since they might provide a stumbling block for the learner? (e. g. the use of make and do in relation to the German term *machen*)
- Which other structures in the target language need to be contrasted with the new feature to avoid mix-ups?

Developing language awareness

These approaches should support learners in developing language awareness that allows them to understand the relationship between form and meaning. Learners need to become *"active explorers of language"* as NUNAN (1999: 138–39) points out: *"Classrooms in which the principle of active exploration has been activated will be characterized by an inductive approach to learning in which learners are given access to data and are provided with structured opportunities to work out rules, principles, and applications for themselves. The idea here is that information will be more deeply processed and stored if learners are given an opportunity to work things out for themselves. Rather than simply being given the principle or rule."*

Problems to be considered

At the same time there are still problems that need to be solved. When students work on tasks they generally rely strongly on a lexicalized system of communication. They mainly use vocabulary and language chunks, and they do not focus on the accurate use of grammar and phonology since this is often not necessary to convey the intended meaning. As a result there may be no structural change in their interlanguages. The task focus on meaning and possible time pressure in negotiating meaning may lead the learner to *"respond with inaccurate use of language or with first language."* And, *"grammar may emerge naturally in first language* [...] *but the grammar of a foreign language is 'foreign', and grammar development requires skilled planning of tasks and lessons, and explicit teaching"* (CAMERON 2001: 108).

Learning-centeredness or the focus on form

While the task-based approach is learner-centred it also needs to be learning-centred. The teacher has to help learners to become aware of their structural problems since a mere focus on meaning does not necessarily support language development. This process of working on discourse functions through the task-based approach is based on a focus on form by way of the activities (see above) of (re)noticing, (re)structuring, and proceduralizing (BATSTONE 1994: 108).

Sequencing activities

This can already be done for young learners as CAMERON (2001: 111–21) shows in her sequencing of activities. For young learners classroom language provides a meaningful discourse context to express language functions and thus may help learners to build their own internal grammars. The teacher can start out with simple management phrases, such as *"give out the scissors"* or *"collect the books"* and then gradually expand language use to support grammar development, such as in *"give out the small scissors"* or *"collect the green writing books"* which help children to notice language use (see CAMERON 2001:103). Children's lexicalized approach to language use can also be supported and developed at the same time by suggesting more accurate forms of language use, as in: *"Child: 'my mummy hospital.' Teacher: 'Oh! Your mummy's in hospital. Why?'"* Apart from helping learners to notice language structure in classroom conversation, teachers can construct guided noticing activities. While listening to a story, for example, learners could use a grid to fill in prepositions that appear in the story in relation to what animals or people do in the story. If 'the cat sits under the table' appears in the story, the learner has to mark the respective field in the grid that connects cat and the icon for under the table.

Proceduralizing tasks

Eventually we want learners to use grammatical forms automatically. For this purpose we have to design proceduralizing tasks that make the use of that grammar point mandatory to fulfil the task goal and thus make learners focus on that aspect of accuracy. By having learners present the description of an animal to the class they will focus on specific vocabulary and grammatical points through repeated rehearsing and perhaps writing down the description. A similar effect is reached when learners work collaboratively to re-construct a text in written form which the teacher has read to the group repeatedly. As CAMERON (2001: 119) explains, *"in Vygotskyan terms, if the text is carefully chosen, learners will be working in their zones of potential development and their peers may scaffold learning in the ZPD."*

From words to grammar

BATSTONE (1994: 104–10) provides a similar sequence of activities and warns us that instead of spending *"a great deal of our time pressing our learners to move off in the opposite direction – from gram-*

mar to lexis" we should help the learners *"shift gradually from words to grammar" through a process of "grammaticization."* They learn how to grammaticize for themselves on the basis of simple language chunks that are given in certain contexts. Instead of having the learner form a correct grammatical sentence from the words *"'arrive Jane leave John'"*, BATSTONE (1994: 104–5) confronts the learner with two different contexts: *"Situation 1: You know that John doesn't like Jane."* And *"Situation 2: John and Jane are good friends, but Jane is feeling ill."* This might lead to sentences such as *"Jane arrived and so John left"* (1) or *"John arrived but Jane had to leave"* (2), allowing learners to notice the different functions of language. Based on this principle more elaborate context-gap activities can be designed, which make learners focus on meaning and form and thus help them develop their discourse competence.

Cultural focus

At the same time this process of grammaticization needs to integrate a cultural focus. The approach of turning learners into active language explorers is exemplified in MÜLLER's approach (1994) of helping learners become intercultural ethnographers who gradually notice and take on the cultural meaning of words. Under the teacher's guidance learners develop cultural curiosity by designing research questions and hypotheses that allow them to gradually become aware of the complex cultural meaning of many words and grammatical functions (for an example, see chap. 4.3). By explicitly establishing relations between words and their cultural backgrounds they engage in cultural awareness building that includes their own and the foreign culture.

6 Conclusion: Current trends and developments

More research on grammar is needed

While advances have been made in the field of vocabulary studies (e.g. COADY/HUCKIN 1997, SCHMITT/MCCARTHY 1997, SCHMITT 2000, NATION 2001), research is not conclusive in the field of grammar (CELCE-MURCIA 1991). Some focus on forms is obviously warranted, but there is still a lot of discussion as to the effectiveness of various approaches to grammar teaching. While *"structured-input practice may provide a useful alternative to production practice"* there is little knowledge on what *"kind of feedback is most effective"* (ELLIS 1998: 47, 53). The lack of clear guidelines for grammar teaching from researchers has led to qualitative studies which look at the behavioural and psychological implications of grammar teaching at the interface of researchers' technical knowledge about grammar and teachers' practical knowledge, thus providing important insights into the actual teaching of grammar. BORG (1998), for example, shows that teacher pre- and in-service training as well as classroom management issues had a powerful influence on the teachers' instructional decisions (see also LARSEN-FREEMAN 2001: 40–41). The role of computer programs to analyse written and especially spoken corpora (concordances; see chap. 4.3) is beginning to produce important results, which might lead to the writing of different grammars that incorporate spoken and written language. One such development is pedagogical grammars which focus on the functional representation of grammar of everyday language use (see ROCHE 2001: 142). The future will see an even stronger emphasis on discourse and the interrelationship between vocabulary and grammar will be strengthened. In terms of developing ICC, there needs to be more research on grammar *"as a resource for choice in the social context"* (BATSTONE 1994: 70). At the same time learners' cultural preferences need to be taken more into consideration (ROCHE 2001: 132).

CHAPTER 4

Language Teaching Contents: Exploring Relevant Areas and Contexts

4.1 Teaching Cultural Studies and Intercultural Learning

1 Introduction: The purpose of intercultural learning

Terminology

Except for the new media, hardly any field of foreign language teaching and learning during the last fifteen years has seen such a comprehensive development as that of teaching culture. The many different terms in use, from *Realienkunde*, *Kulturkunde* and *Landeskunde* to Cultural Studies, intercultural learning, and intercultural communicative competence (ICC) highlight the multiplicity of concepts that have dominated the discussion.

The process of ICC

If our main aim as language teachers is to enable learners to develop ICC (see chap. 2.1), then the way towards this goal can be described as intercultural learning (see RÖTTGER 1996: 157). Culture learning, or learning about culture is a process. Learners in the foreign language classroom bring a lot of cultural schemata and values from their L1 culture. At the same time they often have stereotypical notions of the foreign language and culture, which originate in their native media. On the other hand they increasingly have experiences through stays abroad or contacts with speakers of English. As teachers we therefore have to deal with heterogeneous experiences and perspectives. In the process we need to offer opportunities to learners to engage with the target culture(s) on all five levels of BYRAM's model of ICC (see chap. 2.1) to eventually enable them to mediate between different cultures.

An example from an e-mail project

At first we will focus on the development from the traditional concept of *Landeskunde* to the concept of intercultural learning. The example of an American/German e-mail exchange (11th grade) will serve as the basis for exploring the concepts. In this exchange the American students had the task of explaining Thanksgiving to their German partners. Here are two examples of what U.S. students wrote:

Tomorrow, the United States is celebrating the holiday Thanksgiving. We celebrate this because this is when America was first discovered by Columbus in 1492. On this date, we eat lots of turkey, potatoes, ham, cranberries, bread, and many other foods. It is truly one of the great holidays celebrated in the United States. (E-Mail 1, American student, grade 11)

We are celebrating Thanksgiving in the United States on Thursday. … The holiday originated with the Pilgrims who came to this country who depended on the Native Americans to teach them how to grow food and prepare it. So it is basically the coming together of two different cultures and nationalities. Years later the white people would infect the Native Americans with their disease which wiped out millions of lives. But we do not celebrate that part. (E-Mail 2, American student, grade 11)

2 Developments in teaching culture: From *Landeskunde* to intercultural communication

Traditional *Landeskunde*

These e-mail letters show that the traditional concept of *Landeskunde* which is based on factual learning about the target cultures' history and their political and social institutions does not ensure the development of ICC. With the help of their English textbooks the learners will quickly find out which of their two partners is correct about Thanksgiving. But what about the claim that Columbus was the one who discovered America (e-mail 1)? And even more important, how can the teacher mediate the conflict that obviously some of the American students, who are native speakers and supposedly cultural experts, are wrong in what they present as cultural knowledge?

Realienkunde* and *Kulturkunde

During the modern language reform movement in the 1880s and 1890s realia and culture *(Realienkunde)* were seen as part and parcel of foreign language teaching (for a historical overview see BUTTJES 1990: 51–60). That approach to foreign language teaching was rejected during World War I, but at the same time, the war renewed the interest in cultural and political aspects. At first teachers supported cultural knowledge in foreign language teaching *(Kulturkunde)*, but in the 1920s culture came to be seen *"as a people's soul and character as expressed in their philosophy, arts, and literature. Any cultural expression was to be reduced to certain national traits of character"* (BUTTJES 1990: 55). These national traits were compared to those of other cultures, a chauvinistic approach which led to *"intercultural distortion and prejudice"* which was quickly taken up by the Nazis as *Wesenskunde* (BUTTJES 1990: 56). While in Germany conservative concepts close to *Kulturkunde* avoided all political and social realities after World War II, developments in the U.S. and Great Britain laid the basis for a new concept.

'C'ulture and 'c'ulture

In 1958 Raymond WILLIAMS challenged the reductive concept of a high elitist culture (Culture with a capital 'C', such as the master works of art and literature) and opposed it with the more comprehensive concept of culture as *"a whole way of life"* (culture with a small 'c'). This includes that part of culture which deals with *"the arts and learning"* (WILLIAMS, in: BACH 1998: 193), but it also incorporates all forms of popular culture, such as dress, hairstyle, youth language or comics.

From *Landeskunde* to cultural studies

This more comprehensive approach to culture necessitated an interdisciplinary approach which included the social sciences, literature, and linguistics. During the next decade British cultural studies focused on the role of working class and youth cultures (see SOMMER 2003). Something similar took place in the U.S. with the development of American cultural studies which looked critically at the construction of myths (e.g. the new American man, or the Pilgrims establishing the city on the hill) that secured the dominance of the white Anglo-Saxon Protestant (WASP) ruling class. In opposition to the older *Landeskunde*, cultural studies deconstructed the myth of a national culture and saw culture *"as a terrain of conflict and contestation"* (STOREY 1996: 2). Consequently the question of power plays an important role and the question is who assigns meaning to cultural symbols and actions. Media and the control of media are decisive in conveying these meanings. While in the 1960s the role of class was an important issue in cultural studies, from the 1970s on gender and ethnicity came to the fore since they had been invisible in earlier cultural studies analyses. As STOREY (1996: 4) further explains: *"cultural texts and practices are not inscribed with meaning, guaranteed once and for all* [...] *it* [meaning] *is always expressed in a specific context, a specific historical moment, within specific discourse(s)."* Teaching cultural studies thus means rejecting binary oppositions (us versus them) and looking at issues from multiple perspectives including a historical one. Culture was no longer seen as a static concept, but as a dynamic one which changed over time. This also led to an integration of all text forms, such as fiction and non-fiction texts (KUNA/TSCHACHLER 1986). Looking at the e-mail texts above from a cultural studies point of view, one can see this process taking place. While the first student presents the U.S. according to the myth of WASP nation-building (discovery by the Europeans, and survival in the wilderness), the second student explains Thanksgiving in the historical frame of native-white contacts and shows how America became a place of contestation among the different groups. Consequently a different set of questions than in a *Landeskunde* framework is triggered: Who really discovered America? Was America 'discovered' at all? What role does Thanksgiving play in the relation between Natives and immigrants? Who helped whom and how did the relationships among the different ethnic groups develop? Such an approach allows the learners to develop a more critical and more comprehensive view of the other culture, and thus facilitates BYRAM's fifth competence, critical cultural awareness. But in terms of the other competences in foreign language learning (see chap. 2.1), it still does not help learners to answer the first e-mail letter.

Intercultural communication and ICC

In the 1970s and 80s researchers began to deal with pragmatic issues of misunderstandings which American diplomats, Peace Corps activists, and businessmen encountered abroad. Intercultural communication was seen as interpersonal interaction, based on a language code, between interlocutors from different groups or cultures. This dynamic process was influenced by expectations and at times stereotypical notions (auto- and hetero-stereotypes; see chap. 2.1) of the other culture which had to be negotiated to establish understanding. Understanding the partner in a communicative situation is a social process which involves empathy, tolerance, culture specific knowledge and appropriate learning strategies to establish common meaning through competent language use. The ultimate aim is the ICC of the intercultural speaker (see chap. 2.1). It is this negotiation of different meanings and the effort one makes to understand the other which is decisive for intercultural learning understanding, and not the ethnic background of the participants (see Hu 1999: 297–98). Even speakers of the same language can encounter problems of intercultural understanding. To take a recent example from German history, even though people from eastern and western Germany share a common language, there have been to this day enormous difficulties of understanding. If we look at the two American e-mails a similar conclusion can be drawn. While one student has grasped the concept of Thanksgiving and its historical repercussions in American history (E-mail 2), the other student – apart from getting his historical facts wrong – is still hooked to the auto-stereotype of Thanksgiving being one of the founding days of a great nation.

3 Issues in cultural studies

A dialogue of texts

The aim of turning language learners into intercultural speakers is often pursued in business communication through specific forms of training, one of them being the discussion of critical incidents. How do you react in a specific situation in a different culture which could cause problems because of one's own cultural background, e.g. invitations or communication between different hierarchical levels in a company? (See Brislin et. al. 1986). Language teaching, on the other hand, has focused on work with literary and other texts. Since texts represent different aspects of a culture they form the basis for the negotiation of meaning. As Buttjes (1990: 60) points out, *"the 'dialogue of texts' between literature and culture has been one of the productive approaches in cultural studies"* (see also the concept of intertextuality in chap. 4.2). Before the development of cultural studies, literary texts were often seen as a closed aesthetic product that had to be interpreted in their own right. But literary texts refer to other literary texts (see, for example, the reference in the title in FAULKNER's novel *The Sound and the Fury* to a text by SHAKESPEARE) and to non-literary texts. Often authors play with these relationships between texts, establishing an intertextual field of meanings in the process. At the same time looking at an event from the point of view of different texts helps establish multiple perspectives and thus allows the learner to understand an event or issue more fully (i. e. looking at the Civil Rights Movement in the U.S. through non-fiction analytical texts, through diaries or songs of the participants, and through literary texts) (see HALLET 2002). This dialogue or multilogue can be one between e-mail texts, or between a film and other texts as will be shown below (see also PIEPHO 2003 and his *Szenariendidaktik* in chap. 2.4).

A broad definition of texts

The process of intercultural learning is based on a multitude of texts. This goes beyond the written text and includes classroom discourse as well as oral texts that learners have produced outside the classroom (e.g. interviews). It covers all written texts from non-fiction to fiction texts. It also includes so-called hybrid text genres, such as hypertexts and texts that integrate oral as well as written characteristics, such as e-mail letters or chats.

Project work and critical cultural awareness

To support the process idea of intercultural learning project work is especially helpful (see chap. 2.4), since learners deal in succession with a number of different texts and produce their own texts in the process. In correspondence and encounter projects, the teacher facilitates the intercultural learning process by designing tasks that focus on critical issues, for example, in the e-mail texts above, and thus help learners to understand the other perspective(s), compare it (them) to their own, and evaluate both critically if necessary (see NÜNNING/NÜNNING 2000). Like in the e-mail exchange above, Canadian (one group) and German learners (two groups) in another e-mail project pursued this intercultural learning process because the project format (in that case 2 ½ months) allowed for extended negotiation (see MÜLLER-HARTMANN 1999a). We will use this example to illustrate the way in which you can raise critical cultural awareness with learners.

The project

After a period of getting to know each other – writing about their interests and hobbies – learners turned to the discussion of MIKLOWITZ's young adult novel *The War Between the Classes* which deals with class and race in American society, and which triggered comparisons between their own cultures. The tasks set by the teacher (learners exchanged chapters of their reading journals and sent each other summaries of the class discussions concerning the novel) led to a dialogue or multilogue among the students on the general issues dealt with in the novel. In the following example the reading of the novel triggered a discussion about the role of Turkish immigrants in German society between the two German groups (classrooms from two German cities participated in the project). This raised students' cultural awareness in both cultures. The learners of German background wrote:

We think that discrimination in Germany you can find in a few places, but the main population has no problem with intercultural understanding, they live in harmony with many different ethnic groups (E-Mail, Learners of German background, Gießen, Germany).

There are serious problems between the so-called "foreigners" and German people. But this comes because both sides make mistakes. You mentioned some of them made by German people, though it is more than just settling the "foreigners" in ghettos... On the other hand, non-German people are not open enough, especially the elderly ones. This is because they are so afraid of being assimilated, that they can't even tolerate the smallest integration, because it's losing one's own identity for them, whereas the problems of the young generation are mainly based on being between two cultures (E-Mail, Turkish student in Ulm, Germany).

The Turkish student critically discusses his partners' terminology (foreigner versus non-German) and concepts concerning the integration of Turkish migrants, presenting a diversified picture in the process. This 'German' discussion then raises awareness on the Canadian side:

During this e-mail exchange I found that at first without realizing we were denying that we had any cultural problems. Then we found that we have a huge problem how the French and English just can't get along (E-mail, Canadian student 1).

I found it surprising that there was a large social rift in your schools mainly between the Germans and the Turks. It is almost an exact parallel to what we have here between the French and the English. I would be interested in knowing more about some of the types of problems that arise (E-Mail, Canadian student 2).

Auto- and hetero-stereotypes

Such incidents, in e-mail texts, chats, face-to-face encounters, and in fictional/non-fictional texts offer the opportunity to deal with auto- and hetero-stereotypes and to come to a critical understanding of the cultures involved. While the learners of German background had to confront their hetero-stereotypes concerning Turkish migrants in Germany, their partners confronted their auto-stereotype of Canadian society being a homogenous one, where French- and English-speaking citizens live in harmony with each other. By setting sensible tasks (analysis of e-mail texts) during this phase of the project, the teacher helped German learners realize their intercultural differences, such as their use of terms, for example. In the following mails the learners of German background did not use the term 'foreigner' anymore but talked of non-Germans instead. Learners in both groups were enabled to perform a change of perspectives through the negotiation of cultural meaning in both societies. They thus developed a 'third place' which integrates the former positions into a new critical cultural awareness (see chap. 2.1). This intercultural learning process only became possible through a multilogue of texts and a close interpretation and comparison of them through tasks. It is more difficult though to initiate such a learning process if the focus is on a single text without establishing the text's intertextual character.

4 How to work with cultural studies texts

Popular culture texts

As an example we would like to focus on popular culture since it plays an important role in a concept of 'c'ulture with a small 'c' for our learners. Texts like soap operas, MTV films, cartoons, and comics influence our learners' world to a large extent. The choice of popular culture texts in the English language classroom therefore obviously supports a 'learner'-centred approach. But generally learners will consider these texts as pure fun, and will not see the ideological subscripts which often carry nationalistic, racist or misogynist messages. Consequently when teaching cultural studies we need a 'learning'-centred approach which means that the teacher guides learners' critical inquiry. As an example we would like to look at the Disney cartoon *Who Framed Roger Rabbit?* (1988, 104 min.), which allows learners to develop a critical look at the historical and popular myths of the Disney company. The film could form the centre piece of a teaching unit on the company and its cultural productions, such as theme parks, comics and films (see also Müller-Hartmann 2000a).

Who Framed Roger Rabbit

Targeting also an adult audience under the Touchstone label, *Who Framed Roger Rabbit?* is a good example of how racist discourses still pervade American society. The film could also stand at the centre of a unit on the image of race in 20th century America, and thus help learners understand this field of cultural conflict. While hailing a revolution in film-making through its extremely skillful combination of real-life actors and cartoon characters, the film, a 'mixed breed' in itself between film noir and cartoon, harps on the differences between the toons (the animated characters) which is a shortened form for car'toons', and the human characters. The use of this term thus recalls one of the most pervasive racist terms in American history used for African-Americans, the term 'coon', a derivative of 'goon', meaning hoodlum or violent man, as well as stupid or silly man.

The plot

In the plot, the bad guy, Judge Doom, wants to destroy toontown to make way for a new freeway and the economic opportunities (gas stations, restaurants etc) that entails. This plot is mirrored by a development in many American cities after World War II when freeways were constructed, not only to make space for a growing car culture, but also to 'wall in' ethnic groups into certain areas of the city.

'Toons' and 'coons'

The toon protagonist is the happy-go-lucky character of Roger Rabbit which recalls the stereotype of African-Americans as sex-maniac dancers and jokers. The theatre tradition of the minstrels (see below for an example) of the turn of the century was the only possibility for blacks to dance and sing in front of a white audience. It was started by white actors who put on black polish and painted big red lips and wide eyes onto their faces to appear as an exaggerated black person. They told hilarious jokes and constantly made fun of themselves (as blacks) as stupid, happy-go-lucky, and thus non-threatening jokers. The white majority could thus laugh away their fears of a possibly menacing black presence in American society (slaves had been free only for a short while and were pushing onto the job market; also, blacks were constantly pictured as rapists who would attack white women if not controlled). 'Coon' was one of the most pervasive terms at the time and was used well into the 1950s by whites for blacks. In Disney's film the 'toons' play the same harmless role, i.e. making people laugh.

Intertextuality and ICC

The film allows many approaches. The teacher can focus on technical innovations (combining human actors with cartoon characters), she can compare the different genres of film noir and cartoon, or she can concentrate on the many allusions made to other films in American film history, and thus establish intertextuality. But a focus on the imagery of race allows for the historical as well as critical approach in terms of race, class and gender that is characteristic of a cultural studies concept. In this case a poem, photos, drawings, a song, a journal cover, non-fictional and other fictional texts create a text universe that facilitates different perspectives on the authentic film text and which allows learners to engage with the different levels of ICC, i.e. the affective level, the cognitive level, the skills level, and critical cultural awareness (see chap. 2.1).

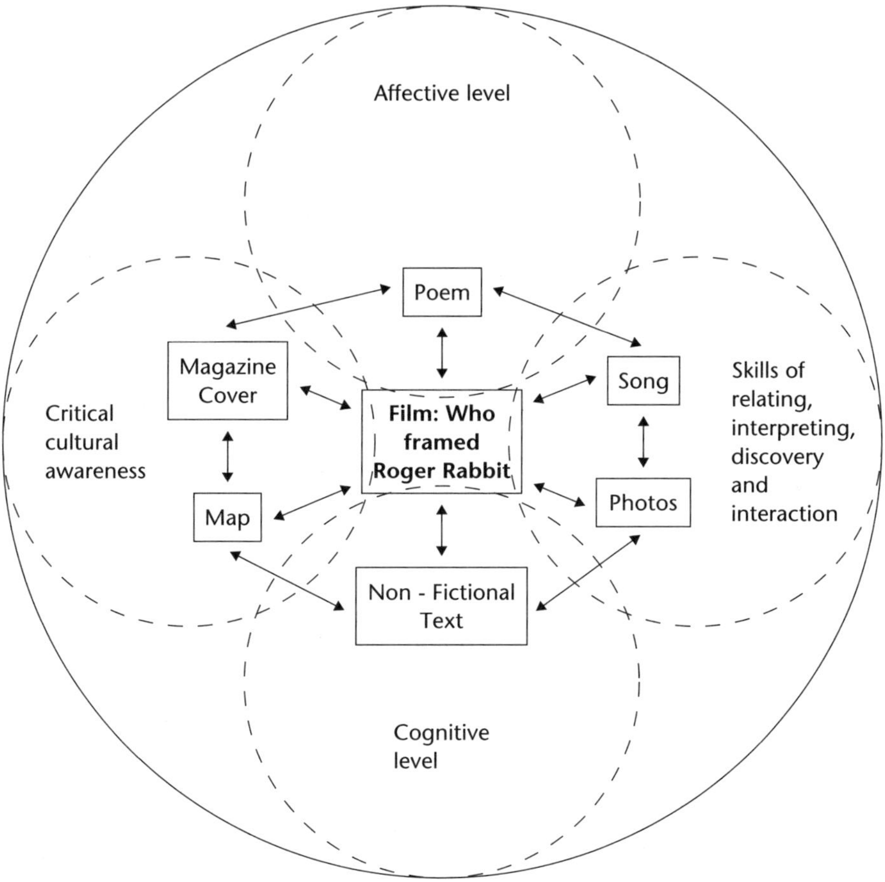

Model 4.1: Establishing intercultural communicative competence through intertextuality

Pre-viewing tasks

As in teaching literature (see chap. 4.2) the task structure follows a pre-, while-, post-viewing structure which first of all allows students to create a field of awareness and curiosity as to the authentic film text. The most important step is to make students aware of the racist terms that existed and still exist (historical perspective). One starting point could be WARD's (1992) poem *Don't Be Fourteen (In Mississippi)* which is based on an actual case of racist stereotyping. The poem tells the story of a 14-year-old black boy who allegedly whistled after a white woman and was sent to prison for that. One of the poem's messages is that black teenagers have to conform to the existing stereotypes (for example, the minstrel type, among others) or otherwise be imprisoned or killed. Here is a verse from the poem:

Don't be fourteen
Black and male in Mississippi,
Have two 20/20 eyes, feet
That fail to buck, wing, and tap,
(WARD 1992: 286)

Black in 'coons' mask
(RIEPE/RIEPE 1992: 109)

Only if blacks look like the minstrel type (20/20 = big eyes), and only if they behave like one, i. e. dancing wildly (buck, wing, tap) do they have a chance to survive in racist Mississippi. To support students' understanding of the poem as well as to make them emotionally aware of the various images that are portrayed in the poem, and to establish links to racist terms in their own surroundings, they could match 1–2 photos or pictures that show racist images (see RIEPE 1992 for examples) with each stanza (affective level). The different products can be compared and discussed in terms of how far these images still exist in today's society (examples from today's advertisement). A song from the 1950s about a black man who was stealing chickens and other things while constantly outrunning the police, further supports this imagery of the minstrel or coon (affective level) doing crazy things.

The coon ran so bloomin' fast
That fire came from his heels;
He scorched the bottom an' burnt the corn
An' cut a road through the farmer's fields.
(LEVINE 1977: 285)

A non-fiction text (BOSKIN 1986, chap. 6), explaining the stereotypes, could then be used to help students understand the pervasiveness of these stereotypes in American society (cognitive level).

While-viewing tasks

With this emotional (visual stimuli) as well as cognitive background (informative text) learners can focus on how the cartoon characters are portrayed in the film during a first viewing of the film. Roger Rabbit's behaviour is very much comparable to the racist descriptions of blacks in the poem and the popular American song from above. The first task would be:

1. How is the cartoon protagonist Roger Rabbit portrayed in the film? Collect examples.
2. Compare your findings with the characters portrayed in the poem and the song.

Learners will re-discover the stereotypes of the poem, song, and photos in the film. In terms of ICC they will develop the skill of interpreting and relating, since they have to relate the different texts (poem, song, drawing, film) to each other and interpret their meaning. By comparing the different texts they will understand the role of these stereotypes in American society and history. A second task focuses on the nightclub scene where the voluptuous mulatta Jessica, Roger Rabbit's wife, sings. She is a mixture of a car'toon' and a human actor because she has a human body drawn in form of a car'toon'. By combining both races (black and white), as well as car'toons' and humans, she merges all white fears (blacks will rape white women – that's why there are mulattas) and desires (the mulatta was considered as a sex object by white men; many slaveowners in the 19th century kept such women as mistresses) concerning blackness in her character. The second task would be:

Watch the nightclub scene and have a closer look at the following aspects:

1. What role do human actors and cartoon characters play in this scene?
2. What is Jessica's role?

Jessica represents the multi-layered stereotype that separates as well as connects black and white worlds. Being the sexual symbol per se, it only makes sense that she is married to Roger Rabbit, an animal that is seen as a symbol for indulgence in sexual activity, recalling once again the racist stereotype of African-Americans' alleged sexual power. The extent to which Jessica has become a popular icon in the U.S. becomes clear through the fact that she appeared on the cover of *Playboy* after the film was published, only this time with a human head and a cartoon body (see FRIEDMAN 1991: 206). The cover picture can be used before showing the nightclub scene or after doing so to trigger a discussion about racial and sexual stereotyping. Thus learners understand the historical role of cultural icons and stereotypes in American society.

Post-viewing tasks

Toontown as a ghetto for the cartoon characters is going to be bulldozed to make way for the freeway plans of Judge Doom. While this plan is finally stopped, it mirrors the development of ghettos that took place in many American cities during mid-century. An understanding of the Judge's plan in the film can thus be compared to a non-fictional text on the construction of freeways. Tasks could be:

1. Make a rough sketch of Hollywood and toontown as presented in the film to get a visual impression of how the two parts are located to each other.

2. Go back to the film to find out how Judge Doom wants to change Hollywood and toontown and draw a new map that represents his plan.
3. Compare his plan to the development that is described in the text "Changing neighbourhoods: Ethnic and Racial Succession in the Urban North and South" (Bayor 1990: 219–36)

Critical cultural awareness

The preceding text 'universe' and the various tasks will allow learners to see the imagery of race critically not only in this Disney cartoon, but also in others and in their own culture (ads) as well. At the same time it prepares them for a possible panel discussion on the question whether such a film should be boycotted or not. This also brings up the issue of the global pervasiveness of Disney products and their role in the learners' culture, helping learners to critically reflect on their own engagement with popular culture products. Last but not least, learners engage in the skills level of real-world interaction by simulating such a panel discussion.

5 Future developments

Institutional constraints

As we have seen, dealing with stereotypes or stereotypical perspectives in the foreign language classroom is a complex undertaking. While institutional constraints (time pressure, small teaching blocks) often keep us from engaging in projects as outlined above, there are hardly any alternatives to this approach, if we want our learners to become intercultural learners. The process of intercultural learning covers many levels and requires different text forms integrating fiction and non-fiction texts (see also Hallet 2002; and Nünning/Nünning 2000: 9). At the same time we need to incorporate authentic voices from the target culture(s) and to help our learners develop a critical view of the cultures involved.

4.2 Teaching Literature and Other Texts

1 Introduction: The purpose of teaching literature

Potential of literary texts

The teaching of literature in foreign language teaching has experienced an enormous boost during the last 20 years. This is due to several factors (see Collie/Slater 1987: 3–6). First of all, literary texts provide authentic material for language learning as well as interesting and therefore motivating content matter. They support extensive reading and the opportunity for many oral and written activities, thus helping to develop the various language skills. Conveying *"an individual awareness of reality"* (Widdowson 1975, in: McKay 2001: 319) of different cultures and ethnic groups, i.e.

their thoughts, ways of living, and value systems, literary texts also represent a rich resource for intercultural learning. Consequently the reading of and working with literary texts facilitates the formation of complex language learner identities. The increased focus on learner-centred teaching went hand in hand with a growing awareness of the importance of the reader's role in the teaching of texts. As BREDELLA (2000: 376–77) points out, the firm establishment of literary texts in the EFL classroom is partly due to the fact that the task-based approach (see chap. 2.4) facilitates this interaction between literary texts and readers of all age groups. This has not always been the case.

2 Developments in teaching literary texts: From close reading to the resistant reader

The literary triangle

The basic triangle of relationships between author, text, and reader – comprised in the social and historical context in which they are placed – has defined over time how literature was taught. While at times author and text were the focus of attention, it is now the reader and his or her relation to the text that is at the centre of the teaching process. In this respect the teaching of literature has always been closely related to developments in the field of literary studies.

Literature with a capital 'L'

Basically, the historical development of teaching literary texts is defined by a movement from integrating classical texts, the 'great' texts of English literature, such as those by SHAKESPEARE (i.e. Literature with a capital 'L', see below), into the language classroom to an increasingly open approach in terms of text selection and reading. Since the late 19th century a restricted canon of literary texts by white, male, and mostly British writers has been taught as works of art that could be analyzed and understood according to certain core meanings. At a time when the grammar-translation method dominated the EFL classroom, SHAKESPEARE and others were considered "the highest form of expression of the target language" (GILROY/PARKINSON 1997: 213). They were read in English but discussed in German.

Efferent and aesthetic reading

While this continued well into the late 20th century, as early as 1938 ROSENBLATT focused on the relationship between reader and text in her approach to teaching literary and other texts. She differentiated between the 'efferent' reading of texts, when the reader's *"attention is primarily focused on selecting out and analytically abstracting the information or ideas or directions for action,"* and the 'aesthetic' approach to reading a text, which focuses on *"the personal associations, feelings, and ideas being lived through during the reading."* As to the prevailing approach at her time she remarked that *"traditional and formalist methods of teaching literature treat it as a body of information to be transmitted, rather than as experiences to be reflected on"* (ROSENBLATT 1938/1995: 32, 292).

New Criticism and close reading

But ROSENBLATT'S approach was only really taken up when the New Criticism (1920–1960) was on the wane again. During that period teaching literature was a matter of close reading that considered only the literary text itself without its contextual influences. This approach was similarly applied in the EFL classroom and found its continuation in the 1970s with WERLICH'S (1986) *Interpretationsgespräch* and FREESE'S (FREESE/GROENE/HERMES 1979) *Fragenkatalog* for the interpretation of short stories. In terms of strictly language-based approaches, it was mirrored by the stylistics approach which dealt with literary texts from a purely linguistic point of view.

Reader-response criticism

The approach described above did not change until the 1970s and 80s with the advent of reception theory and reader-response criticism. These moved away from an attempt at providing an objective and thus rather closed view of literary readings to a subjective and more open view which focused on the relationship between the text and the reader. Both ISER (1980) and FISH (1980) have demonstrated how the reader constantly makes inferences, processes information, and adjusts his point of view when reading a text (see also chap. 3.1.4), all of which are influenced by his or her experiences. As GILROY and PARKINSON (1997: 216) point out, *"his* [sic] *varying viewpoint produces contradictions and uncertainties, 'gaps of indeterminacy'* [why does the character X act that way?], *which the reader must resolve and fill to actualise meaning in the text."* The reader, i.e. learner, thus becomes a very active agent in the dialogue between text and reader.

Learner-centred and creative tasks

Whereas earlier approaches were characterized by clear teacher-centred teaching, the learner is now the focus of attention. To help the learner realize the potential of the text, the text variety is increased in the classroom, including literary texts for young adults, comics etc. At the same time learner-centred tasks support and structure the reading process (for examples see below). While class discussions are also changing in this direction, as BRUSCH'S *Rezeptionsgespräch* (1986) and NISSEN'S *Lerngespräch* (1982) have shown, the most pervasive influence in this area has come from creative tasks. They have opened the way for a clearly structured process-oriented approach to teaching literature on the basis of pre-, while-, and post-reading tasks (for an example see below). Since tasks are also product-oriented (see chap. 2.4) this led to a large variety of oral and written learner products, allowing learners to relate to the text on a personal level, and voice their personal perspectives on a text individually or in pairs or groups (see COLLIE/SLATER 1987 and CASPARI 1994 generally for tasks on literature, DUFF/MALEY 1989 on poetry, and MALEY/DUFF 2001 on drama). The tasks also support a process approach that reflects the general phases of reception when a learner reads a text. At first readers *"feel like reading"* because the text interests them (motivation), then they develop a relationship to the story, i.e. they are *"getting into the story"*. In a third phase they enter the world of the text, *"getting lost in the book"*, aesthetically distancing themselves from their own world but also reflecting on what they read, before in a last phase they develop a *"sense of an ending"* which is supported or refuted by the text (BENTON/FOX 1985, in: DELANOY 1996). By supporting the personal reading experience of the learners the teacher's role changes as well. As in other contexts of the EFL classroom (see chap. 4.1) he or she becomes more of a facilitator who provides rich learning environments through a wide selection of authentic texts, and the design of learner-centred tasks.

Intercultural learning

With the 1990s the potential of literature for intercultural learning became clear. As KRAMSCH (1993: 8) has pointed out, if language *"is seen as social practice, culture becomes the very core of language teaching."* Teaching foreign literature, which already represents linguistic otherness, is ideal since it allows learners to experience other cultures and value systems. In the process of relating their own values and world view(s) to those of the text, comparing and contrasting them, learners might change and co-ordinate perspectives and thus begin to understand the other culture (BREDELLA 2002: 14–18; see also HUNFELD 1998 and chap. 2.1 and 4.1). This dialogue between text and reader is supported by text selections and tasks that facilitate negotiation of meaning between the foreign culture represented in the text and the learners' own culture (for an example see below). As BREDELLA (2000: 378) stresses, *"of special significance for intercultural understanding are post-colonial and minority texts, because these often dramatise intercultural conflicts and reveal causes for misunderstanding and misrecognition of others."*

Cultural studies

The relationship to the cultural studies approach is obvious (see chap. 4.1). BREDELLA (2000: 378) points out: *"Literary texts depict, for example, what it means to be a child, a woman, or a member of a minority, and what it means to be in love or to experience death in the foreign culture. Such an understanding of literary texts opens up a new perspective for the relationship between literary texts and cultural studies or Landeskunde."* While the actual reading experience should be in the forefront, often texts might be too difficult to understand or, as KRAMSCH (1993: 131–37) has shown, students' experiences do not help them in understanding the different world views represented in the text. At that point background reading is necessary since it supports understanding and eventual student response. Bredella and Delanoy (1996: xii) affirm that *"we must activate the students' prior knowledge but we must also give them the opportunity to reflect critically on their frame of reference and this can be done by offering them cultural and historical knowledge which allows them to see things from a different perspective."* Informed by literary theories such as New Historicism, this contextual approach extends the hermeneutic or reader-centred concepts to include factors such as *"the class-, race- and gender-related implications of aesthetic communication"* (Delanoy 1996: 78). This also demands a critical reading of texts since we want learners to develop a critical intercultural competence as well.

Intertextuality

The addition of other texts and the way texts relate to each other leads to the concept of intertextuality. Hallet (2002: 29) establishes the relationship between intertextuality or the interplay of texts and cultural studies: *"Da Intertextualität eine allen Texten innewohnende Eigenschaft ist, befindet sich jeder Text* [...] *beständig im Austausch mit anderen Texten. Aus dieser Zirkulation von Bedeutungen in Diskursen und aus den damit verbundenen Textbeziehungen entsteht kulturelle Bedeutung."* This includes all kinds of texts, and it includes the learner and his or her identity, since by choosing texts (for example, from the Internet), by responding to texts or by creating their own texts they develop their linguistic and cultural identities. The free play of texts characterizes the foreign language classroom, *"in dem sich die Texte aller Interaktionspartner (Textvorlagen, Lehrende, Lernende) in einem komplexen und komplizierten Geflecht von Bedeutungen bewegen, indem die tatsächlichen oder angenommenen Texte der Interaktionspartner (deren Erwartungen, Ziele usw.) jeweils auch Teile der eigenen Texte sind. Da alle beteiligten Texte unablässig interagieren, sind diese nicht als fixe Entitäten, sondern als Prozesse zu denken"* (Hallet 2002: 29–30). This understanding of texts and working with texts exemplifies the rich learning environment teachers try to facilitate through tasks. Hallet (2002: 144–45) has provided a list of tasks that support the interactive play with literary texts.

Reordering und *jigsaw*-Techniken	Ein Einzeltext wird in verschiedene Teiltexte (Sätze, Zeilen etc.) zerlegt. Die Schüler müssen durch die Herstellung von Beziehungen einen sinnvollen Text herstellen.
Gap-filling	Unvollständige Texte (z. B. halbe oder verkürzte Gedichtzeilen) müssen ergänzt werden.
Jumbled pictures	Bildvorlagen werden in eine sinnvolle Reihenfolge gebracht und dienen als Vorlage für einen neuen Text, z. B. eine Erzählung.
Illustration	Eine Textvorlage wird mit selbst hergestellten oder selbst beschafften Bildern (Zeichnungen, Fotos usw.) illustriert.
Texte ergänzen und fortsetzen	Ein unvollständiger oder an einer bestimmten Stelle unterbrochener Text wird von den Lernenden vervollständigt oder fortgesetzt. Es kann scih um sehr kurze (z. B. Überschriften) oder auch umfangreiche Textproduktion handeln (z. B. zu einer Erzählung eine neue Episode erfinden).
Texte aus einer anderen Perspektive gestalten	Aus einer in der Vorlage nicht zur Geltung kommenden Perspektive (einer Figur, aber auch eines 'sprechenden' Tieres oder Gegenstandes) entsteht ein neuer Text, der 'blinde Stellen' der Textvorlage ausfüllt.
Visualisierung von Sprachtexten	Verbalsprachliche Texte werden in eine bildliche Darstellungsform überführt (Zeichnung, Foto, Video usw.).

Table 4.1: Creative work on literary texts (HALLET 2002: 144–45)

A literary reading model

DELANOY'S (2002: 7–12) model of literary readings includes the concepts described above. One axis describes the relationship between the literary text and tasks, i. e. the way interaction in the classroom between texts and learners is structured and facilitated by the teacher.

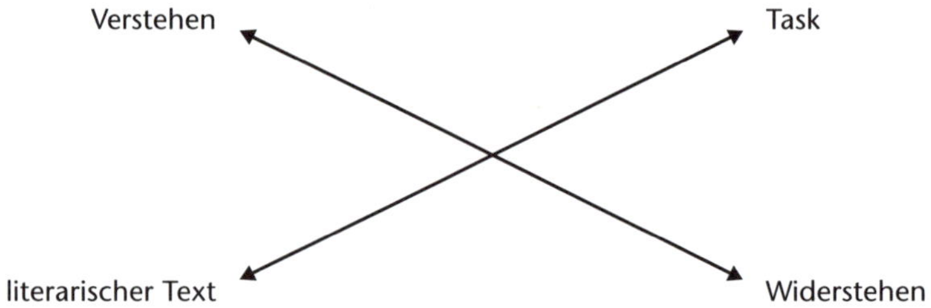

Model 4.2: Reading and working with literary texts (Delanoy 2002: 7)

The other axis represents the continuum from trying to understand other cultures through literary texts to resisting the text's or the author's representation of reality. This *"reading against the grain"* (Fetterley 1978, in: Delanoy 2002: 104), when for example a male-dominated text world is questioned from a woman's point of view, allows our learners to become critical readers, the process of which has again to be supported by tasks. In looking at Delanoy's model it is therefore helpful to imagine the reader at the crossing of the axes, at the centre of the reading process of literary and other texts.

3 Issues: Keeping the reader at the centre

Literary and non-literary texts

If we work on the basis of intertextuality, which is characterized by an increasing use of multi-modal texts, then the differentiation between literary and non-literary texts no longer holds true in terms of their use in the classroom. If we look at texts from the degree of the reader's involvement, one could say with Rosenblatt that texts find themselves on a continuum between efferent and aesthetic readings. As Miller has pointed out, *"literary and non-literary discourse differ in degree but not in kind. The newspaper article, the essay and the short story are on a continuum from single-voiced to double-voiced discourse"* (Miller 1992, in: Kramsch 1993: 131). This is what McRae in 1991 *"termed literature with a small 'l'"*, which includes *"advertisements, jokes, puns, newspaper headlines, examples of verbal play"* (McRae 1991, in: Carter/McRae 1996: 7). Working in the frame of reader response we also need to add the learners' own texts, such as their own rap songs or e-mail texts, which become the centre for the presentation of self or intense negotiation.

Canon discussion

While there is an unlimited number of texts to choose from for the foreign language classroom, for a long time the same books have been read and taught over and over again, even though curricula generally no longer restrict teachers in their choice of texts. Student teachers who have been taught the top five novels *(Lord of the Flies, Brave New World, Animal Farm, The Catcher in the Rye*, and *1984* see NÜNNING 1997, and MÜLLER-HARTMANN 2000b) during the last 25 years in school, basically expect and choose the same authors in their teacher education courses at the university, thus perpetuating the cycle when they start teaching. As NÜNNING (1997: 6) points out these texts mainly cover a few decades in the 20th century and mostly represent white male British writers. Women writers are missing as well as earlier writers and writers from other national or ethnic literatures. While this situation still reflects large-scale practice in schools, developments in the last 15–20 years have extended the canon into fields like gender study, postcolonial literatures and multi-ethnic literature(s) that give voice to those identities which have been suppressed by dominant ideologies.

Young adult literature

Texts for young adults or adolescents, the publication of which experienced a sharp increase since the 1960s, make up another field that has increased the text pool for teaching EFL learners. These books deal with issues teenage readers are concerned with, such as generational conflicts, peer pressure, first love, and the development of one's identity. Learners of this age find them especially accessible in a phase of transition during which reading books supports their process of identity formation (see HESSE 2002: 25–34, HALLET 2002: 34). Unlike easy readers or other simplified texts they provide authentic full-length novels or plays that can be read from lower secondary classes on, providing exactly the kind of subject matter and character relationships which may trigger student-centred responses (see BUSHMAN/BUSHMAN 1997).

Different Interests

Children's literature

With the extension of EFL into the primary school, literary texts have been used from the very beginning. Texts such as fairy-tales, or stories that contain strong repetitive elements (e.g. doing three tasks to defeat the giant etc) are extremely supportive of the language learning process. Since young learners grow up with stories in their L1, they are aware of the model text types such as fairy-tales, which supports their understanding of the storyline and allows them to focus on the language features. In stories, such as *The Very Hungry Caterpillar*, repetition ('I am still hungry') not only facilitates understanding of the structure of the story, it also supports the learning of language chunks. The storytelling approach enables coverage of the whole language curriculum (see the storyline approach in chap. 2.4) since interactive storytelling sessions create communicative situations for all the basic language functions (for example, imperatives such as 'I Want a Cat!' or questions such as 'Is that you Elmer?' in books by ROSS and MCKEE) (see CAMERON 2001: 159–79, ELLIS/BREWSTER 1991).

4 How to work with literary and other texts

Product-based and process-based approaches

We differentiate between product-based and process-based approaches to teaching texts. The product-based approach sees the text as an object of study and it requires learners to acquire a number of analytic techniques to interpret the text as an object of art. This is not very conducive to the language learning process since it usually does not involve the reader with his or her personal responses to the literary text. As CARTER and MCRAE (1996: xxii) have pointed out, instead of viewing *"literature as a sacrosanct object for reverential, product-centred study,"* teachers should facilitate a process-oriented approach. This implies that many strategies from the language learning classroom can be applied to the text (such as prediction and role-play). The literary text is open for manipulation (it can be cut apart and puzzled together again, it can be rewritten in a different genre) and learners are involved through learner-centred activities *"to develop their perceptions of it and to help them explore and express those perceptions"* (ibid.). Since there are many ways of reading and interpreting a text, learners assume a greater autonomy in voicing their views, often supported by pair and group work. This approach is exemplified by pre-, while-, and post-reading tasks (see example below for a number of suggestions on learner-centred tasks).

Pre-, while-, and post-reading tasks

Pre-reading tasks are designed to make learners curious about the literary text, to build up expectations and a field of awareness for what the story possibly has to offer (e.g. working with the title, chapter headings, images on the title page, possible character lists). This helps them with the reading process, when they can test their predictions against the actual text. While-reading tasks support the reading process through guiding questions, charts that trace the development of plot and characters, or prompts (see LEGUTKE/MÜLLER-HARTMANN 2001) that help to organize the discussion of longer texts. This process can also be supported by a reading journal in which learners collect their reading impressions, thoughts, and questions during the reading process at home or in class and which – having been individually designed by the learners – is the basis for discussions in class (see MOSNER 2001). This ensures that not just the teacher's but the learners' views on the text are brought out into the open. The while-reading phase would also be the place for more focused interpretation tasks that deal more in detail with narrative issues, such as the narrator's perspective, the setting, narrating and acting time, the plot, the characters, and stylistic and linguistic means (see MCKAY 2001: 321–26 for an example, see also NÜNNING/NÜNNING 2001). Post-reading tasks are especially helpful in facilitating learners' communicative proficiency. The previous discussion of the text serves as a spring board for more open oral or writing tasks that allow learners, for example, to speak more freely and spontaneously in the context of role-plays and roundtable discussions, or to write in different genres (see chap. 3.1.1).

Creative tasks to support ICC

Before we give an example of how to apply these methodological approaches to a short story, we would like to focus on one specific field of literary task design, which is becoming increasingly important in developing intercultural communicative competence by reading literary texts. Based on the various facets of intercultural learning (see chap. 2.1), CASPARI (2001) identifies four phases which generally match with the concept of pre-, while-, post-reading phases:

MOTIVATION

1. The pre-reading phase specifically focuses on the learner's willingness to engage with the otherness of the text (language, unusual structure, topics etc), thus making learners aware of multiple perspectives on a text.
2. A second phase, which extends into the while-reading phase, makes learners aware of their own cultural perspectives and experiences in relation to the world created by the text, by writing a reading journal (see above), by choosing music or pictures that could go with the text, or by filling gaps that the text offers.
3. In the third phase (during the while-reading phase) tasks are designed that help learners engage with the perspectives of characters in the text, thus facilitating a change of perspective. This involves close reading and understanding of the text, supported by creative tasks that make the text 'strange' (text puzzles, gaps, the original text has to be rediscovered in a merged text version), allowing learners to test their hypotheses against the text's and the characters' actions, i. e. comparing their solutions to those of the text. Here the teacher can supply linguistic, literary or cultural background knowledge to help learners to change perspectives. Role-plays, speaking from a different perspective, taking a character's perspective and defending his/her views are possible tasks.
4. In the fourth phase, generally the post-reading phase, learners need to relate their own views to those of the characters, coordinating perspectives, by comparing views, by contradicting, and/or reading and speaking against the grain of the text (see above) and by accepting differences to their own views. Possible tasks here are changing the action or characters, adding parts that have been omitted from the text, evaluating the text, or playful activities with linguistic or literary elements (especially in working with poetry).

Self Reflection

An example: Walker's *The Flowers*

By using WALKER's short story *The Flowers* (1973) which can be employed in classes 9 to 13, we will try to show the different possibilities of working with a literary text. In the story, set on a sharecropper's farm in the American South in the 1950s, Myop, a ten-year-old black girl, sets out on her morning walk into the surrounding woods. While she is walking across her parents' small farm the mood of the story is light, she is singing a song, collecting flowers – the world looks bright. When she moves deeper into the woods, the mood begins to change. It gets gloomier and the well-known agricultural products of her parents' farm, such as cotton and squash, are replaced by strange flowers and plants. The climax is reached when she suddenly steps into the decaying skeleton of a man who hanged himself or was hanged, shown by the remains of a noose. Myop does not seem particularly shocked by this. Having collected flowers on her walk, she finally lays them down at the dead man's side as if she was at a funeral and the last line reads: *"And the summer was over."*

Reading a text in a foreign language

The story exemplifies the problems EFL learners encounter when reading foreign literature. It is quite dense in terms of vocabulary and the cultural references to the American South, such as sharecropping, cotton etc are not necessarily known to them. The author's possibly intended meaning eludes them since they usually do not know WALKER and the only hints that this story could be about race relations (WALKER's work mainly deals with the effects of racism on African-Americans), and that the dead man could have been lynched, is a reference to Myop's 'dark hand'. While some of the unknown words could be annotated to help with a first reading, the following tasks present varied ways of dealing with a literary text, including the promotion of ICC.

Pre-reading tasks

A brainstorming on the basis of the title (What do you associate with the word 'flowers'?) allows students to predict what the story could be about. Since the function of flowers at a funeral rarely comes up, their expectations are called into question which makes them read the story carefully and causes bewilderment at Myop's actions in the second part. Another task would be the selection of pictures that could represent somebody called Myop (French 'myope' = short-sighted), thus focusing on her age, gender, and cultural background.

While-reading

More form-focussed tasks here work together with taking characters' perspectives to allow learners to see the world through Myop's eyes. A close reading of the text, supported by tasks such as looking for all the different kinds of plants in the text as well as adjectives or adverbs that describe the mood, produces an awareness of the perfect structure of the story (temporal set-up: morning-noon-afternoon; mood: light – gloomy- light again; spatial set-up:

civilization – wilderness – civilization, exemplified by plants of the field and those of the woods, and Myop's final gesture of laying down the flowers. All these movements signify her move from childhood to beginning adulthood (and the initiation into the problems of her society and ethnic group) and thus supports the process of reading and linguistic understanding. Taking Myop's position (Why was she not afraid when she stepped into the skeleton?) and especially that of the dead man (What happened to him? Write an obituary for him.) allows learners to think about the role of characters and their development, and brings up the question of their relationship in the cultural framework of the text. Here additional texts about the American South, triggered by a task that turns learners into cultural detectives, looking for hints at the cultural frame of the story (e.g. sharecropper's cabin, squash, cotton etc), provides possible literary and cultural background knowledge that extends the basis for interpreting the story, and supports intertextual play in the classroom.

Post-reading tasks

Finally learners need to co-ordinate their perspectives (Did the man hang himself? Was he killed? By whom? What impact does the discovery have on Myop?) taking account of the cultural background information they have discovered by looking at other texts (see above). Open tasks that promote learners' writing and speaking abilities could focus on Myop and her family (learners could write a conversation between Myop and family members when she comes home), Myop and societal representatives, for example, a policeman she tells about the discovery (police question Myop about the dead man), or the teacher could have learners write non-literary texts in the form of newspaper articles on the discovery.

Telecommunication and literary texts

On a different level, such a text can be used to initiate real mediation between non-native and native speakers when learners communicate via e-mail about it (MÜLLER-HARTMANN 1999b, see also CHRISTIAN 1997 who focuses on creative writing in such a project). When *The Flowers* became the focus of an exchange between American and German university students, the different cultural assumptions led to cultural misunderstandings, since the German learners, who had assumed the American students to be experts due to their Southern origin, were not satisfied with their interpretation of the text. The Americans' immediate focus on race relations was questioned by the Germans since they did not have the same cultural background knowledge. Discussions ensued and eventually enabled both sides to change and co-ordinate their different perspectives.

Hypertext

By creating a hypertext (see chap. 4.3), learners can combine their various interpretations of the text by adding new texts from the internet to the story or by writing their own texts about the story, changing and/or extending it in the process. That way they can develop intertextual references which reflect the process-oriented approach of interpreting the literary text from different points of view. This project-oriented approach allows learners to deal playfully with the text while at the same time producing complex language forms and other text genres. This could include pictures of Myop and the countryside (How do students imagine her/it?) as well as audio-recordings of a conversation between Myop and her family when she comes home (see MÜLLER-HARTMANN 2000d).

5 Future developments

Text choice

The fact that the top five novels (see above) have dominated the EFL classroom for so long shows that the opening of the canon has not necessarily led to a change in the 'hidden curriculum'. While schoolbook publishers have begun to extend their text pool by including ethnic literatures as well as young adult literary texts (see HESSE 2002, MÜLLER-HARTMANN 2000b), and while the possibility of ordering material over the internet has greatly improved the availability of these texts, it is not clear what effect this has had on the actual teaching situation.

Empirical research

In the field of teaching texts surprisingly little empirical research has been carried out. The last extensive look at the situation in German schools is over ten years old (see BENZ 1990). While we do not have an overview of what is happening in the German EFL classroom in terms of text selection and general methodology when dealing with texts, there have been empirical studies on specific aspects of teaching texts which reflect the growing interest in intercultural learning and young adult literature. KÜPPERS (1999) offers insights into the rather disappointing proficiency in reading in upper-level EFL courses, BURWITZ-MELZER (2003) shows the potential of literary texts for intercultural learning in lower intermediate courses, and HESSE (2002) presents a convincing model for writing on the basis of young adult literary texts.

Cultural studies and intertextuality

The development towards a multimodal and intertextual approach in the framework of a cultural studies paradigm will largely determine the use of texts in the future EFL classroom. The availability of unlimited-text resources on the internet and the increasing media literacy on the part of the learners will strengthen reader response by allowing learners to access, compare, and produce texts more easily, and thus facilitate the development of learner autonomy.

4.3 Media in the English Language Classroom

1 Introduction

Different media

In this chapter we will deal with one of the most important changes in the field of foreign language learning and teaching during the last ten years, the integration of the new media into the foreign language classroom. Media have always formed part of the foreign language classroom because they help teachers to create a more authentic English speaking atmosphere. While it probably sounds somewhat technical, we may differentiate between personal media, i. e. the teacher and the learners, and non-personal or instructional media, i. e. technical and non-technical media, such as the textbook, the board or maps. Media are also differentiated according to the different senses they relate to, the visual (blackboard, photos, worksheets, overhead transparencies, slides etc.), the auditory (audio-cassettes, CDs, etc.) and the audiovisual (films, videos, DVDs etc.) (see FREUDENSTEIN 1995: 288). The focus here will be essentially on technical non-personal media and their role in language teaching.

Media and the degree of simulation

The traditional forms of media such as the textbook as a basic medium for language instruction, the board, the poster, and flashcards have long been used by the teacher as tools to present language in simulated learning environments. Technical media, such as the audio-cassette, the film, as well as satellite and cable TV have improved the creation of simulated environments by bringing native speakers in voice and image into the classroom. In terms of language learning these media have extended the repertoire by allowing students to improve their listening skills, and their proficiency in non-verbal communication by watching native speakers on film. They have also extended learners' knowledge of the target culture. However, the invention of the personal computer and its relatively fast development into a multimedia machine has the potential both to offer an even more authentic learning environment, and to turn the teacher-centred classroom into a more learner-centred one in the process. One of the major functions of the computer is still to present language input, but what is new is that it allows learners to communicate with other foreign language learners or native speakers of English worldwide. It enables them to do research using the internet's unlimited store of authentic materials, which hones their skills in reading and increasingly in listening. Also, by producing multimedia texts, learners develop their writing, publication and presentation skills, as well as their technical skills in using the different tools.

The role of the teacher

Earlier approaches have looked at different media as a replacement for the teacher (see KERN 1996: 107–08), but experience and research have shown that the teacher, while increasingly playing the role of advisor, is decisive in designing these often complex learning environments, and in initiating and monitoring the learning processes that develop. At the same time the electronic media may be a powerful motivational tool in the language learning process, facilitating a more learner-centred classroom (see HANSON-SMITH 2001: 109 for a research overview).

Electronic literacy

With the advent of the electronic media and its growing importance in the workplace and at home, teachers' and learners' proficiency in using these tools have come to the fore. Being able to use technology has become a key qualification, leading to a new concept of literacy. Different terms are used to describe this skill, such as information, computer or media literacy (see HENDRICKS 2000, WARSCHAUER 1999). Computer literacy is often seen as just developing the technical skills it takes to use a computer. SHETZER and WASHINGTON's definition of electronic literacy (2000: 173) though comprises more and is essential for computer-mediated language learning: "[...] *an electronic literacy framework considers how people use computers to interpret and express meaning. Electronic literacy thus involves what has been called information literacy – the ability to find, organize, and make use of information – but electronic literacy is broader in that it also encompasses how to read and write in a new medium.*" They propose a three-tier structure to their concept of electronic literacy, i.e. communication, construction of texts and websites, and research. They stress the importance of communicating in a meaningful way with learners worldwide. This generally involves collaboration on the local and the virtual level and hence supports a sociocultural approach to language learning (see chap. 2.1).

Multi-literacies

To develop ICC, though, we still need to go one step further. The native speaker model (often based on the British English Standard) was abandoned because of the multiplicity of different 'Englishes' world-wide (which learners may access via telecommunication). This resulted in an even broader view of literacy which the New London Group, an international team of interdisciplinary researchers, has termed *multiliteracies* (COPE/ KALANTZIS 2000: 3–8). They point out that there is a *"multiplicity of communications channels and media"*, which forces our learners to learn how to deal with different modes of communication beyond the mere *"written-linguistic"* one. The hypertext and interactive multimedia integrate visual, textual, audio and spatial patterns of meaning. Since a hypertext is three-dimensional – the two-dimensional text surface we see on the screen as well as the links that lead to other texts – it is also spatial. These various representations of linguistic and cultural contexts require learning to go beyond the learning of linguistic features of a language and include the learning about different cultural backgrounds. *"Increasing local diversity and global connectedness"* and the use of English as a lingua franca (English as a language used by people who have different first languages) force us *"to negotiate differences every day, in our local communities and in our increasingly globally interconnected working and community lives"* (COPE/KALANTZIS 2000: 3–8). The necessity of developing multiliteracies (see example below) thus goes hand in hand with an ICC, highlighting the importance of integrating the new media into the foreign language classroom.

Questions of media use

After a historical overview we will turn our attention to the potential the media offer to support EFL teaching and learning today. The use of media in the classroom, whether technical or non-technical, traditional or modern, always generates the same questions: How does the use of the medium support language learning? What tasks can be designed? How does the role of the learner and the teacher change?

2 Historical development: From tutor to tool

Behavioural paradigm

The use of electronic media in computer assisted language learning (CALL) has been determined by the various approaches to language learning and by technical developments. In the 1950s and 1960s drill and practice tutoring programs were used which provided learners with feedback in small discrete learning steps. This was an attempt to objectify the learning process by using the computer as a mechanical tutor which provided repeated drills and direct right or wrong feedback without any further comment:

Computer: *Fill in the correct form of the past tense or present perfect tense: I ________ in London since 1999. (to live)*
Learner: *I lived in London since 1999.*
Computer: *Wrong.*

These programs basically copied the existing structuralist approach to teaching and did not fully exploit the interactive potential of the computer, i. e. they did not analyse the learner input in a more intelligent way, and the use of language was largely unimaginative and lacked any form of creativity. The best manifestation of these learning environments is the language lab that was set up in the late 1960s and 70s. Today more sophisticated and interactive language learning programs have been developed (see for example RÜSCHOFF/WOLFF 1999: 79–87 on a program called *English*

Coach) that present interactive learning environments with more complex feedback features and a generally more flexible and creative task structure, but *"until recently, these programs tended to be technically unsophisticated, generally allowing only one acceptable response per item"* (KERN/WARSCHAUER 2000: 8–9).

Communicative language teaching

With the advent of the communicative approach the learner moved into the centre, and media were designed to provide opportunities for using the foreign language as a means of communication. One approach was based on the idea of combining various media in a teaching situation to support language learning. These combinations included film, video, cassette, slides etc. and together with the textbook a complex learning environment was established. Learners worked with different text genres which generated a real-world situation that needed little simulation. Classroom management of the different media presented teachers with a real challenge as this meant carrying around cassette recorders and pushing TV sets and video recorders, which were often not available in combination (LEGUTKE/MÜLLER-HARTMANN/ULRICH 2000: 53–54). But the development of the personal computer combined these different elements since pictures, audio files, movies, and texts were made available through just one machine. Learners now had their personal computers, even though it was only in the late 1990s that computers were set up in sufficient numbers in German schools through the program 'Schulen ans Netz'. During this period a number of software programs for language learning were developed as well as authoring tools for the teacher to design her own materials (for the possible combination of the computer as tool and tutor see RITTER 1998). But, as KERN and WARSCHAUER (2000: 10–11) point out, *"despite the apparent advantages of multimedia CALL, today's computer programs are not yet intelligent enough to be truly interactive."* And they add that although they might *"provide an effective illusion of communicative interaction"*, learners still act *"within a closed system"* which guides them in terms of the interaction by what the designers of the programs have chosen to provide. In the following example of a storyboard program learners have to reconstruct a conversation (replace the XXX) by guessing the possible solutions:

"Excuse me!"

"XXX?"
"Could XXX tell me XXX way XX XXX station, XXXXXX?"
"Certainly. Turn right XXXX XXX leave XXX school. Turn right XXXX XX XXX end XX XXXXXX Street [...]. *XXX station XX XX XXX end XX XXXX XXXX."* [...]
"XX XX XXX?"

"XX'X XXXXX five XXXXXXX' walk."
"XXXXX XXX,"
"XXX'X mention XX!"
(from RÜSCHOFF/WOLFF 1999: 97)

While this program attempts to provide a communicative situation and makes learners think about lexical, semantic, and grammatical aspects, as well as questions of topic, content and register, there is no negotiation of meaning since the program provides a set form of interaction. It has to be pointed out, though, that if learners work in pairs or small groups, there can be quite a high degree of negotiation of the tasks set by language software in front of the computer among the learners. This leads us to the sociocultural approach.

Sociocultural language teaching

In the 1990s the continuous development of the personal computer into a complex multimedia machine supported a sociocultural approach to language learning (see chap. 2.1). Since *"reading and writing came to be viewed as processes embedded in particular sociocultural contexts,"* which helped *"learners to become part of literate communities through extensive discussion of readings and the linking of reading and writing"*, the computer facilitated interaction and negotiation of meaning with other learners (KERN/WARSCHAUER 2000: 5–6). This process was supported by the development of a number of telecommunication technologies, such as e-mail (which had already existed since the early 1960s), the Internet (available since the 1980s), and the development of the world wide web (WWW) in the 1990s. These services enabled learners to contact other language learners and to access authentic materials worldwide. Now learners were able to use the foreign language in e-mail projects, for example (see chap. 2.1 and 4.1), to exchange information about each other's lives, and to negotiate scoiocultural meaning when discussing similarities and differences of their cultures. This new dimension of communicative language learning via computer found expression in a change of concept from the old tutorial CALL (see above) to that of *"computer-mediated collaborative learning"* (CMC) (WARSCHAUER 1997). It has recently been subsumed under the term of network-based language teaching (NBLT) environments (WARSCHAUER/KERN 2000). In NBLT environments learners work together with others on topic-based projects, such as discussing homelessness in their respective cultures and doing internet research on the topic. This can be done in an e-mail project, or learners can ask specialists for information to help them do the project. NASA, for example, provides access to specialists if schools have questions about their space program, or Vietnam veterans can be contacted online to provide their view on the Vietnam War. These learning environments are characterized by a number of principles that not only provide more authentic opportunities for input and production, but also lead to new roles for teachers and learners.

3 Principles of network-based language learning environments

Communication channels and time and place independence

Basically there are two different modes of communication: asynchronous (communicating at different times, e. g. e-mail, forums) and synchronous (communicating in real time, e. g. chat, videoconference etc.). In contrast to the communication between two people the computer allows many-to-many communication via an e-mail list, a chatroom (see http://www.icq.com or http://schmooze.hunter.cuny.edu:8888/) or a computer conferencing software (see http://bscw.gmde.de or http//www.softarc.com [commercial]). Hence language input and language production increase because all the learners in a classroom can communicate simultaneously with each other and other computer users outside the classroom. As long as learners have access to a computer they can communicate whenever and from wherever they like, making computer use independent of time and place. Learners can communicate around the clock, they can mail or chat from school, home or from an internet café. This also allows combinations between the traditional classroom and other learning environments, such as the computer lab and home. Consequently the local classroom may be extended into many directions, to the learners' home as well as to classrooms world-wide.

Language production

Since CMC is text-based, the multiplicity of communication channels enables learners to read and write more EFL texts. Also, in e-mail and chat communication new hybrid text genres develop which integrate features of oral and written communication. In a chat between German and English learners (8th grade) the oral character of the written communication becomes obvious (MareikeF is the teacher):

14:41:52 *[MareikeF] Hello Hannah and Ali, how are you? Glad you joined us.* ☺
14:42:31 *[Hannah&Ali] Hello, Hannah isn't here, it's just alice.*
14:42:34 *[Uwe&Thomas] servus*
14:42:52 *[Uwe&Thomas] ahhh … good morning*
14:43:16 *[MareikeF] Sorry, I thought your name was Ali* ☹

Turn-taking differs from face-to-face communication, too. Consider the following sequence from the above chat. The two groups were discussing the young adult novel *Holes* by SACHAR which deals with a camp of juvenile delinquents. After a first exchange about the weather and hobbies, Uwe and Thomas initiate the discussion about the book:

14:47:38 [Tim&Jony] Nobody can not like football
14:47:43 [Uwe&Thomas] Let's talk about bootcamps now ….

While in the classroom choice of topic is often controlled by the teacher who structures communication following the IRE sequence (see chap. 2.2), in CMC the learners may control turn-taking to a much larger extent. In a chat all participants are potentially equal, as everybody can initiate a turn. This can be seen in the following example. The teacher does not give the explanation, but keeps in the back and just intervenes to pass the turn on to the learners.

14:55:07 [Uwe&Thomas] i think psychologic headwashing could help more than boot camps
14:56:14 [Tim&Jony] What is Psychologic headwashing?
14:58:22 [Hannah&Ali] What is brainwashing?
14:58:51 [MareikeF] Uwe and Thomas, do you want to answer Alice's question?
14:59:37 [Max&Leonar] it's when someone talks to you really intensive and changes all your minds to what he wants

If there are more than two people in the chat, communication may often be characterized by parallel conversations. This allows learners to produce more extensive pieces of discourse, increasing their language production and language use. Research has also shown that learners produce a higher amount of discourse varieties in synchronous communication. They often produce language that *"is lexically and syntactically more complex"* (Warschauer 1997: 474), as can be seen in the chat example. CMC facilitates negotiation of meaning because of the opportunity of increased interaction. Since computers allow the storage and analysis of texts, they also offer learners the opportunity to notice language functions through the use of concordances, for example. Concordances list the possible usages of a word or structure in everyday spoken and written language and therefore may enhance processing of language (for an example see below; and chap. 3.2). By using these possibilities, learners develop language awareness.

Research orientation

The hypermedial structure (combination of texts, pictures, audio and video files) of the WWW facilitates collaborative research projects and the publication of learner texts for a world-wide audience. The proliferation of authentic English texts, the availability of specialists in almost every field, and the possibility of finding appropriate and authentic material for every age level make the WWW a welcome source of content-based material. For young language learners, for example, texts that English speaking primary schools have published on their servers provide appropriate language and content level. The major medium of today's language classes, the textbook, can thus be extended and critically analyzed through data found on the WWW, since often the textbook material is out of date or has been specifically written for the classroom and may therefore not be very authentic. While learners can research their own texts, they also become authors in their own right when they publish project results or other texts.

Intercultural communicative competence

For the first time native speakers and learners of other languages are directly connected to the local classroom, without actually being present in person (e.g. language assistants, exchange students). CMC enhances language production, provides meaningful contexts of interaction and thus offers a qualitatively different approach to the development of an intercultural communicative competence (see chat example above). Through contact with speakers from other cultures learners enter a negotiation process where different cultural practices can be compared and discussed (see chap. 2.1 and 4.1 for examples from e-mail projects).

Task-based language learning

Network-based language learning can lead to very complex learning environments where learners use different localities, the classroom, the computer lab and their study at home to communicate with one or more classrooms abroad. While such an authentic learning environment needs real-world tasks that make sense to all participants involved (see chap. 2.4), it also calls for clear structures and guidelines to initiate and monitor the learning processes. The tasks-as-workplan will often be changed in action, not only because learners work in pairs and groups and thus determine their own agenda, but also because the logistics of working with electronic media calls for great flexibility. Computers might crash, partners do not provide the expected answers, or the appropriate material cannot be found in restrictive 45 minutes slots. However, well-set tasks can lead learners onto a path of discovery, allowing them to develop project knowledge in the process since telecommunication favours this approach to language learning.

Roles of learners and teachers

All of the above has far-reaching consequences for the roles of teachers and learners. On the one hand, the use of the computer leads to an individualization of learning processes since learners can work at their own pace and proficiency level when, for example, working with language software. On the other hand, telecommunication facilitates collaborative learning in the local classroom and with other learners, fostering communication independent of the teacher. In both these respects, as well as by offering free text choice and a high amount of personal text production, and last but not least because of the often higher technical expertise of learners, the development of autonomy is supported. Authoring products with other learners for a world wide peer audience (e. g. creation of websites) enhances discussion and reflection and may boost motivation. Teachers have to design, initiate and monitor these complex learning processes, hence they have to undertake a variety of new tasks to enhance learners' interaction in CMC learning environments. Project-oriented learning and a stronger individualization of the learning processes demand more specific planning as well as increased flexibility. The teacher will need to become a facilitator, *"[who] manages the interaction, usually in the background, by relating individual comments, by suggesting a different interpretation of an idea, or by clarifying a position and so forth"* (AHERN 1998: 230; see also chat example above). Increased interaction among all participants in CMC environments, the intensified search for materials, and the necessity to design meaningful tasks offer new opportunities for a negotiated curriculum between learners and teacher since the full potential of CMC will only be realized in close cooperation (see BREEN 1987).

4 Integrating media into the English language classroom

Examples of media use

As outlined above, media can be used in many different ways in the foreign language classroom. The following suggestions concentrate on specific forms of integration, such as tasks that have a specific language focus, the watching of films, the presentation of group work results, or communication with other learners. While they are presented separately to give a structured overview, all of the different media functions can be combined in more complex projects, such as intercultural e-mail projects or internet research projects.

Watching films

Since (video) films represent another form of text, the general task structure is that of working with literary texts (see chap. 4.1 and 4.2). We also distinguish pre-, while-, and post-viewing activities. At the same time, working with films offers additional approaches, such as the manipulation of sound and image by turning off the sound and having learners find a text for the sequence being presented, or by freezing important scenes to have learners speculate on characters' actions and the continuation of the story-line, or to study non-verbal communication. STEMPLESKI and TOMALIN (1990: 3–4) present a whole range of varied activities. While films and documentaries allow detailed study and comparison of cross-cultural differences and similarities, music video clips offer another chance of motivating learners (see *Der Fremdsprachliche Unterricht Englisch* 2002).

Analyzing and practicing

Language learners may analyze the texts they find on the WWW or the texts they receive from other learners according to the language functions, and compare them to their own language use in, for example, e-mail texts. ECK, LEGENHAUSEN and WOLFF (1995: 141–68) have shown how the use of concordance software allows learners to analyse not only the different styles of e-mails written by themselves and their native project partners, but also how intercultural differences and similarities can be detected. The German students were especially surprised about the differences between authentic daily language use in America and their own school English in that the American students' English was much more informal and colloquial than their own. In terms of intercultural learning the analysis showed that while the German students put stress on mentioning their age in the introduction letters, 40% of the American students leave it out and describe their height, and the colour of hair and eyes instead (e.g. *auburn hair, radiant red hair, blond hair, hazel eyes, poppy dog eyes* etc., see ECK et. al. 1995: 150), something their German partners neglect.

Presenting results

Apart from the textbook the 'blackboard' is still the most often used medium in the foreign language classroom. It allows the quick presentation and structuring of important aspects of instruction and its results, and can be put to flexible use by writing or drawing on it or by combining it with other media, such as posters or flashcards that are stuck on the board. The same is true of 'transparencies' which can be prepared beforehand and consequently allow a wider range of representations. If used in an appropriate way both media facilitate learner-centred teaching since learners can come to the board or overhead projector to present their findings from work at home or group work, thus intensifying interaction among students. When presenting the results of a larger classroom project, a power point presentation is a modern option, demanding a certain degree of computer literacy and the ability to carefully combine oral presentation and visual support so that neither redundancy nor information overload result. 'Posters' on the other hand cannot be changed and they remain in place over a longer period of time, such as grammar posters or posters representing classroom language. They support language production in the classroom since learners can look at them when they are unsure of a phrase. Combining all of these various possibilities of representing results of individual and collaborative work is the construction of 'websites' by learners. It is here that learners can show their proficiency in the field of multiliteracies, combining the various forms of media usage. Since there are a number of relatively simple tools that allow the construction of websites without knowing hypertext mark-up language (html), the representation of project work is possible via websites. At the same time this allows learners to reach a potentially world-wide audience (for examples see KALLENBACH/RITTER 2000 and www.englisch.schule.de).

Communicating with other learners

E-mail projects, combined with synchronous chat facilitate real-world communication among learners from different backgrounds and cultures. In these projects learners not only practise language use in a real-world situation, they also engage in intercultural learning through the negotiation of meaning. E-mail projects can be organized for all levels of language learning, from simple exchanges about pets and hobbies to highly political projects such as the peace projects represented by CUMMINS and SAYERS (1995) on the list I*EARN (http://www.iearn.org/. See chap. 2.1 and 4.1 for examples. See also DONATH 1996, CHRISTIAN 1997, MÜLLER-HARTMANN/RICHTER 2001).

5 Conclusion: Current trends and developments

The new media and English

As WARSCHAUER (2001: 212) points out, *"electronic literacies are important in many languages, but in none more so than English since an estimated 85 per cent of the electronically-stored information in the world is in the English language."* This leads him to conclude that while on-line communication has been increasingly used to teach foreign languages, it *"is a major new medium of English-language communication and literacy in its own right, and one that is likely to affect the development of TESOL* [Teaching English to Speakers of Other Languages] *in important ways that we cannot yet predict."* In terms of technology one can agree with HANSON-SMITH (2001: 112) who says that *"the move from wired to wireless communications and the consolidation of telecommunications into combined telephone-internet-television access will not drive pedagogy in quite the same way as the move to the personal computers has done."* Still, new forms of using tone and voice will change the text-based nature of foreign language learning and will provide important stimuli not only for reading and writing, but also for listening and speaking.

Digital divide

There is still a digital divide in terms of computer access between technology-rich and technology-poor countries. The same problem exists within many countries between poor and rich people. At the same time schools are often the only places that provide online access for students whose parents are unable to provide computer access.

Qualification of teachers

But access is only the basic requirement. Teachers' resistance to the use of the new media, often due to institutional and curricular hindrances, remains an important issue. One of the most pressing needs in this regard is the qualification of teachers in pre- and in-service teacher training in combination with school development (LEGUTKE & MÜLLER-HARTMANN/SCHOCKER-V. DITFURTH in press, SCHNOOR 2000). WARSCHAUER/KERN (2000: 12, 15) conclude that after the euphoria concerning virtual environments the need for a pedagogy of network-based language learning remains an important issue, as is the need for more qualitative research to find out how the electronic media are actually integrated into the foreign language classroom.

4.4 Acknowledging, Promoting and Assessing Achievement

1 The context

Different views on testing

You may have experienced in your own school-days an approach to assessment that asked you to demonstrate what you had learned at the end of a textbook unit (= a product-oriented approach to assessment) and to have your performance assessed in relation to the level of achievement of your fellow students, where the distribution of marks in a class was expected to correspond to the bell curve (= a norm-referenced approach to assessment). In contrast to this limited view of testing, this chapter takes a wider perspective. It focuses on the relationship between testing, teaching and learning because assessment practices determine to a large extent what is being taught and learned – a phenomenon known as backwash (or washback) effect. CAMERON illustrates the power of assessment over teaching and learning with various examples from different language learning contexts and concludes: *"It would seem reasonable to require assessment to serve teaching, by providing feedback on pupils' learning* […]. *In practice, the scenario is quite different: assessment seems to 'drive' teaching by forcing teachers to teach what is going to be assessed.* […] *The testing practices and the syllabus together determine what a child will experience in lessons, with little room for taking account of his or her individual needs"* (CAMERON 2001: 215). As language learning occurs in socio-cultural contexts, what is assessed and how it is assessed depends on the administrative requirements of the school as an institution (see chap. 2.5), the necessity for teachers to prepare their students for a final externally set exam, or the culturally defined attitudes towards testing. But of course there are choices as we will see. Even though context features may restrict teachers' possibilities, their role in assessment is nonetheless central: they determine the quality of personal relationships in their classrooms and therefore contribute both to a relaxed language learning atmosphere and to a positive attitude to testing: *"People vary widely in their reactions to tests. Some like the sense of challenge; others find it unpleasant.* […]

The 'amount' of unpleasant stress associated with a test depends on various factors at least some of which may be under the control of the teacher: how well the learners are prepared for it and how confident they feel of success; what rewards and penalties are associated with success or failure [...]*; and so on"* (UR 1996: 36). Whatever the limiting or supporting context variables may be, seen in this wider perspective, assessment may serve a multitude of purposes. The following list gives you an idea of what is currently discussed.

2 General purposes of testing

Purposes: aims of assessment

An obvious purpose of testing is what REA-DICKINS describes as bureaucratic: teachers provide information on the attainment standards achieved by individual students as these are specified in a particular curriculum, so that students may be screened and placed (REA-DICKINS 2001: 451). Another purpose is the monitoring of student progress in relation to learning goals specified in a curriculum or in a textbook for formal certification. Other purposes are pedagogically motivated: the focus of assessment may be to support learning. To do so, teachers develop an awareness in the learner of what is being learned. In this case a teacher is working with her students and is including their perspectives, for example through collecting best work samples in individual student portfolios or by providing feedback in student-teacher conferences: "[A]*ssessment for learning thus motivates learners to become engaged in the interaction through which they are enabled to develop skills of reflection* [...]*, as well as providing them with an ability to reflect metacognitively on their own learning"* (REA-DICKINS 2001: 452–3).

Purposes: point in time of assessment

Another useful distinction to clarify the various purposes of assessment is to look at the point in time when the assessment is administered. You may either give an assessment at the end of a teaching sequence, for example at the end of a textbook unit, which 'sums up' what a student has learned during that course and which is therefore referred to as 'summative' assessment, or you may provide assessment procedures while doing your coursework to get ongoing feedback from your students on their development and progress. This is called 'formative' assessment, meaning that you are trying to find out if your teaching has a forming influence on learning. As a consequence of the formative assessment of skills, teachers may decide to give extra practice if results are not satisfactory. We will now turn to the specifics of assessing (foreign) language performance. There are two basic questions we need to ask: What is assessed? And how can language performance be interpreted and assessed appropriately?

3 Developments in language-related purposes of assessing modern languages

What counts as appropriate evidence for the mastery of the target language has been influenced by various developments. These will be discussed below.

a) Language policy and features of a specific teaching/learning context: Negotiating standards, areas and procedures for assessment

Language policy: The Common European Framework of Reference for Languages

The COUNCIL OF EUROPE publication *Common European Framework of Reference for Languages: Learning, teaching, assessment* (2001) is a politically powerful paper which is bound to affect language assessment purposes and practices in Europe. It aims to provide a common framework and to set common standards for the traditionally different assessment practices around Europe to enable comparisons across different systems of qualifications. It sets out to set these standards for all European languages. To do so, it describes six different levels of language proficiency (from A1 to C2) for the different content areas and communicative language competences (e. g. vocabulary range, grammatical accuracy, sociolinguistic appropriateness). It provides descriptors for these different aspects of proficiency and relates them to each of these particular competences and levels (see CEF chap. 5). It also describes appropriate communicative activities for each level of proficiency (e. g. asking for clarification, information exchange, reading for information; (see CEF chap. 4). Despite its drawbacks (see critical evaluation in BAUSCH et al 2003), the value of the *Common European Framework* is that it can be used as a basis for educational policy decision makers and for teams of language teachers to negotiate and to agree on commonly accepted, context-specific and therefore context-appropriate standards of assessment.

b) Developments in applied linguistics: Taking account of the complexity of language and language learning

Discrete vs. integrative assessment formats

Developments in modern language assessment have also been influenced by the many changes in the way we view language and language learning. LARSEN-FREEMAN (1998: 4) provides an excellent survey of developments in linguistics (from structural, generative, social/functional, discourse/text/corpus to critical) and of changes in ideas of language acquisition (habit formation in behaviourism, rule formation in cognitivism, interactionism, constructivism, experiential; see graph in chap. 1). She concludes that in order to get a whole picture of what language and language learning involves, we need to be aware of the complexity and wholeness of what language proficiency entails rather than look for a 'correct' representation of its parts. This has lead to the development of forms of assessment that go beyond the testing of discrete aspects of language and focus instead on test formats that are integrative and take account of the complexity of language and language learning.

c) Developments in the field of educational measurement: From assessing discrete items to assessing complex skills

Designs

In the last fifty years there have been considerable developments in assessment design formats that are available for teachers. General trends may be presented as follows, even though this categorization is of course simplified and there are overlaps.

Discrete Point Testing

The 1960s were defined by Discrete Point Testing in discrete item test formats (LADO 1961). Assessment focuses on discrete aspects of language that have been taught. Each test item is intended to measure only one linguistic element of the same type. This may be an aspect of one of the subskills (pronunciation, vocabulary, grammar) or of one of the four skills (listening, writing, reading, speaking). This approach is based on the assumption that the sum of discrete, isolated elements gives feedback on language competence. It therefore represents a simplistic idea of what language performance means. You find a comprehensive survey of the different types of tasks in DOYÉ (1986).

Skill-Based Testing

Skill-Based Testing in integrative and open-ended test formats were used in the 1970s. Tests that assess one or more levels of language (phonology, morphology, lexicon, syntax, or discourse) and/or one or more language skills (reading, writing, speaking, and listening) have come to be called integrative tests (BAILEY 1998: 245). Typically these tests include a variety of procedures such as dictation, gap-texts, or guided interviews. An example from our English language learning context is the centrally set final exam for *Realschulen* in *Baden-Württemberg*.

Communicative Testing

Communicative Testing in task-based and criterion-referenced test formats then came to the fore in the 1980s. The general focus of assessment shifted from testing language 'knowledge' to testing language in 'use'. Therefore, tests focused on communicative, integrated 'real-life' tasks (for examples see BYGATE et. al. 2001). This has led to a criterion-referenced approach to testing: You compare a learner's performance against a set of commonly accepted criteria of how performance can be described. To do so, you discuss and agree on criteria that demonstrate successful performance with your colleagues, involving your learners in this process (for examples see BAILEY 1998: 208; LEGUTKE / THOMAS 1991: 245 & 247).

There are basically two procedures that you can follow to establish criteria that describe successful performance.

a. You describe the response you expect from a task you set in a test to get feedback from your learners (*Erwartungshorizont*). Then you match your learners' performance against the expected feedback on the task.
b. You develop various descriptors that you put on a scale. You then place a learner at the appropriate place on the scale according to his or her performance (for an example see descriptors for spoken fluency in the Council of Europe framework, the Oral Assessment Criteria Grid (SCHNEIDER/NORTH 2000: 345) or O'MALLEY in CAMERON (2001: 223–4).

Complex-competence testing

Language learning is now seen as a complex competence involving the assessment of non-language related skills. In institutional contexts language competence develops as a result of social processes where the teacher and other learners play an important part (i. e. as partners in communication or as collaborators during group work activities). Development and demonstration of language competences involves the successful use of various skills and techniques (i. e. the skill to use a dictionary to look up the meaning of unfamiliar words or visualizing techniques to illustrate a poster that learners need to support presentation of a talk). The list of skills and techniques which support language development and production is endless but, they have to be developed and assessed if we want to do justice to the complexity of the process. We have only just begun to devise tools that allow us to assess complex competences and current publications on assessment focus very much on these issues. The following examples give you an idea of what is involved. Paired or grouped tests of spoken language are something of a challenge when administered with a large group of learners. FOOT (1999), EGYÜD and GLOVER's response (2001) to the issues raised by FOOT and NUNN's (2000) suggestions for designing rating scales for small-group interaction gives you an excellent idea of some of the issues and the solutions being currently discussed (an excellent example for a rating scale that covers the interactive ability to participate in keeping a conversation going in terms of turn-taking and negotiation can be found in NUNN (2000: 172–3). GRUNDER and BOHL (2001) have published a research report on their experiences with new forms of assessing topic-based projects. They aim to integrate the assessment of content-related, socio-communicative and methodological-strategic competences. Two of the reported case-studies refer to projects in English as a foreign language. For example, they illustrate their attempt to find criteria to assess autonomous learning (2001: 127) and to develop criterion-referenced observation sheets to assess presentations in English (2001: 152).

4 Features of 'good' assessment practice

Traditional features of test quality: validity & reliability

The quality of assessment practices has traditionally been described by two related concepts: validity and reliability. 'Validity' asks if a test actually assesses what it claims or intends to assess. CAMERON (2001: 224–5) illustrates this principle with the following examples taken from the group of young learners. "[I]*f we claim to have assessed a child's 'writing skills' but only give a mark for spelling and neatness, and omit discourse level skills of organisation and sequencing, this would not be valid assessment.* [...T]*he assessment of young children's, mostly oral, language learning is not validly done through pencil and paper tests that require written responses.*" 'Reliability' examines if a test produces 'reliable' that is consistent results even though a test is administered on different occasions or by different people. CAMERON points out a resulting dilemma because validity and reliability "*can be conflicting needs for assessment techniques and procedures. The most reliable assessments will be pencil and paper tests in which each item measures only a single aspect of a skill and which give each testee a numerical mark. But the most valid assessments will be those that collect a lot of information about performance on several aspects of a skill. When validity is increased, reliability decreases*" (CAMERON 2001: 225). Therefore, the two potentially conflicting principles need to be suitably balanced, which can best be achieved when site-specific test designs are negotiated between teams of teachers responsible for the same group of learners.

Objectivity in testing?

Having said this, we need to be aware of the fact that there is no such thing as objectivity in testing a phenomenon as complex as language performance: „*Die Definition der Leistung muss von den Beteiligten, ganz besonders von Lehrerinnen und Lehrern, geleistet werden. Jede Definition stellt eine subjektive Gewichtung bestimmter Leistungsmerkmale dar. Leistung ist dadurch niemals wertfrei, ebenso wenig ist sie völlig objektivierbar.* [...] *Der Leistungsanspruch ist unterschiedlich, zur Verringerung dieser Unterschiede sind kollegiale Vereinbarungen notwendig.* [...] *Die traditionelle* [...] *Zensurengebung wird von Eltern, Lehrerinnen und Lehrern sowie von Schülerinnen und Schülern oftmals unhinterfragt als objektiv angesehen.* [...] *Es ist daher umso dringlicher, die mangelnde Wertfreiheit jeder Leistung zu betonen*" (GRUNDER/BOHL 2001: 30–31). KLIPPERT therefore defines 'quality in assessment' as „*weitestgehend informierte Subjektivität*" (personal communication).

Feasibility

This takes us to another principle, that of feasibility: "*Assessors operate under time pressure. They are only seeing a limited sample of performance and there are definite limits to the type and number of categories they can handle as criteria*" (COUNCIL OF EUROPE 2001: 178). For an assessment tool to be practical, selection is crucial – or, as JOHNSON puts it: "*Testing is sometimes the art of the possible*" (JOHNSON

2001: 306). As a consequence, what counts as appropriate assessment needs to be negotiated by teachers working in the same context against standards that have been commonly agreed on.

5 Conclusion: Current trends and developments

Learner involvement

- Promoting learner and teacher awareness of language development and monitoring progress through various formative assessment strategies that are based on observation and description (REA-DICKINS 2001: 457). Teachers will have to become more involved in their learners' language development and they will need to know about procedures that help them *to notice* and to monitor what a learner does when s/he is engaged in an activity and to adjust their teaching accordingly.

Focus on testing language in use

- Choosing tasks for assessment that focus more on communicative skills-based tasks such as interaction and oral discourse skill (REA-DICKINS 2000: 388) than they do now. Referring to classroom-based research in the assessment of languages with young learners, REA-DICKINS and RIXON (1999) observed *"a mismatch* [...] *between curricular aims, pedagogy, and test content"* and concluded that it presented something of a challenge *"to find procedures that capture* [...] *the dimensions of language and language use"* one actually wishes to capture, such as the cultural and the social/communicative dimensions of language use (1999: 96). The most frequently used test format was paper-and-pencil, discrete point testing with very few focusing on the assessment of spontaneous speech.

Self- and peer assessment

- Supporting learners to self-assess and peer assess their language development by using portfolios and other supportive ways to assess language learning (BAILEY 1998: 215–221; GENESEE/UPSHUR 1996; REA-DICKINS 2000: 391; examples of peer assessment in FROESE 1998: 18; BAILEY 1998; GEIST 1998; HARRIS 1997: 16; HARRIS/MCCANN 1994: chap. 3; MACHT/NUTZ 1999; WESKAMP 1996).

Tools for testing complex competences

- Developing feasible tools that allow teachers to assess complex competences that include communicative language competence, social competences and competences in related methods and media-based skills – competences you develop in project-work and other forms of autonomous and co-operative learning (for examples see KLIPPERT 1998: 67; GRUNDER/BOHL 2001: Fallstudie 4; HECHT/GREEN 1987).

- Developing criteria that allow assessing intercultural communicative competences (Byram 1997) in a terminology that can actually be understood and used by learners to evaluate their own progress.

Testing ICC

4.5 Content and Language Integrated Learning (CLIL)

1 Introduction

CLIL and bilingual education

Content and language integrated learning (CLIL), i.e. the teaching of different subject areas, such as geography, biology, or art in a foreign language, is one of the most promising approaches to developing intercultural communicative competence and promoting multilingualism in the European framework. It encourages a learner-centred and task-based approach to language learning. The concept of CLIL and the term itself grew out of the debate surrounding bilingual education, the various manifestations of which are context and therefore also culture specific. Natural bilingualism refers to children who grow up with two languages in their family, to people who live in a bilingual society such as that of parts of Canada, or in a context of immigration. Bilingual education, on the other hand, deals with questions of integration into a monolingual (USA) or bilingual culture (Canada) by learning a second language (L2) (Bach 2000: 16). Canadian programs, for example, are generally immersion programs, where at least 50% of instruction of the content matter is in the language which is not the L1 for the majority of the population, i.e. French. There are also wider definitions of the concept of immersion (see Zydatiss 2000: 26–27). For the European context we differentiate between three basic types of bilingualism (based on Niemeier 2000: 33):

Parallel bilingualism:	Territorial bilingualism:	Functional bilingualism:
Languages are used side by side (e.g. Luxemburg)	In a country certain languages are used in certain areas (e.g. Canada or Belgium)	In countries which only have one official language, but which want the population to have some knowledge of a foreign language (i.e. foreign language learning in Germany)

Consequently, in the German foreign language classroom bilingual education is geared towards a higher competence in EFL or another foreign language, and is thus an additive form of bilingualism where an L2 is added to the existing L1(s). Since the term bilingualism might be misleading because it suggests a similar competence in two languages, which would raise expectations that cannot be met in foreign language teaching, the discussion of terminology centres on the relation between the teaching of the foreign language and the subject matter. While the often-used term 'content-based language learning' puts the focus on the learning of the foreign language through content matter, CLIL (the German equivalent is *Bilingualer Sachfachunterricht*) stresses the fact that content matter is taught in a foreign language and that competence both in the content matter and in the foreign language/culture are goals of the learning process.

2 Developments and forms of CLIL

From a focus on French to English

The majority of programmes in Germany in the 1970s and 1980s were French, with a strong focus on social studies subjects, such as history, political science, and geography which have dominated the curriculum ever since. The situation began to change in the 1980s so that by today the majority of programmes in Germany are English ones. In 1998 out of 366 secondary schools 250 schools offered English and 84 schools French programmes. The other schools offered programmes in eight other foreign languages (Helbig 2003: 181). CLIL is also being established in primary schools (see Zydatiss 2000). In Germany teachers usually teach both the foreign language and the content subject, thus making organization of a CLIL curriculum in the individual schools much easier than in other European countries where teachers only teach one subject. Basically three general models of bilingual education can be found in Germany.

Bilingual schools

There are immersion programs in Germany in the form of bilingual or bicultural schools in which learners of two or more different L1s learn together. The best-known examples are the European schools which offer various subject areas taught in a foreign language which are often phased differently than in the most common form of CLIL (see also Rymarczyk 2003: 29–36).

CLIL

While there is a large degree of flexibility from school to school, some general guidelines can be established. In most schools CLIL starts in year seven and lasts until year ten. Depending on the school, students can continue CLIL in the upper level courses by taking a CLIL *Grundkurs* in one of the subjects on offer, which has to be continued until year 13 and then forms part of the *Abitur*. Learners are prepared for CLIL by taking two additional hours of English classes in years five and six before CLIL starts in year seven, usually with geography. It is then followed by history and/ or political science. There are schools though that also start with biology followed by a subject in the social sciences. RYMARCZYK (2003: 82–90) makes a strong case for having learners start with more contextualized subjects, such as art, music or sports, to ease learners into the new curriculum.

Englisch als Arbeitssprache (EAA)

In the early 90s during a phase of greater autonomy and profile-building many Austrian schools (14,6 % of all schools in 1996/97) initiated a programme called *Englisch als Arbeitssprache* to avoid the confusion around the term bilingual. While the goal is the same as in the CLIL programmes outlined above, this approach is characterized by its high level of flexibility which allows the individual school to set up different kinds of programmes, ranging from short project phases of one-two weeks in various subjects to the full-scale teaching of the subjects in English over several years. Through these small-scale modules schools avoid exaggerated demands, which might otherwise lead to a decrease in motivation on the learners' part (ABUJA 1999: 3–4). These flexible forms have led to proliferation of EAA approaches in Austria (ABUJA 1999). During the last few years this modular approach has taken root in Germany as well, as can be seen, for example in the CLIL modules that are being taught in the *Realschule* in Baden-Württemberg (see also RYMARCZYK 2003: 43–45).

3 Purposes of CLIL

Promotion of multilingualism and multiculturalism

The purpose of CLIL is clearly to promote multilingualism and –culturalism (see MEISSNER/REINFRIED 1998, AGUADO/HU 2000) in a European context by finding new ways of teaching foreign languages.

CLIL tries to reach that goal by improving learners' competences and flexibility in the target language under conditions imposed by the subject area (KRECHEL 1999). This integration of content and foreign language learning supports the development of an intercultural communicative competence since content material is culturally coded, such as primary sources in the subject of history. Learners need to negotiate the different perspectives of their own and the foreign culture that are represented in the materials and are thus learning to become intercultural mediators. A unit on British imperialism in South Africa, for example, could have an ICC focus (see HALLET 1998: 123–24). Reading excerpts from MAN-

DELA's autobiography *Long Walk to Freedom*, learners realize how his experience of starting in a British school, which was accompanied by being given a new name and a school uniform, led to a complete break with his own culture. By comparing it to their own school experience, which might have been quite different or for some students even similar, learners have to deal with multicultural issues. In terms of learning-centredness CLIL thus promotes cultural awareness as well as language awareness, since learners need to learn how to consciously apply language learning strategies and study skills when, for example, dealing with complex texts in the subject matter. While MANDELA's autobiographical text might be relatively easy to understand, additional informational texts on British imperialism in South Africa will be more demanding in terms of language complexity.

4 Major principles of CLIL

Task-based approach and authenticity

In CLIL the focus is not on language learning, but on working on the content matter of the particular subject. The language is used in an authentic way as the medium to solve subject- and thus task-based problems. This functional use of language allows learners to take risks when negotiating content in communicative situations.

Learner-centredness and learning-centredness

Texts, topics and materials are selected to establish a rich learning environment in which learners can pursue questions that are relevant for them. The increased use of multimedia materials and the access learners have to the internet increase the pool of materials. By making it easier for them to get access to materials, these new media increase learners' chances of autonomously choosing relevant materials, for example in project-based scenarios. This 'learner-centredness' of CLIL is combined with a clear 'learning-centredness', since the integration of subject matter and foreign language learning forces learners to develop study skills and strategies that enable them to deal with cognitively demanding texts.

Intercultural communicative competence

At the same time CLIL seems to be especially supportive of developing intercultural communicative competence. *"For example, learners studying the history curriculum through English would be introduced not only to the national curriculum of their country for history but would study alternative interpretations of the same event"* (BYRAM 1997: 114). An example would be how the British government saw the menace of Sadam Hussein, which was in part due to their close partnership with the U.S., and how this compares to the official German view. A closer look at other groups in both countries who supported or opposed the Iraq war leads to multiple perspectives on this recent historical issue. Comparisons like these could support possible revisions of one's own society's views on historical events and concepts while allowing learners to understand the perspectives of other cultures.

Code-switching

Language learning in CLIL in the beginning is characterized by code- switching, since learners want to get a message across but they often do not have the language proficiency. Thus receptive skills are more important at first and tolerance of mistakes is another characteristic of early CLIL. While BUTZKAMM argues for an intensive usage of L1 alongside the foreign language, others have shown that while learners code-switch because the necessary vocabulary is missing, they still try to express themselves in the foreign language. The rich learning environment offers opportunities for learners to express themselves even with a rather restricted L2 proficiency (GROENE 2003; RYMARCZYK 2003).

5 Issues

Bilingual triangle

The relationship between the foreign language and the subject has been the most controversial issue. HALLET (1998), who rejects the use of content subjects in favour of a mere training of translation competence in the foreign language, suggests an integrated model that uses the foreign language to process and integrate knowledge of one's own culture, the target culture and a field that is being defined through an 'interlanguage' and 'interculture'. Those are phenomena that the learner will compare and contrast across cultures, such as global warming, peace-keeping missions or laws of nature. With this model for the social studies subjects HALLET supports the idea of an intercultural speaker who is able to mediate between cultures and languages. HALLET's model makes a case for intercultural learning, but it does not clarify the issue on the language level.

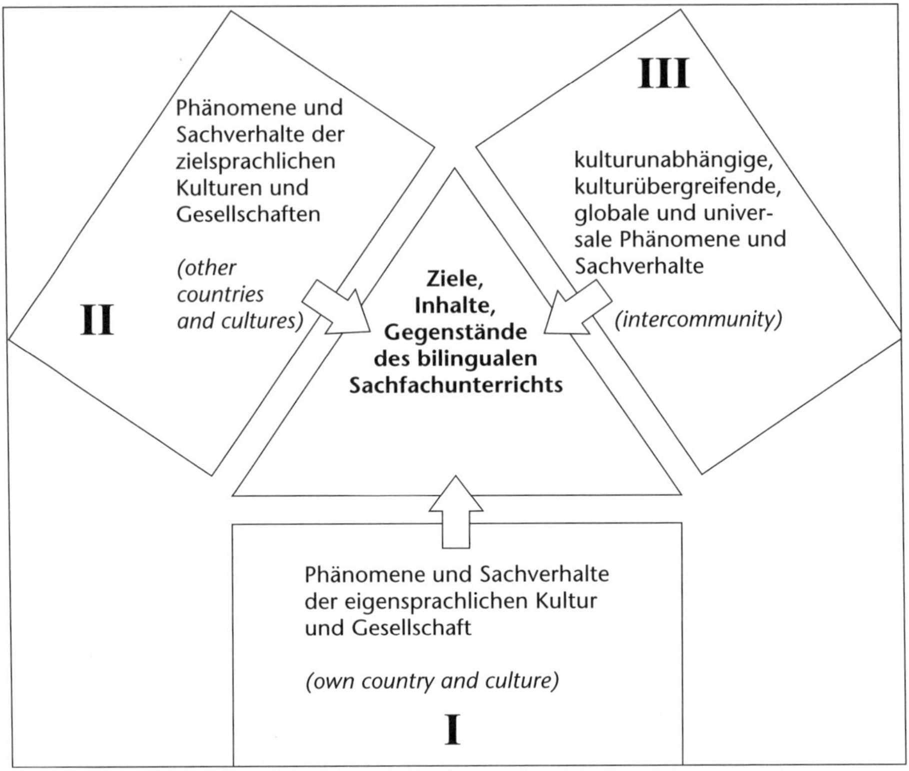

Model 4.3: The bilingual triangle (HALLET 1998: 119)

Relationship between subject matter and the foreign language

While there seems to be a consensus that integration on the level of methodology is necessary (see HELBIG 2003) the role of the foreign language is another issue. So far foreign language methodology has instigated and dominated the development of CLIL. THÜRMANN (2000) and others argue from the subject matter and demand a clear set of language functions to be able to help teach the subject matter (e.g. identify – classify/define – describe – explain – conclude/argue – evaluate). VOLLMER (2000), on the other hand, supports more language learning in CLIL so that foreign language learning and subject learning are more integrated, making the explicit transfer of language functions between subjects unnecessary (see RYMARCZYK 2003: 45–48). Despite this controversy RYMARCZYK (2003: 48) stresses the fact that language functions need to be connected to the content demands of the subject matter. While she makes suggestions for art and English, LAMSFUSS-SCHENK (2002) focuses on the teaching of history in CLIL and its potential for intercultural learning and awareness-building.

Extension of subjects and different phases

RYMARCZYK (2003: 89) calls for a different phasing of CLIL and additional subjects to further integrate language learning and content learning and to help reduce the discrepancy between the foreign language competence of learners and their cognitive abilities in the content subjects. She argues for an integration of less cognitively demanding and more contextualized subjects earlier in the learners' career – such as art, music and sports – which involve the senses in a more holistic way and keep up motivation. At the same time study skills in dealing with longer texts and language competence would be gradually developed for more demanding subjects that come later such as history. An early start in these subjects would even reduce the necessity of providing extra English lessons in years five and six.

Focus on grammatical form and code-switching

Research in Canadian immersion programmes has shown that while learners' receptive skills were well developed, there was a lack in accuracy in their productive skills (THÜRMANN 2000). While more elaborate language production needs to be enhanced, the early start with more contextualized subjects, supported by visual materials and an experiential and holistic approach to learning, also helps with the problem of code-switching and the focus on form. While learners should be allowed to decide when they enter the discussion (silent period), research shows that they are usually eager to express themselves in the foreign language. GROENE (learn-line), for example, points out that her learners in a year seven geography class are often quiet because they do not want to make contributions in the L1 since they still lack sufficient knowledge in English so they do not participate. At the same time she relates that learners do not worry about accuracy when they want to make a contribution. Since it is mostly the words that are missing and not the grammar, she as a teacher supports them quickly with the necessary terms when needed. RYMARCZYK (2003: 268–69) supports this view in her qualitative research on art lessons in a sixth grade class. In her study learners tried to communicate non-verbally as well as on the basis of minimal verbal contributions, all the while being supported by subject-related media.

L: *[…] How can we mix colours? – On the pad? […]*
S: *In this here. (Zeigt auf Mischparzellen des Farbkastendeckels)*
L: *Yes, here. (L hebt den Kasten hoch.) In the lid of your water-colour box. Here you can mix your colours* (RYMARCZYK 2003: 187).

As learners gain more confidence in expressing themselves in English, lexical and grammatical growth can be detected without any explicit language support. While learners do need language support in the lexical field to improve reading and negotiating skills, the importance attributed to the L1 (see BUTZKAMM, learn-line) seems to be exaggerated when measures such as a different choice of subjects in the different phases of CLIL are established. Instead of opposing L1 and foreign language RYMARCZYK (2003: 34, 272) suggests a continuum between non-verbal/minimally productive and verbally productive to gauge the level of language activity.

Material

The discrepancy between language proficiency and the often high cognitive demands of authentic materials is still a major problem. Textbooks from the other culture do not present a solution since the vocabulary is usually too difficult or tasks are too complex. When CLIL was introduced teachers had to produce their own materials and they still do, but with the advent of the Internet, access to authentic materials has become much easier, and there is a growing pool of institutionally produced materials (see http://www.learn-line.nrw.de/angebote/bilingual).

6 Features of good practice

Methods' transfer

Many of the features of good practice already outlined in other chapters apply to CLIL, such as those for intercultural communicative competence, task-based learning, project-based learning, and language as discourse, the latter with a special focus on the lexical approach. At the same time there are specific aspects that need to be taken into consideration to facilitate learning of often highly complex and cognitively demanding subject matter in English (based on RYMARCZYK 2003: 272):

- The use of media should support the creation of a rich learning environment where learners have access to many forms of non-lingual information concerning the subject matter at hand, such as pictures, maps, graphs, movement.
- Learners should be allowed to take advantage of a silent period, i. e. learners decide themselves when they want to participate verbally in English.
- The likelihood that learners will only produce minimal output during the initial stages of language acquisition should be realized, instead of asking for longer grammatical expressions.
- Tasks should be designed that allow learners to express themselves in a non-verbal way, i. e. in the form of pictures/paintings, through music or movement.
- To support more extensive oral participation, learners can prepare oral presentations individually in written form, or orally with fellow learners (e. g. discussion sheet).

CLIL – the first steps

When learners start out with CLIL a number of steps can be taken to make the transition work more smoothly (see HELLEKJAER 1999). To avoid cognitive overload, one should not start with two CLIL subjects at the same time and starting with more contextualized subjects such as art is a good idea. The use of the L1 should be allowed more extensively to help learners getting used to the new teaching approach. The first lessons should be simple and clearly structured. Apart from providing spontaneous language support (bridging/prompting), the teacher could work with word lists (topic specific lists and phrases for classroom discourse), explain key words, and use pre-reading strategies to help learners understand the texts. While learners often stumble across missing words, the more severe problem is the lack of cultural knowledge when learners try to make inferences; this is something the teacher has to provide.

Study skills and language

Once learners have managed the first steps, they are confronted with integrating general and subject-specific study skills with specific language functions.

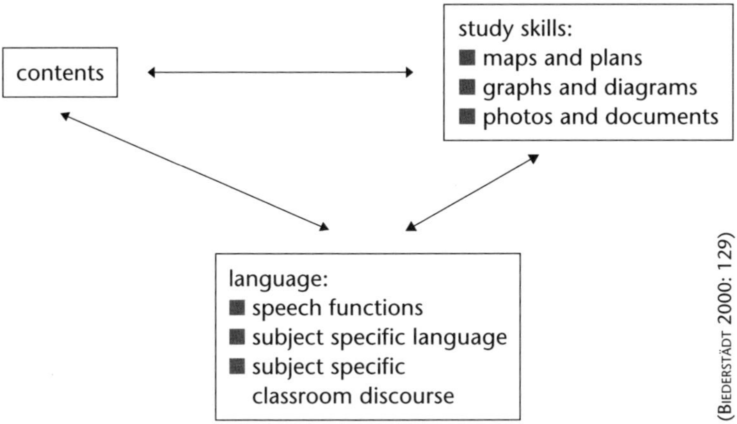

(Biederstädt 2000: 129)

Model 4.4: The relationship between contents, study skills and language

Receptive skills

Intensive work with texts necessitates receptive and productive skills which learners can already practise in the foreign language classes when reading young adult literature, for example. When learners work with texts in the content fields they need content-based reading strategies (see also chap. 3.1). They must be able to scan the text and to do a close reading of a text. As Krechel (1999: 195) points out, *"the task is to extract the most important information as quickly as possible against the background of a content question from the subject area."* He suggests a basic model of three phases to help learners identify and situate the topic, describe the context and the developments, work out relationships of cause and effects, and evaluate the message of the text (Krechel 1999: 195–96):

Phase 1: Grasping the information via 'islands of comprehension'
Phase 2: Understanding the details
Phase 3: Checking, revising and supplementing the information

In more general terms, learners need a number of study skills for working with texts (based on KRECHEL 1999: 196–97):

1. Inferencing the meaning of words (knowledge of word formation rules is important here).
2. Working with dictionaries and other tools, such as theme-based vocabulary books or class files.
3. Note-taking and visualizing techniques, such as underlining, explaining symbols, noting important information on a second sheet. Visualizing techniques would include making drawings, sketches of areas or regions, as well as organigrams to show content structures or causal relations. These techniques can be applied to texts, but also to working with graphs, tables, diagrams, statistics, and maps.

Productive skills

The discussion of specific subject matter requires the productive skills of describing, explaining, comparing, drawing conclusions, evaluating, and assessing. These general functions find their way into writing tasks, such as *"labelling diagrams or maps* [...]*; making collages and wall newspapers; producing summaries of information; explaining maps, diagrams or statistics; preparing statements, reports or references; newspapers articles; travelogues; brief presentations; talks"* (KRECHEL 1999: 198–99). To help learners with these demands, model texts are helpful. As to oral activities, CLIL classrooms provide a wealth of authentic communicative situations, such as *"exchanging information and opinions relevant to the subject area in classroom discussions, in talks, in planning games, in discussion groups, in panel discussions, in round-table discussions, or during and following a talk."* In these situations students need the following speech acts among others (KRAMSCH, in: KRECHEL 1999: 199–200):

- *taking the initiative/initiating an exchange*
- *making suggestions*
- *presenting facts*
- *expressing one's own opinion*
- *interrupting, correcting, giving support*
- *giving signals of approval, disapproval, showing understanding*
- *evaluating, judging, criticizing statements made by others*

Some of these speech acts are especially important for developing ICC such as paraphrasing a complex sentence in a discussion, acting as an interpreter when comparing primary sources in the L1 and English, or negotiating the outcome when comparing texts or concepts. Learners thus hone their skills on multiple levels when they engage in CLIL tasks.

7 Current trends and developments

Integration of methodologies

In the future, flexible CLIL modules will be used on an even wider scale in schools since they offer an alternative to full-scale and often costly programs. This way more space can be given to supporting the development of multilingualism through other subjects and languages. This makes the integration of content subjects and EFL on the methodological level even more important to avoid time-intensive preparatory phases. The idea of starting out with highly contextualized subjects such as art while cutting down on the additional foreign language lessons in year five and six seems to be a promising approach (RYMARCZYK 2003: 274–76). The suggested approach based on art also highlights the fact that one general integrated methodology is not the answer, but that context- and school-based solutions have to be found (HELBIG 2003: 185). At the same time individual content subjects have to provide more specific methodologies (LAMSFUSS-SCHENK 2002). The concepts of CLIL should also be taken into consideration for a general methodology on multilingualism, to develop multilingual and multicultural competences.

Teacher education

While the demand for CLIL teachers is constantly rising, only universities in Bochum, Bremen, Dortmund, and Wuppertal as well as the Universities of Education in Karlsruhe and Freiburg *(Europaschullehramt)* offer specific teacher education programmes so far. Apart from general theoretical knowledge about bilingual education, the profile for CLIL teachers includes competences related to the EFL terminology of subject content and its specifically culturally oriented perspective, i. e. CLIL teachers need to be intercultural mediators themselves. More specific programmes are needed that include phases abroad to allow student teachers to learn about the cultural perspectives in the relevant subject matters.

Action research

The field of CLIL is characterized by an increasing research focus. So far research in Austria has shown that while the amount of content had to be reduced somewhat with a stronger focus on exemplary learning and competences in opposition to mere content knowledge, the programmes result in a higher competence in the foreign language and an increase in language flexibility (ABUJA 1999: 9). As ABUJA (1999: 10) points out more qualitative research needs to be done in the field of methodology to understand the use of L1 in CLIL and the integration of internet-based materials, and to further promote the integration of content and foreign language methodologies. Changes brought about by early foreign language learning in the primary school, which is based on the concept of integrated learning, can only be speculated about at this point. It will lead to new curricular structures in secondary education, though, which will most certainly further CLIL as well at that level.

4.6 Teaching English in the Primary Classroom

1 The context

Situation in Germany

Developments in introducing English as a compulsory subject in primary education in Germany point in the following direction: *"Die derzeitige Entwicklung (zeigt), dass in allen Ländern der Fremdsprachenunterricht in der Primarstufe deutlich ausgeweitet wird. Dies betrifft vorrangig die Jahrgangsstufen 3 und 4, in einigen Ländern auch die Jahrgangsstufen 1 und 2. Einigkeit herrscht in einer zunehmenden Zahl von Ländern darin, dass neben dem Begegnungskonzept das eher systematische und themenorientierte Fremdsprachenlernen auf der Grundlage eines (Rahmen-)Lehrplans mit ergebnisorientierter Progression ebenfalls die grundschulspezifische, handlungsorientierte und anschauliche Vermittlung vorsieht"* (REPORT OF THE KULTUSMINISTERKONFERENZ, 2002).

Primary specific teaching

The same paper emphasizes that the teaching of foreign languages at primary level follows its own methodology and principles. But what is it that makes the teaching of a foreign language primary-specific? According to CAMERON, *"Children are often more enthusiastic and lively,* [...] *want to please the teacher rather than their peer group,* [...] *will have a go at an activity even when they don't quite understand why or how. However, they also lose interest more quickly and are less able to keep themselves motivated on tasks they find difficult,* [...] *they do not have the same access as older learners to metalanguage that teachers can use to explain about grammar* [...]*, often seem less embarrassed than adults at talking in a new language, and their lack of inhibition seems to help them get a more native-like accent"* (CAMERON 2001: 1).

Learning-centred perspectives

Generalisations about children such as these should not hide the fact that every child is different and has an individual learning potential. Differences arise from their linguistic, psychological and social development. This is why CAMERON puts the learning potential of children at the centre of her framework for teaching young learners and distinguishes between a 'learner-centred' and a 'learning-centred' perspective on teaching: In a *learner*-centred approach, the teacher may just follow what seem to be the immediate needs of the child and in doing so, she may be wasting *learning* potential as she does not move the child towards increasingly demanding challenges: *"I have seen too many classrooms where learners are enjoying themselves on intellectually undemanding tasks but failing to learn as much as they might. The time available* [...] *is too short to waste on activities that are fun but do not maximise learning"* (CAMERON 2001: 2). What can we learn from research into children's language learning?

2 Assumptions about how children learn foreign languages and their implications for appropriate methodology

Primary specific learning

Primary specific materials and activities are based on assumptions about how children learn foreign languages. But although the field of teaching English to young learners has expanded considerably in the last decade, it is only just beginning to be researched. This is why CAMERON (who to our knowledge provides the only methodological approach to teaching young learners which is based on research into language learning of that age) draws on work from beyond language classrooms: child development (developmental psychology), learning theory, first language development and the development of a second language in bilingual contexts (see CAMERON 2001: chap. 1). We will refer in the following chapters to her book, in which she draws implications for appropriate learning at primary level from research results in these disciplines.

Children actively try to construct meaning

Since PIAGET's research on children's mental development we know that young children learn and develop by working with objects or ideas, trying to solve problems and making sense of their experiences. In doing so, they actively construct their own knowledge. Teachers therefore need to provide opportunities for children to develop their language competence through tasks and activities that actively involve learners because they perceive them as stimulating. Here is an example from a primary course-book of an activity for a 1st year whose purpose it is to consolidate language learned in a unit on pets. To do so, learners are making a class chart of favourite pets. These are the notes (in summary) given in the teacher's guide (see *My class activity* in *Magicland, Class Book 1*, p. 10):

- Tell the class about your favourite animal. Show them a picture and say: *This is my favourite animal. It's a cat.* Ask individual children what their favourite animal is.
- Explain that they are going to make a class chart like the children in the book – to find out what their favourite animals are.

- Drawing activity. Children draw a picture of their favourite pet. They can choose from those they have learned in class or you may teach new vocabulary as necessary.
- When pupils have finished their drawings, hold some of them up and ask: *What's Peter's favourite animal?* Pupils guess: *It's a (fish).*
- Attach the class pet chart to the wall. Check new vocabulary for animals your learners wanted you to include. Add an extra column for the pictures of other animals. Ask: *What are our favourite animals?*. Pupils stick their pictures onto the chart in the correct column. There is some small talk each time, i.e. *What's your favourite animal? It's a dog/cat/tortoise. It's big/small,* etc.
- Talk about the chart, using as much English as possible. Use mime and gesture to demonstrate meaning as far as possible. *Who has got a dog? My dog is big. Is this your cat? Is he small? Is your rabbit friendly?* etc.

In the task example above, learners are actively involved because the activities relate to their own worlds. The activities encourage their personal participation through tasks which allow personal response and individualized language input.

Children learn by solving problems

The following activity is also taken from a year 1 primary English course *(Pebbles)*. Learners are asked to listen to a conversation of children in a playground and to point to the 4 pictures that illustrate the conversation in their textbooks while they listen (a 'listen and point' activity). This task directs their attention to what they hear, but probably fails to involve them as they may not perceive it as a challenge to do the task. A minor change of focus of task could turn this into a problem-solving activity which would support learning. If the teacher introduced the listening activity by saying: 'Eddie and Rose are making some new friends'. [repeat in L1, whisper: 'Sie lernen neue Freunde kennen']. But: 'What are their names? Can you [emphasize 'you'] find out? I'm sure you can. Listen to this' – she would then face them with a problem they can solve by listening to the conversation.

Children need enough time to process new language

Younger children internalise the structure of the target language more slowly than older learners because their cognitive development is not yet complete. Effects of instruction are usually delayed, that means that young learners are not able to produce language that teachers have presented and that has been practised more or less immediately (see description of the so-called PPP approach to language learning in chap. 3.2.). It takes constant revision of new language items in varying contexts until learners will eventually be able to confidently reproduce new language in spontaneous speech: *"Acquisition results from the gradual and dynamic process of internal generalisation rather than from instant adjustments to the learner's internal grammar. It follows that learners cannot be expected to learn a new feature and be able to use it in the same lesson. They might be able to rehearse the feature, to retrieve it from short-term memory or to produce it when prompted by the teacher or the materials. But this does not mean that learning has taken place. I am sure most of you are familiar with the situation in which learners get a new feature correct in the lesson in which it is taught but then get it wrong the following week. This is partly because they have not yet had enough time, instruction and exposure for learning to have taken place"* (TOMLINSON 1998: 16). Teachers need to offer ample practice opportunities of new language items in varying contexts to be able to contribute to the restructuring of students' internal grammar – gradually. This is, of course, a general principle in language learning but it applies particularly to young learners.

Children seem to pay more attention to sound and prosody. But they need to get support to notice

The relationship between a learner's age and their success in language learning has been a lively topic of debate in language acquisition research. The so-called Critical Period Hypothesis suggests that young learners' pronunciation achievement is superior to that of older learners who almost inevitably have a noticeable 'foreign accent' (see CAMERON 2001: 60–68). Meanwhile research has found out that it is more complex than this. Undoubtedly, children's capacity for the imitation of sounds which they hear around them is usually well developed but not all children imitate to the same extent. In studies of immersion language learning younger children (7–8 years) seem to pay more attention to sound and intonation patterns (study of HARLEY et al 1995 in CAMERON 2001: 15). At the same time, children *"are generally less able to give selective and prolonged attention to features of learning tasks than adults, and are more easily diverted and distracted by other pupils. When faced with talk in the new language, they try to understand it in terms of the […] cues of their first language and also pay particular attention to items of L2 vocabulary that they are familiar with (Harley 1994; Schmidt 1990). These findings […] give further empirical support to the idea that teachers can help learners by focusing their attention on useful sources of information in the new language"* (CAMERON 2001: 15). This is why teachers need to offer exposure to examples of oral language and to focus on explicit and direct attention on new elements of language so that learners 'notice' the differences between the two languages. Support is particularly important when children learn how to produce new and unfamiliar sounds.

Children cannot give prolonged attention to tasks

Course books need to provide a variety of different activities to stop learners from getting diverted and distracted by the other children in the classroom, which easily happens with young learners. Most primary course books currently on the market take account of this.

Children need to work with materials which achieve impact

TOMLINSON (1998) in his summary of the basic principles of second language acquisition relevant to the development of materials for the teaching of languages, says that materials need to achieve impact on learners. They must have *"a noticeable effect on learners, that is when the learners' curiosity, interest and attention are attracted. If this is achieved there is a better chance that some of the language in the materials will be taken in for processing"* (TOMLINSON 1998: 7). According to TOMLINSON, materials can achieve impact through novelty, variety, attractive presentation and appealing content. BUZAN (in STEINBACH 1995: 13) follows the same line of argument in his research on the factors that contribute to remembering new words in child foreign language teaching. Words need to be presented in contexts that are unusual, or absurd, or exaggerated, or they need to be presented with a sense of humour or trigger creativity. The impact of materials on learners also depends on whether learners perceive a task as personally relevant, meaningful and useful to them. This is why textbooks need to include what NUNAN has called *target tasks* or *real word tasks* (NUNAN 1999: 24–26). These relate to learners' own lives and interests and are rehearsals for performance outside of the classroom to mirror the things people do in everyday life. To give an example: when you teach numbers you may involve learners in a role-play about making a telephone conversation (example taken from the primary EFL course *Playway to English 3, Rainbow Edition, Pupils' Book*, p. 8):

Mike: Ann?
Ann: Yes, Mike.
Mike: What's your telephone number?
Ann: 584390
Mike: 584390 (writing)
Thanks, Ann.
Ann: All right!

3 Purposes and contents of learning English at primary level and their implications for appropriate methodology

Multitude of purposes

The teaching of English to children involves educational, motivational and linguistic/content-related purposes. These include the following:

- to develop and sustain positive attitudes towards learning foreign languages (plurilingualism as an educational value)
- to sensitise learners to the similarities and differences between languages (language awareness)
- to develop an attitude of openness towards other languages and cultures to prevent prejudice (intercultural competences)
- to develop language learning competences and strategies (i. e. how to remember new words, how to promote talking)
- to develop a basic communicative competence in the target language based on purposeful listening, and to learn about the lives of people living in different cultures (see report KULTUSMINISTERKONFERENZ 2002).

Features of methodology

There is not the space to discuss primary-specific procedures in detail, but they will include the following features which you find in most materials and course-books produced for this level (for a detailed discussion of these see SCHMID-SCHÖNBEIN 2001).

Tasks and activities

Tasks need to involve learners (see above), have a clear purpose and clear language learning goals (for a detailed discussion of defining tasks for young learners see CAMERON 2001, chap. 2.6). At primary level tasks may include games and craft activities as these are everyday activities that children pursue. Language is generated naturally this way and it is meaningful to children and provides them with a fun and stimulating context for language production.

Language and content

Teachers need to choose activities and content that are appropriate for children's age and socio-cultural experience. But it is difficult to define what children will use the foreign language for at that age. Language will need to grow with the children, that is, teachers will have to provide a useful basis for learners' possible needs in their adolescent or adult lives (see CAMERON 2001: 30–1).

Focus on oral skills

Children need to become familiar with the sound of the new language and they need to develop the confidence to produce spoken language. Learning how to read and write in the foreign language is of secondary importance, as children's L1 literacy development is still in progress and L2 reading and writing may interfere with it. This is why there is a focus on listening – to stories, dialogues, songs, and chants – and on doing role-plays, singing songs, and even performing mini plays.

4 Issues

Assessment and self-assessment

Children can develop their self-awareness of the learning process and are capable of reflecting about what they have done and how well they have done it (De Leeuw 1997). Legutke and his team have developed a portfolio for language learners at primary level and they are researching its effects (see Legutke 2003). Hopeful as results are, more research needs to be done to find out how this tool may be efficiently integrated in a school context where the time frame available is very limited. If achievement at this level is to be assessed is contentious (some states have decided to introduce testing in years 3 and 4). The content to be assessed and the procedures to be used need to be compatible with what teachers and learners can realistically achieve in the limited time available. This presents a real challenge as it is predominantly the oral skills that are to be assessed (for a convincing manageable approach see Becker et. al. 2003).

Time and quality of exposure

Exposure time is crucial for the quality of language development in a foreign language. Teachers need to develop realistic ideas about what may be achieved in the limited time available at this level. What needs to be developed are 'can do' standards which describe language performance and which are derived from experience with practice. This has yet to be done. The same is true for the quality of exposure. With the enormous demand for qualified primary EFL teachers, there is a danger that teachers are not qualified adequately. They need a profound language and methodological competence which cannot be acquired in 'crash-courses' as are offered by some states to make ends meet (for ideas on appropriate contents and procedures of primary teacher education see Klippel 2003; Schocker-v. Ditfurth 2003).

Transition from primary to secondary level

Teaching foreign languages at primary level follows its own principles and methodology, as we have seen. If differs from secondary EFL teaching even though there are common concerns and principles. This may cause problems when learners move on to secondary school. KAHL and KNEBLER (1996) in their study found out that generally children leave primary school with a high motivation to learn languages, with clearly identifiable language skills, and with a positive attitude to the English language. They use the foreign language without being afraid of making mistakes, they like to experiment with the language and try to get their meanings across even though they often lack the appropriate linguistic means to do so. This is due to the particular social culture of the primary classroom where communication is naturally supported by peers and understanding and talking are not seen as primarily individual but social acts that are achieved in a co-operative endeavour (LEGUTKE 2000).

Teachers at secondary level need to know about the particularities of language learning in the primary context to value and appreciate learners' competences and ways of learning and to develop from there. If this is not the case, valuable knowledge, skills, and attitudes developed at that level may be lost. Teachers need to build on familiar activities, routines, competences and topics and develop language learning from there. Transition conferences and the portfolio (LEGUTKE/LORTZ 2002) are means to achieve this.

Bibliography

(The books recommended in the paragraphs giving information on further reading, along with several other works which are recommended for frequent use, are marked with a ◆.)

ABUJA, Gunther: „Die Verwendung einer Fremdsprache als Arbeitssprache: Charakteristika ‚bilingualen' Lernens in Österreich." In: *Zeitschrift für Interkulturellen Fremdsprachenunterricht* 4.2 (1999), 14 pp. Avail.: http://www.spz.tu-darmstadt.de/projekt_ejournal/JG_04_2/beitrag/abuja2.htm (15.12.03).

AEBERSOLD, Jo Ann & Mary Lee FIELD: *From Reader to Reading Teacher. Issues and Strategies for Second Language Classrooms.* Cambridge: Cambridge UP 1997.

AGUADO, Karin & Adelheid HU (Eds.): *Mehrsprachigkeit und Mehrkulturaliät. Dokumentation des 18. Kongresses für Fremdsprachendidaktik.* Bln: Pädagogischer Zeitschriftenverlag 2000 (= Beiträge zur Femdsprachenforschung).

AHERN, Terence C. W.: "Groups, Task, and CMC: Designing for Optimal Participation." In: *Wired Together: The Online Classroom in K-12. Vol. I: Perspectives and Instructional Design.* Eds.: Z. L. BERGE & M. B. COLLINS. Cresskill, NJ: Hampton Press 1998. P. 221–232.

AITCHINSON, Jean: *Introducing Language and Mind.* Ldn.: Penguin 1992.

ALDERSON, Charles J.: *Assessing Reading.* Cambridge: Cambridge UP 2000.

ALLWRIGHT, Dick: "The Importance of Interaction in Classroom Language Learning." In: *Applied Linguistics* 5 (1985), P. 156–171.

◆ ALTRICHTER, Herbert & Peter POSCH: *Lehrer erforschen ihren Unterricht. Eine Einführung in die Methoden der Aktionsforschung.* Bad Heilbrunn: Klinkhardt 1994.

ANDERSON, Anne & Tony LYNCH: *Listening.* Oxford: Oxford UP 1988.

BACH, Gerhard: „Interkulturelles Lernen." Lernen - Lehren - Forschen." In: BACH/NIEMEIER 2000. P. 11–23.

BACH, Gerhard: „Bilingualer Unterricht: In: *Englisch lernen und lehren.* Ed.: J.-P. TIMM. Bln.: Cornelsen, 1998. P. 192–200.

◆ BACH, Gerhard & Susanne NIEMEIER (Eds.): *Bilingualer Unterricht. Grundlagen, Methoden, Praxis, Perspektiven.* Franfurt: Lang 2000 (= Kolloquium Fremdsprachenunterricht, Bd.5)

◆ BAILEY, Kathleen M.: *Learning about Language Assessment. Dilemmas, Decisions, and Directions.* Pacific Grove: Heinle & Heinle 1998.

◆ BATSTONE, Rob: *Grammar.* Oxford: Oxford UP 1994 (= Language Teaching: A Scheme for Teacher Education).

BAUSCH, Karl-Richard, Herbert CHRIST, Frank G. KÖNIGS & Hans-Jürgen KRUMM (Eds.): *Der gemeinsame europäische Referenzrahmen für Sprachen in der Diskussion. Arbeitspapiere der 22. Frühjahrskonferenz zur Erforschung des Fremdsprachenunterrichts.* Tübingen: Narr 2003.

◆ BAUSCH, Karl-Richard, Herbert CHRIST & Hans-Jürgen KRUMM (Eds.): *Handbuch Fremdsprachenunterricht.* 4. Auflage. Tübingen: Francke 2003.

BAYOR, Ronald H.: "Changing Neighborhoods: Ethnic and Racial Succession in the Urban North and South." In: *From 'Melting Pot' to Multiculturalism. The Evolution of Ethnic Relations in the United States and Canada.* Ed.: V. G. LERDA. Roma: Bulzoni Editore 1990. P. 219–236.

BECKER, Carmen, Anette CLAUS, Günter GERNGROSS & Herbert PUCHTA: *Playway 3 Rainbow Edition. Show What You Know.* Rum/Innsbruck: Helbling & Klett 2003.

BELL, Steve: "Storyline as an Approach to Language Teaching." In: Die *Neueren Sprachen* 94.1 (1995), P. 5–25.

BENZ, Norbert: *Der Schüler als Leser im fremdsprachlichen Literaturunterricht.* Tübingen: Narr 1990.

BIEDERSTÄDT, Wolfgang: „Möglichkeiten und Grenzen des Englischen als Arbeitssprache im Geographieunterricht der Klassen 7–10." In: BACH/NIEMEIER 2000. P. 127–135.

BLOCK, David: "Globalization and language teaching." In: *ELT Journal* 58.1 (2004), P. 75–76.

BORG, Simon: "Teachers' Pedagogical Systems and Grammar Teaching. A Qualitative Study." In: *TESOL Quarterly* 32. 1 (1998), P. 9–38.

BOSKIN, Joseph: *Sambo. The Rise and Demise of an American Jester.* Oxford: Oxford UP 1986.

Bredella, Lothar: "Literary Texts." In: Byram 2000. P. 375–382.

◆ Bredella, Lothar: *Literarisches und interkulturelles Verstehen*. Tübingen: Narr 2002.

Bredella, Lothar: "Literaturwissenschaft." In: Bausch/Christ/Krumm 2003. P. 54–60.

Bredella, Lothar & Werner Delanoy: „Introduction." In: *Challenges of Literary Texts in the Foreign Language Classroom*. Eds.: L. Bredella & W. Delanoy. Tübingen: Narr 1996. P. vii-xxviii.

Breen, Michael P.: "The Social Context for Language Learning – A Neglected Situation?" In: *Studies in Second Language Acquisition* 7 (1985), P. 135–158.

Breen, Michael P.: "Learner Contributions to Task Design." In: Candlin/Murphy 1987. P. 23–46.

Breen, Michel P.: "Navigating the Discourse: On What is Learned in the Language Classroom". In: *Learners and Language Learning. Proceedings*. Eds.: G. Jacobs et al. RELC Seminar 1997. Singapore: RELC 1998.

Breen, Michael P.: "Overt Participation and Covert Acquisition in the Language Classroom." In: *Learner Contributions to Language Learning. New Directions in Research* Ed.: M. P. Breen. Harlow: Pearson Education 2001a. P. 112–140.

Breen, Michael P.: "Syllabus design." In: Carter/Nunan 2001b. P. 151–159.

Breen, Michael P. & Christopher N. Candlin: "The Essentials of a Communicative Curriculum in Language Teaching." In: *Applied Linguistics* 1.2 (1980), P. 89–112.

Brislin, Richard W., Cushner, Kenneth, Cherrie, Craig & Mahealani Yong: *Intercultural Interactions. A Practical Guide*. Beverly Hills: Sage 1986.

Brusch, Wilfried: *Text und Gespräch in der fremdsprachlichen Erziehung*. Hbg.: ELT 1986.

Buck, Gary: *Assessing Listening*. Cambridge: Cambridge UP 2001.

Burwitz-Melzer, Eva: *Allmähliche Annäherungen: fiktionale Texte im interkulturellen Fremdsprachenunterricht der Sekundarstufe I*. Tübingen: Narr 2003.

◆ Bushman, John H. & Kay Parks Bushman: *Using Young Adult Literature in the English Classroom*. 2nd. ed. Englewood Cliffs: Prentice Hall 1997.

Buttjes, Dieter: "Culture in German Foreign Language Teaching: Making Use of an Ambiguous Past." In: *Mediating Languages and Cultures: Towards an Intercultural Theory of Foreign Language Education*. Eds.: D. Buttjes, & M. Byram. Clevedon: Multilingual Matters 1990. P. 62–47.

Butzkamm, Wolfgang: „Zum Sprachwechsel im bilingualen Sachfachunterricht." In: *learn-line* http://www.learn-line.nrw.de (15.12.03).

Bygate, Martin: "Speaking." In: Carter/Nunan 2001. P. 14–20.

◆ Byram, Michael: *Teaching and Assessing Intercultural Communicative Competence*. Clevedon: Multilingual Matters 1997.

Byram, Michael (Ed.): *Routledge Encyclopaedia of Language Teaching and Learning*. Ldn.: Routledge 2000.

Byram, Michael: "Assessment and Testing." In: Byram 2000. P. 48–53.

Byram, Michael, Adam Nichols & David Stevens (Eds.): *Developing Intercultural Competence in Practice*. Clevedon: Multilingual Matters 2001.

◆ Cameron, Lynne: *Teaching Languages to Young Learners*. Cambridge: Cambridge UP 2001 (= Cambridge Language Teaching Library).

Candlin, Christopher N.: "Communicative Language Teaching Revisited." In: *Kommunikativer Fremdsprachenunterricht: Rückblick nach vorn*. Eds.: M. K. Legutke & M. Schocker-v. Ditfurth. Tübingen: Narr 2003. P. 41–58.

Candlin, Christopher N. & Dermot Murphy (Eds.): *Language Learning Tasks*. Englewood Cliffs, NJ: Prentice-Hall International 1987 (= Lancaster Practical Papers in English Language Education, Vol. 7).

Carter, Ronald & Michael McCarthy: *Vocabulary and Language Teaching*. Ldn.: Longman 1988 (= Applied Linguistics and Language Study).

◆ Carter, Ronald & John McRae (Eds.): *Language, Literature and the Learner. Creative Classroom Practice*. Ldn.: Longman 1996.

Carter, Ronald & David Nunan (Eds.): *Teaching English to Speakers of Other Languages*. Cambridge: Cambridge UP 2001.

◆ Caspari, Daniela: *Kreativität im Umgang mit literarischen Texten im Fremdsprachenunterricht. Theoretische Studien und unter-*

richtspraktische Erfahrungen. Ffm.: Lang 1994.

CASPARI, Daniela: „Fremdverstehen durch literarische Texte – der Beitrag kreativer Verfahren." In: *Bausteine für einen neokommunikativen Französischunterricht. Lernerzentrierung, Ganzheitlichkeit, Handlungsorientierung, Interkulturalität, Mehrsprachigkeitsdidaktik.* Eds.: F.-J. MEISSNER & M. REINFRIED. Tübingen: Narr 2001. P. 169–184.

CASPARI, Daniela: *Fremdsprachenlehrerinnen und Fremdsprachenlehrer – Studien zu ihrem beruflichen Selbstverständnis.* Tübingen: Narr 2003.

CELCE-MURCIA, Marianne: "Grammar Pedagogy in Second and Foreign Language Teaching." In: *TESOL Quarterly* 25.3 (1991), P. 459–480.

CHRISTIAN, Scott: *Exchanging Lives: Middle School Writers Online.* Urbana, IL: National Council of Teachers of English 1997.

COADY, James & Thomas HUCKIN: *Second Language Vocabulary Acquisition. A Rationale for Pedagogy.* Cambridge: Cambridge UP 1997.

◆ COLLIE, Joanne & Stephen SLATER: *Literature in the Language Classroom. A Resource Book of Ideas and Activities.* Cambridge: Cambridge UP 1987.

COOK, Guy: *Applied Linguistics.* Oxford: Oxford UP 2003.

COPE, Bill & Mary KALANTZIS: "Introduction: Multiliteracies: the Beginnings of an Idea." In: *Multiliteracies. Literacy Learning and the Design of Social Futures.* Eds.: B. COPE & M. KALANTZIS. Ldn.: Routledge 2000. P. 3–8.

COUNCIL OF EUROPE: *Linguistic Content, Means of Evaluation and their Interaction in the Teaching and Learning of Modern Languages in Adult Education.* Strasbourg: Council of Europe 1971.

◆ COUNCIL OF EUROPE (Ed.): *Modern Languages: Learning, Teaching, Assessment. A Common European Framework of Reference.* Cambridge: Cambridge UP 2001.

CROOKES, Graham & Susan M. GASS (Eds.): *Tasks in a Pedagogical Context. Integrating Theory and Practice.* Clevedon: Multilingual Matters 1993.

CUMMINS, Jim & Dennis SAYERS: *Brave New Schools. Challenging Cultural Illiteracy Through Global Learning Networks.* NY: St. Martin's Press 1995.

DAM, Leni: "How Do We Recognize an Autonomous Classroom?" In: *Die Neueren Sprachen* 93.5 (1994), P. 503–527.

DELANOY, Werner: "The Complexity of Literature Teaching in the Language Classroom." In: *Challenges of Literary Texts in the Foreign Language Classroom.* Eds.: L. BREDELLA & W. DELANOY. Tübingen: Narr 1996. P. 62–90.

DELANOY, Werner: *Fremdsprachlicher Literaturunterricht. Theorie und Praxis im Dialog.* Tübingen: Narr 2002.

DE LEEUW, Howard : *English as a Foreign Language in the German Elementary School.* Tübingen: Narr 1997.

DER FREMDSPRACHLICHE UNTERRICHT ENGLISCH: *Musikvideoclips.* 36, 60, (6) (2002).

DÖRNYEI, Zoltan: *Motivational Strategies in the Language Classroom.* Cambridge: Cambridge UP 2001a.

◆ DÖRNYEI, Zoltan: *Teaching and Researching Motivation.* Ldn.: Longman 2001b.

DONATH, Reinhard: *E-Mail-Projekte im Englischunterricht.* Stg.: Klett 1996.

DONNERSTAG, Jürgen: "Literary Reading and Intercultural Learning – Understanding Ethnic American Fiction in the EFL-Classroom." In: *Amerikastudien/ American Studies* 37.4 (1992), P. 595–611.

DOYÉ, Peter: *Typologie der Testaufgaben für den Englischunterricht.* München: Langenscheidt-Longman 1986.

◆ DUFF, Alan & Alan MALEY: *The Inward Ear. Poetry in the Language Classroom.* Cambridge: Cambridge UP 1989.

DUXA, Susanne: „Interaktive Übungen." BAUSCH et al 2003. P. 305–308.

ECK, Andreas, Lienhard LEGENHAUSEN & Dieter WOLFF: *Telekommunikation und Fremdsprachenunterricht: Informationen, Projekte, Ergebnisse.* Bochum: AKS-Verlag 1995.

EGYÜD, Györgyi & Philip GLOVER: "Oral Testing in Pairs – a Secondary School Perspective." *ELT Journal* 55, 1 (2001), P. 70–76.

EHLERS, Swantje: „Übungen zum Leseverstehen." In: BAUSCH et al 2003. P. 287–292.

ELLIS, Rod: "Teaching and Research: Options in Grammar Teaching." In: *TESOL Quarterly* 32.1 (1998), P. 39–60.

ELLIS, Rod: "Task-based Research and Language Pedagogy." In: *Language Teaching Research* 4.3 (2000), P. 193–220.

ELLIS, Rod: "The Metaphorical Constructions of Second Language Learners." In: BREEN 2001. P. 65–85.

ELLIS, Gail & Jean BREWSTER: *The Storytelling Handbook. A Guide for Primary Teachers of English*. Ldn.: Penguin 1991.

ESSER, Ruth: „Übungen zum Schreiben." In: BAUSCH et al. 2003. P. 292–295.

ESTAIRE, Sheila & Javier ZANÓN: *Planning Classwork. A Task-Based Approach*. Oxford: Heinemann 1994.

Europäische Kommission (Eds.): *Weißbuch zur allgemeinen und beruflichen Bildung. Lehren und Lernen. Auf dem Weg zur kognitiven Gesellschaft*. Luxembourg: Amt für Veröffentlichungen der Europäischen Gemeinschaft, 1996.

European Council of Cultural Co-Operation: "The Celebration of Linguistic Diversity." 2001. Avail.: http://culture.coe.int/AEL2001EYL (17.02.2004).

EYRING, Janet L.: "Experiential and Negotiated Language Learning." In: *Teaching English as a Second or Foreign Language*. Ed.: M. CELCE-MURCIA. 3rd. ed. Ldn.: Heinle & Heinle 2001. P. 333–344.

FISH, Stanley: *Is There a Text in This Class? The Authority of Interpretive Communities*. Harvard: Harvard UP. 1980.

FOOT, Michael C.: „Relaxing in Pairs." In: *ELT Journal* 53.1 (1999), P. 36–41.

FREEMAN, Donald: "Second Language Teacher Education." In: CARTER/NUNAN 2001. P. 72–79.

FREEMAN, Donald & Karen E. JOHNSON: "Reconceptualizing the Knowledge-Base of Language Teacher Education." In: *TESOL Quarterly* 32.3 (1998), P. 397–417.

FREESE, Peter, Horst GROENE & Liesel HERMES: *Die Short Story im Englischunterricht der Sekundarstufe II. Theorie und Praxis*. Paderborn: Schöningh 1979.

FREUDENSTEIN, Reinhold: „Funktion von Unterrichtsmitteln und Medien: Überblick." In: *Handbuch Fremdsprachenunterricht*. Eds.: K.-R. BAUSCH, H. CHRIST & H.-J. KRUMM. 3. überarb. Aufl. Tübingen: Francke 1995. P. 288–291.

FRIEDMAN, Lester D.: *Unspeakable Images. Ethnicity and the American Cinema*. Urbana: University of Illinois Press 1991.

FROESE, Wolfgang, Axel PLITSCH, Gitta SELLIN & Thomas UNRUH: *Englischprojekte Klasse 7*. Stg.: Klett 1998.

FULLAN, Michael: *Change Forces. Probing the Depths of Educational Reform*. Ldn.: Falmer Press 1993.

GABEL, Petra: *Lehren und Lernen im Fachpraktikum Englisch. Wunsch und Wirklichkeit*. Tübingen: Narr 1997.

GEIST, Hanne: „Anforderungsprofil für einen guten Schüler. Selbstevaluation als gemeinsame Reflexion von Lehrenden und Lernenden." In: *FS Deutsch*, Sonderheft Benoten und Bewerten (1998), P. 32–35.

GENESEE, Fred & John A. UPSHUR: *Classroom-Based Evaluation in Second Language Education*. Cambridge: Cambridge UP 1996.

GERNGROSS, Günter: „Lernstandsfeststellung. Es ist Zeit für eine Diskussion, die den Unterrichtsalltag nicht aus den Augen verliert." In: *Primary English*. 2 (2004), P. 8–12.

GERNGROSS, Günter & Herbert PUCHTA: *Playway to English 3 - Rainbow Edition. Pupils' Book*. Innsbruck & Leipzig: Helbling & Klett 2001.

GILROY, Marie & Brian PARKINSON: "Teaching Literature in a Foreign Language." In: *Language Teaching* 29 (1997), P. 213–225.

GOWER, Roger, Diane PHILLIPS & Steve WALTERS (Eds.): *Teaching Practice Handbook*. New Ed. Oxford: Macmillan Heinemann 1995.

◆ GRABE, William & Robert B. KAPLAN: *Theory and Practice of Writing*. Harlow: Pearson Education 1996 (= Applied Linguistics and Language Study).

◆ GRABE, William & Fredricka, L. STOLLER: *Teaching and Researching Reading*. Harlow: Pearson Education 2002.

GROENE, Helga: "'We SPEAK English in Our GEOGRAPHY class, and We LEARN English in Our ENGLISH Class.' Beobachtungen an Lernern in der Praxis." In: *Learnline, Arbeitsbereich: Bilingualer Unterricht*. 6 pp. Avail.: http://www.learn-line.nrw.de (15.12.03).

◆ GRUNDER, Hans-Ulrich & Thorsten BOHL (Eds.): *Neue Formen der Leistungsbeurteilung in den Sekundarstufen I und II*. Hohengehren: Schneider 2001.

HALLET, Wolfgang: „The Bilingual Triangle. Überlegungen zu einer Didaktik des bilingualen Sachfachunterrichts." In: *Praxis des neusprachlichen Unterrichts* 45 (1998), P. 115–125.

◆ HALLET, Wolfgang: *Fremdsprachenunterricht als Spiel der Texte und Kulturen. Intertextualität als Paradigma einer kulturwissenschaftlichen Didaktik.* Trier Wissenschaftlicher Verlag 2002 (= Studies in English Literary and Cultural History Band 6).

HANCOCK, Penny, Susannah REED & Marita SCHOCKER-V. DITFURTH: *Magicland. Class Book 1.* München: Langenscheidt 2003.

◆ HANSON-SMITH, Elizabeth: "Computer-assisted Language Learning." In: CARTER/NUNAN 2001. P. 107–113.

HARRIS, Michael: "Self-assessment of Language Learning in Formal Settings." In: *ELT Journal* 55.1 (1997), P. 12–20.

HARRIS, Michael & Paul MCCANN: *Assessment.* Oxford: Macmillan/Heinemann 1994.

HECHT, Karlheinz & Peter Stuart GREEN: „Analyse und Bewertung von mündlichen Schülerproduktionen." In: *Praxis des neusprachlichen Unterrichts* (1987), P. 3–11.

◆ HEDGE, Tricia: *Teaching and Learning in the Language Classroom.* Oxford: Oxford UP 2000 (= Oxford Handbooks for Language Teachers).

HELBIG, Beate: „Bilinguales Lehren und Lernen." In: BAUSCH et al. 2003. P. 179–186.

HELLEKJAER, Glenn Ole: "Easy Does It: Introducing Pupils to Bilingual Instruction." In: *Zeitschrift für interkulturellen Fremdsprachenunterricht* 4.2 (1999), 8 pp. Avail.: http://www.ualberta.ca/~german/ejournal/hellek1.htm (15. 12. 03).

HENDRICKS, Wilfried (Ed.): *Neue Medien in der Sekundarstufe I und II.* Bln.: Cornelsen: Scriptor 2000.

HERMES, Liesel & Friederike KLIPPEL (Eds.): *Früher oder später? Englisch in der Grundschule und Bilingualer Sachfachuterricht.* München: Langenscheidt 2003.

◆ HESSE, Mechthild: *Jugendliteratur als Schreiblehre. Untersuchungen zum Verhältnis von Lesen und Schreiben im Englischunterricht der Sekundarstufe I.* Tübingen: Narr 2002.

HU, Adelheid: „Interkulturelles Lernen. Eine Auseinandersetzung mit der Kritik an einem umstrittenen Konzept." In: *Zeitschrift für Fremdsprachenforschung* 10.2 (1999), P. 277–303.

HUNFELD, Hans: *Die Normalität des Fremden.* Waldsteinberg: Heidrun Popp 1998.

ISER, Wolfgang: "Interaction Between Text and Reader." In: *The Reader in the Text: Essays on Audience and Interpretation.* Eds.: S.R. SULEIMAN & I. CROSSMAN. Princeton: Princeton UP 1980. P. 106–119.

*I*EARN* http://www.iearn.org/ (15. 12. 03).

JODY, Marilyn & Marianne SACCARDI: *Using Computers to Teach Literature. A Teacher's Guide.* Sec. ed. of *Computer Conversations,* rev. and upd. Urbana, IL: National Council of Teachers of English 1998.

JOHNSON, Karen: "The Emerging Beliefs and Instructional Practices of Preservice English as a Second Language Teachers." In: *Teaching &Teacher Education* 10. 4 (1994), P. 439–452.

◆ JOHNSON, Karen: *Understanding Communication in Second Language Classrooms.* Cambridge: Cambridge UP 1995.

JOHNSON, Keith: *An Introduction to Foreign Language Learning and Teaching.* Harlow: Longman/Pearson 2001.

KAHL, Peter W. & Ulrike KNEBLER: *Englisch in der Grundschule – und dann? Evaluation des Hamburger Schulversuchs Englisch ab Klasse 3.* Berlin: Cornelsen 1996.

◆ KALLENBACH, Christiane & Markus RITTER: *Computer-Ideen für den Englischunterricht. Anregungen und Beispiele für den Software- und Internet-Einsatz Klassen 5 bis 10.* Bln.: Cornelsen 2000.

KAST, Bernd: *Fertigkeit Schreiben.* München: Langenscheidt 1999.

KEH, Claudia L.: "Feedback in the Writing Process: a Model and Methods for Implementation." In: *Power, Pedgagogy & Practice.* Eds.: T. HEDGE & N. WHITNEY. Oxford: Oxford UP 1996. P. 294–306.

KERN, Richard: "Computer-Mediated Communication: Using E-Mail Exchanges to Explore Personal Histories in Two Cultures." In: *Telecollaboration in Foreign Language Learning. Proceedings of the Hawai'i Symposium.* Ed.: M. WARSCHAUER. Honolulu: University of Hawai'i Press 1996. P. 105–120.

KERN, Richard & Mark WARSCHAUER: „Introduction: Theory and Practice of Network-based Language Teaching." In: WARSCHAUER/KERN 2000. P. 1–19.

KIEWEG, Werner: „Alternative Konzepte zur Vermittlung der Grammatik." In: *Der Fremdsprachliche Unterricht Englisch* 4 (1996), P. 4–12.

KLIPPEL, Friederike: "Teaching in English – Teacher Language in Primary School." In: HERMES/KLIPPEL 2003. S. 53–68.

KLIPPEL, Friederike: *Keep Talking. Communicative Fluency Activities for Language Teaching*. Cambridge: Cambridge UP 1984.

KLIPPERT, Heinz: *Teamentwicklung im Klassenraum. Übungsbausteine für den Unterricht*. Weinheim und Basel: Beltz 1998.

KOCHER, Doris: *Das Klassenzimmer als Lernwerkstatt. Medien und Kommunikation im Englischunterricht nach der Storyline-Methode*. Hbg.: Kovac 1999.

KRAINER, Konrad & Peter POSCH (Eds.): *Lehrerfortbildung zwischen Prozessen und Produkten. Hochschullehrgänge „Pädagogik und Fachdidaktik für LehrerInnen" (PFL): Konzepte, Erfahrungen und Reflexionen*. Bad Heilbrunn: Klinkhardt 1996.

◆ KRAMSCH, Claire: *Context and Culture in Language Teaching*. Oxford: Oxford UP 1993.

KRECHEL, Hans-Ludwig: "Methodological Aspects of Content-Based Language Work in Bilingual Education." In: *The Construction of Knowledge, Learner Autonomy and Related Issues in Foreign Language Learning*. Eds.: B. MISSLER & U. MULTHAUP. Tübingen: Stauffenberg 1999. P. 193–202.

KREEFT PEYTON, Joy: "Theory and Research: Interaction via Computers." In: *CALL Environments. Research, Practice, and Critical Issues*. Eds.: J. EGBERT & E. HANSON-SMITH: Alexandria: TESOL Publication 1999. P. 17–26.

KRUMM, Hans-Jürgen: „Lehr- und Lernziele." In: BAUSCH et al 2003. P. 116–121.

KRUMM, Hans-Jürgen & Eva-Maria JENKINS: *Kinder und ihre Sprachen – lebendige Mehrsprachigkeit*. Wien: Eviva 2001.

KÜPPERS, Almut: *Schulische Lesesozialisation im Fremdsprachenunterricht. Eine explorative Studie zum Lesen im Englischunterricht der Oberstufe. Unterrichtsbeobachtungen, Interviews und Fallanalysen*. Tübingen: Narr 1999.

KULTUSMINISTERKONFERENZ (KMK): *Bericht: Fremdsprachen in der Grundschule – Sachstand und Konzeptionen. Beschluss der Kultusministerkonferenz vom 1. 3. 2002* (www.kmk.org, 29.08.03).

KUNA, Franz & Heinz TSCHACHLER (Eds.): *Dialog der Texte. Literatur und Landeskunde. Beiträge zu Problemen einer integrativen Landes- und Kulturkunde des englischsprachigen Auslands*. Tübingen: Narr 1986.

KURTZ, Jürgen: *Improvisierendes Sprechen im Fremdsprachenunterricht. Eine Untersuchung zur Entwicklung spontansprachlicher Handlungskompetenz in der Zielsprache*. Tübingen: Narr 2001.

LADO, Robert: *Language Testing*. Ldn.: Longman 1961.

LAMSFUSS-SCHENK, Stefanie: „Bilingualer Geschichtsunterricht: Die Perspektive des Sachfaches." In: *Neusprachliche Mitteilungen aus Wissenschaft und Praxis* 55.2 (2002), P. 87–96.

LANTOLF, James P. "Second Language Learning as a Mediated Process." In: *Language Teaching* 33 (2000), P. 79–96.

LARSEN-FREEMAN, Diane: "Teacher Education in an International Context: Aspects of Language Acquisition, Linguistics, and Language Teaching Methodology." In: *Fremdsprachen lehren lernen – Lehrerausbildung in der Diskussion. Dokumentation des 17. Kongresses für Fremdsprachenforschung der DGFF.* Eds.: L. HERMES & G. SCHMID-SCHÖNBEIN. Bln.: Pädagogischer Zeitschriften Verlag 1998. P. 1–12.

LARSEN-FREEMAN, Diane: "Grammar." In: CARTER/NUNAN 2001. P. 34–41.

LARSEN-FREEMAN, Diane & Michael H. LONG: *An Introduction to Second Language Acquisition Research*. Ldn.: Longman 1991.

LEGUTKE, Michael K.: "Room to Talk. Experiential Learning in the Foreign Language Classroom." *Die Neueren Sprachen*, 92, 4 (1993), P. 306–331.

LEGUTKE, Michael K.: „Handlungsraum Klassenzimmer *and beyond*." In: TIMM 1998. P. 93–109.

LEGUTKE, Michael K.: „Fremdsprachen in der Grundschule: Brennpunkt Weiterführung." In: *Kognitive Aspekte des Lehrens und Lernens von Fremdsprachen*. Ed.: C. RIEMER. Tübingen: Narr 2000.

LEGUTKE, Michael K.: „Redesigning the Foreign Language Classroom: A Critical Perspective on Information Technology and Educational Change." In: *Innovation and Language Education*. Eds.: C. DAVISON, V. CREW & J. HUNG. Hong Kong: The University of Hong Kong, Department of Curriculum Studies, Faculty of Education 2001. P. 35–51.

LEGUTKE, Michael K.: „Neue Wege für die Lernstandsermittlung im fremdsprachlichen Unterricht der Grundschule? Anmerkungen zum Junior-Portfolio für Sprachen." In: HERMES/KLIPPEL 2003. P. 69–86.

LEGUTKE, Michael K. & Wiltrud LORTZ: *Mein Sprachenportfolio.* Ffm: Diesterweg 2002.

LEGUTKE, Michael K. & Andreas MÜLLER-HARTMANN: "Vom Lerneinstieg zum *prompt*: Die Arbeit mit einer literarischen Ganzschrift in Klasse 9/10." In: *Der fremdsprachliche Unterricht-Englisch* 35, 52 (3) (2001), P. 25–29.

LEGUTKE, Michael K., Andreas MÜLLER-HARTMANN & Marita SCHOCKER-V. DITFURTH: "Preparing Teachers for Technology-supported ELT." In: *Kluewer International Handbook of Education*, in press.

LEGUTKE, Michael K., Andreas MÜLLER-HARTMANN & Stefan ULRICH: „Neue Kommunikationsformen im fremdsprachlichen Unterricht." In: *Kommunikationsformen im Wandel der Zeit. Vom mittelalterlichen Heldenepos zum elektronischen Hypertext.* Eds.: G. FRITZ & A. H. JUCKER. Tübingen: Niemeyer 2000. P. 51–73.

LEGUTKE, Michael K. & Wolfgang THIEL: *Airport: Ein Projekt für den Englischunterricht in Klasse 6.* Wiesbaden: Hessisches Institut für Bildungsplanung und Schulentwicklung (HIBS) 1983.

◆ LEGUTKE, Michael K. & Howard THOMAS: *Process and Experience in the Language Classroom.* 1991. Harlow: Longman 1993.

LEVINE, Lawrence W.: *Black Culture and Black Consciousness.* Oxford: Oxford UP 1977.

◆ LEWIS, Michael: *The Lexical Approach. The State of ELT and a Way Forward.* Hove: Language Teaching Publications 1993.

◆ LIGTBOWN, Patsy M. & Nina SPADA: *How Languages Are Learned.* Rev. ed. Oxford: Oxford UP 1999.

LITTLE, David: "Words and Their Properties: Arguments for a Lexical Approach to Pedagogical Grammar." In: *Perspectives on Pedagogical Grammar.* Ed.: T. ODLIN:. Cambridge: Cambridge UP 1994. P. 99–122.

◆ LYNCH, Toni: "Teaching Listening." In: *Communication in the Language Classroom.* Ed.: T. Lynch. Oxford: Oxford UP 1996. P. 87–103.

MACHT, Konrad & Martin NUTZ: „Schülerselbstbewertung." In: *Der fremdsprachliche Unterricht Englisch* 1 (1999), P. 40–45.

MACKEY, William Francis: "Applied Linguistics." In: *Readings for Applied Linguistics. The Edinburgh Course in Applied Linguistics.* Eds.: J.P.B. ALLEN & S. PIT CORDER. Vol. 1 (1973). P. 247–255.

MALEY, Alan: "Literature in the Language Classroom." In: CARTER/NUNAN 2001. P. 180–185.

MALEY, Alan & Alan DUFF: *Drama Techniques in Language Learning. A Resource Book of Communication Activities for Language Teachers.* Cambridge: Cambridge UP 2001.

MCKAY, Sandra Lee: "Literature as Content for ESL/EFL." In: *Teaching English as a Second or Foreign Language.* 3rd ed. Ed.: M. CELCE-MURCIA. Heinle & Heinle 2001. P. 319–332.

MCKAY, Sandra Lee: "The Cultural Bias of Teaching English as an International Language." In: *TESOL Matters* 13.4 (1 & 6) (2003).

MEDGYES, Peter: *The Non-Native Teacher.* Ldn.: Macmillan 1994.

MEDGYES, Peter: "Review of 'The Cambridge Guide to Teaching English to Speakers of Other Languages'." In: *ELT Journal* 56.1 (2002), P. 87.

MEISSNER, Franz-Joseph & Marcus REINFRIED (Eds.): *Mehrsprachigkeitsdidaktik. Konzepte, Analysen. Lehrerfahrungen mit romanischen Fremdsprachen.* Tübingen: Narr 1998 (= Giessener Beiträge zur Fremdsprachendidaktik).

MIKLOWITZ, Gloria: *The War Between the Classes.* 1985. Stg.: Klett 1996.

◆ MORROW, Keith (Ed.): *Insights from the Common European Framework.* Oxford: Oxford UP 2004.

MOSNER, Bärbel: *Das Leser-Tagebuch im Englischunterricht am Beispiel von Shakespares ‚Romeo and Juliet.'* Ffm.: Lang 2000.

MÜLLER, Bernd-Dietrich: *Wortschatzarbeit und Bedeutungsvermittlung.* Bln. 1994 (= Fernstudieneinheit 8 im Fernstudienprojekt „Deutsch als Fremdsprache und Germanistik").

MÜLLER-HARTMANN, Andreas: „Auf der Suche nach dem ‚dritten Ort': Das Eigene und das Fremde im virtuellen Austausch über literarische Texte." In: *Interkultureller Fremdsprachenunterricht.* Eds.: L. BREDELLA & W. DELANOY. Tübingen: Narr 1999a. P. 160–182.

MÜLLER-HARTMANN, Andreas: „Die Integration der neuen Medien in den schulischen Fremdsprachenunterricht: Interkulturelles Lernen und die Folgen in E-mail-Projekten.“ In: *Fremdsprachen Lehren und Lernen* 28 (1999b), P. 58–79.

MÜLLER-HARTMANN, Andreas: „'Disney Is Safe for Kids; or Is It?' Eine kritische Betrachtung der Walt Disney Company im Englischunterricht.“ In: *Der Fremdsprachliche Unterricht – Englisch* 34, 43 (1) (2000), P. 18–23.

MÜLLER-HARTMANN, Andreas: „Multiethnische Literatur der USA im Englischunterricht." In: *Praxis des neusprachlichen Unterrichts* 47.2 (2000b), P. 115–124.

MÜLLER-HARTMANN, Andreas: "The Role of Tasks in Promoting Intercultural Learning in Electronic Learning Networks." In: *Language Learning & Technology* 4.2 (2000c), P. 129–147. http://llt.msu.edu (15.12.03).

MÜLLER-HARTMANN, Andreas: „'What Happened to the Dead Man?' Students Discuss Alice Walker's Short Story 'The Flowers' via E-mail." In: *Englisch betrifft uns* 2 (2000a), P. 10–16.

MÜLLER-HARTMANN, Andreas: „'And How Does the Story Continue?' Der Hypertext als neue, elektronisch basierte narrative Form." In: *Der Fremdsprachliche Unterricht Englisch* 37, 61 (1) (2003), P. 32–36.

MÜLLER-HARTMANN, Andreas & Michael K. LEGUTKE: „Lernwelt Klassenzimmer – Internet.“ In: *Der Fremdsprachliche Unterricht Englisch* 35, 49, (1) (2001), P. 4–11.

MÜLLER-HARTMANN, Andreas & Annette RICHTER: "From Classroom Learners to World Communicators." In: *Der Fremdsprachliche Unterricht Englisch* 35, 45, (6) (2001), P. 4–15.

◆ MUKHERJEE, Joybrato: *Korpuslinguistik und Englischunterricht. Eine Einführung*. Ffm.: Lang 2002 (= Sprache im Kontext, Bd. 14).

NATION, I.S.P.: *Learning Vocabulary in Another Language*. Cambridge: Cambridge UP 2001 (= The Cambridge Applied Linguistics Series).

NATION, Paul & Jonathan NEWTON: "Teaching Vocabulary." In: COADY/HUCKIN 1997. P. 283–254.

NATION, Paul & Robert WARING: "Vocabulary Size, Text Coverage and Word Lists." In: SCHMITT/MCCARTHY 2000. P. 6–19.

NATTINGER, James: "Some Current Trends in Vocabulary Teaching." In: CARTER/MCCARTHY 1988. P. 62–82.

NIEMEIER, Susanne: „Bilingualismus und ‚bilinguale‘ Bildungsgänge aus kognitivpsychologischer Sicht.“ In: BACH/NIEMEIER 2000. P. 27–49.

NISSEN, Rudolf: „Phasen und Formen des textverarbeitenden Lerngesprächs im Englischunterricht.“ In: *Neusprachliche Mitteilungen aus Wissenschaft und Praxis* 35 (1982), P. 114–125.

NÜNNING, Ansgar: „‚Nur nicht gleich interpretieren!‘ Kreative und produktionsorientierte Zugangsmöglichkeiten bei der Textarbeit.“ In: *Fremdsprachenunterricht* 39, 48 (2) (1995), P. 102–106.

NÜNNING, Ansgar: „Literatur ist, wenn das Lesen wieder Spaß macht.“ In: *Der fremdsprachliche Unterricht Englisch* 31, 27 (3) (1997), P. 4–13.

NÜNNING, Ansgar & Andreas H. JUCKER: *Orientierung Anglistik/ Amerikanistik. Was sie kann, was sie will*. Reinbek: Rowohlt 1999.

NÜNNING, Vera & Ansgar NÜNNING: „British Cultural Studies konkret. 10 Leitkonzepte für einen innovativen Kulturunterricht.“ In: *Der Fremdsprachliche Unterricht Englisch* 34, 43 (1) (2000), P. 4–9.

NÜNNING, Vera & Ansgar NÜNNING: *Grundkurs anglistisch-amerikanische Literaturwissenschaft*. Stg.: Klett 2001 (= Uni Wissen).

NUNAN, David: *Designing Tasks for the Communicative Classroom*. Cambridge: Cambridge UP 1989.

NUNAN, David & Lindsay MILLER (Eds.): *New Ways in Teaching Listening*. Alexandria, VA: TESOL 1995.

◆ NUNAN, David: *Second Language Teaching & Learning*. Boston: Heinle & Heinle 1999.

NUNN, Roger: "Designing Rating Scales for Small-Group Interaction." In: *ELT Journal* 54.2 (2000), P. 169–178.

OXFORD, Rebecca L.: "Language Learning Strategies." In: CARTER/NUNAN 2001. P. 166–172.

OXFORD, Rebecca L.: "Language Learning Strategies in a Nutshell: Update and ESL Suggestions." In: RICHARDS/RENANDYA 2002. P. 124–119.

PIEPHO, Hans-Eberhardt: *Lerneraktivierung im Fremdsprachenunterricht - „Szenarien“ in Theorie und Praxis*. Hannover: Diesterweg/Schroedel/Klinkhardt 2003.

PRABHU, N.S.: *Second Language Pedagogy.* Oxford: Oxford UP 1987.

PRABHU, N.S.: "There Is no Best Method – Why?" In: *TESOL Quarterly* 24.2 (1990), P. 161–176.

QUETZ, Jürgen: "Fremdsprachliches Curriculum." In: BAUSCH et al 2003. P. 121–127.

Rahmenrichtlinien Englisch Hessen: Avail.: http://lernen.bildung.hessen.de/english/materialien/rplan/ (1. 2. 2004).

REA-DICKINS, Pauline: „Classroom Assessment." In: *Teaching and Learning in the Language Classroom.* Ed.: T. HEDGE. Oxford: Oxford UP 2000. P. 375–401.

REA-DICKINS, Pauline: "Mirror, Mirror on the Wall: Identifying Processes of Classroom Assessment." In: *Language Testing* 18.4 (2001), P. 429–462.

REA-DICKINS, Pauline & Shelagh RIXON: "Assessment of Young Learners' English: Reasons and Means." In: *Young Learners of English: Some Research Perspectives.* Ed.: S. RIXON. Ldn.: Longman, 1999. P. 89–101.

REID, Joy: "Writing." In: CARTER/NUNAN 2001. P. 28–33.

◆ RIBE, Ramon & Núria VIDAL: *Project Work. Step by Step.* Oxford: Heinemann 1993.

RICHARDS, Jack C.: "The Ideology of TESOL." In: CARTER/NUNAN 2001. P. 213–217.

RICHARDS, Jack C. & John and Heidi PLATT: *Dictionary of Language Teaching & Applied Linguistics.* Harlow: Longman 1992.

RICHARDS, Jack C. & Willy A. RENANDYA (Eds.): *Methodology in Language Teaching: An Anthology of Current Practice. Cambridge:* Cambridge UP 2002.

RICHARDS, Jack C. & Theodore S. RODGERS: *Approaches and Methods in Language Teaching.* 2nd ed. Cambridge: Cambridge UP 2001.

◆ RICHARDS, Jack, Richard SCHMIDT, Heidi PLATT & Marcus SCHMIDT. *Dictionary of Language Teaching and Applied Linguistics.* 3rd. ed. Harlow: Pearson Education 2002.

RIEPE, Regina & Gerd RIEPE: *Du Schwarz – Ich Weiss. Bilder und Texte gegen den alltäglichen Rassismus.* Wuppertal: Hammer 1992.

RITTER, Markus: „Der Computer im offenen Klassenzimmer – wie sich Tutor- und Toolfunktionen (einstweilen) verschränken lassen." In: *Fremdsprachen lehren lernen – Lehrerausbildung in der Diskussion.* Eds.: L. HERMES & G. SCHMID-SCHÖNBEIN. Bln.: Pädagogischer Zeitschriftenverlag 1998. P. 241–253.

ROCHE, Jörg: *Interkulturelle Sprachdidaktik. Eine Einführung.* Tübingen: Narr 2001 (= Narr Studienbücher).

RÖTTGER, Evelyn: „Überlegungen zum Begriff des interkulturellen Lernens in der Fremdsprachendidaktik." In: *Zeitschrift für Fremdsprachenforschung* 7.2 (1996), P. 155–170.

ROSENBLATT, Louise M.: *Literature as Exploration.* 5th ed. 1938. NY: The Modern Language Association of America 1995.

ROST, Michael: *Listening in Language Learning.* Harlow: Pearson Education 1990.

ROST, Michael: *Introducing Listening.* Ldn.: Penguin 1994.

ROST, Michael: "Listening." In: CARTER/NUNAN 2001. P. 7–13.

◆ ROST, Michael: *Teaching and Researching Listening.* Harlow: Pearson Education 2002.

RUBIN, Jerry: "Learner Strategies: Theoretical Assumptions, Research History and Typology." In: *Learner Strategies for Learner Autonomy.* Eds.: A. WENDEN & J. RUBIN. Ldn.: Prentice Hall International 1987. P. 15–30.

RÜSCHOFF, Bern & Dieter WOLFF: *Fremdsprachenlernen in der Wissensgesellschaft. Zum Einsatz der Neuen Technologien in Schule und Unterricht.* Ismaning: Hueber 1999.

◆ RYMARCZYK, Jutta: *Kunst auf Englisch? Ein Plädoyer für die Erweiterung des bilingualen Sachfachkanons.* München: Langenscheidt-Longman 2003 (= Münchner Arbeiten zur Fremdsprachen-Forschung 6).

SAVIGNON, Sandra J.: "Communicative Language Teaching for the Twenty-First Century." In: *Teaching English as a Foreign Language.* Ed.: M. CELCE-MURCIA. 3rd. ed. Boston: Heinle & Heinle 2001. P. 13–28.

◆ SCHMID-SCHÖNBEIN, Gisela: *Didaktik: Grundschulenglisch.* Bln.: Cornelsen 2001.

◆ SCHMITT, Norbert: *Vocabulary in Language Teaching.* Cambridge: Cambridge UP 2000 (= Cambridge Language Education).

SCHMITT, Norbert & Michael MCCARTHY: *Vocabulary; Description, Acquisition and Pedagogy.* Cambridge: Cambridge UP 1997.

SCHNEIDER, Günther & Brian NORTH: *Fremd-*

sprachen können – was heißt das? Skalen zur Beschreibung, Beurteilung und Selbsteinschätzung der fremdsprachlichen Kommunikationsfähigkeit. Chur/Zürich: Rüegger 2000.

SCHNOOR, Detlev: „Neue Schulen und die Innovationsfähigkeit von Schulen.“ In: *Neue Medien in der Sekundarstufe I und II*: Ed.: W. HENDRICKS. Bln.: Cornelsen Scriptor 2000. P. 50–62.

◆ SCHOCKER-V. DITFURTH, Marita: *Forschendes Lernen in der fremdsprachlichen Lehrerbildung. Grundlagen, Erfahrungen, Perspektiven.* Tübingen: Narr 2001.

SCHOCKER-V. DITFURTH, Marita: „Fremdsprachenlehrerausbildung für die Primarstufe: Erfahrungen mit praxisbezogenen und teilnehmerorientierten Didaktikseminaren." In: HERMES/KLIPPEL. 2003. P. 87–100.

SCHOCKER-V. DITFURTH, Marita: *Learning to listen. Authentic Texts and Learner-centred Tasks.* Bln.: Cornelsen 1997. (Klasse 9)

SCHOCKER-V. DITFURTH, Marita: *Learning to Listen. Authentic Texts and Learner-centred Tasks.* Bln.: Cornelsen 1999. (Klasse 10)

SCHOCKER-V. DITFURTH, Marita: *Unterricht verstehen. Erfahrungswissen reflektieren und den eigenen Unterricht weiterentwickeln. Medienpaket zur Förderung reflektierter Unterrichtspraxis.* München: Goethe Institut Inter Nationes 2002. [Buch und Video zum Buch]

SCHÖN, Donald A.: *The Reflective Practitioner: How Professionals Think in Action.* NY: Basic Book 1983.

SCOVEL, Thomas. *Psycholinguistics.* Oxford: Oxford UP 1998.

SHETZER, Heidi & Mark WARSCHAUER: "An Electronic Literacy Approach to Network-based Language Teaching." In: *Network-based Language Teaching: Concepts and Practice.* Eds.: M. WARSCHAUER & R. KERN. Cambridge: Cambridge UP 2000 (= The Cambridge Applied Linguistics Series).

SINCLAIR, John & Malcom COULTHARD: *Towards an Analysis of Discourse.* Oxford: Oxford UP 1975.

◆ SKEHAN, Peter: *A Cognitive Approach to Language Teaching.* Oxford: Oxford UP 1998.

SMITH, Geoff P. "Music and Mondegreens: Extracting Meaning from Noise." *English Language Teaching Journal* 57, 3 (2003), P. 113–121.

SOMMER, Roy: *Grundkurs Cultural Studies/Kulturwissenschaft Großbritannien.* Stg.: Klett 2003 (= Uni Wissen).

STEINBACH, Gudrun: "Words are Like Flowers ...“ In: *Der fremdsprachliche Unterricht Englisch* 1 (1995), P. 12–16.

◆ STEMPLESKI, Susan & Barry TOMALIN: *Video in Action.* NY: Prentice Hall 1990 (= Language Teaching Methodology Series).

STENHOUSE, Lawrence: *An Introduction to Curriculum Research and Development.* Ldn.: Heinemann 1975.

STEVICK, Earl W.: *Memory, Meaning, & Method. A View of Language Teaching.* Boston, MA: Heinle & Heinle 1996.

STOLLER, Fredericka L.: "Project Work: A Means to Promote Language and Content." In: RICHARDS/RENANDYA 2002. P. 107–119.

STOREY, John: *Cultural Studies and the Study of Popular Culture: Theories and Methods.* Athens: University of Georgia Press 1996.

THOMPSON, Geoff: "Some Misconceptions about Communicative Language Teaching.“ *English Language Teaching Journal,* 50, 1 (1996), P. 9–15.

THÜRMANN, Eike: „Eine eigenständige Methodik für den bilingualen Sachfachunterricht?“ In: BACH/NIEMEIER 2000. P. 75–93.

TIMM, Johannes-Peter: *Englisch lernen und lehren. Didaktik des Englischunterrichts.* Bln.: Cornelsen 1998.

TOMLINSON, Brian (Ed.): *Materials Development in Language Teaching.* Cambridge: Cambridge UP 1998.

TRIBBLE, Christopher: "Five Electronic Learners' Dictionaries.“ In: *English Language Teaching Journal* 57.2 (2003), P. 182–197.

UNDERHILL, Nick: *Testing Spoken Language.* Cambridge: Cambridge UP 1987.

UNDERWOOD, Mary: *Teaching Listening.* Ldn.: Longman 1989.

UR, Penny: *A Course in Language Teaching.* Cambridge: Cambridge UP 1996.

VAN EK, J.: *The Treshold Level.* Strasbourg: Council of Europe 1975.

VOLLMER, Helmut J.: „Förderung des Spracherwerbs im bilingualen Sachfachunterricht.“ In: BACH/NIEMEIER 2000. P. 139–158.

VYGOTSKY, Lev S.: *Mind in society. The Development of Higher Psychological Processes.* Cambridge: Harvard UP 1978.

WALKER, Alice: "The Flowers." In: *In Love & Trouble. Stories of Black Women*. Ed.: A. WALKER. San Diego: Harcourt Brace Jovanovich 1973. P. 119–129.

WALLACE, Catherine: *Reading*. Oxford: Oxford UP 1992.

WALLACE, Catherine: „Reading." In: CARTER/NUNAN 2001. P. 21–27.

◆ WALLACE, Michael J.: *Training Foreign Language Teachers. A Reflective Approach*. Cambridge: Cambridge UP 1991.

WALTER, Catherine: "Review of *Teaching and Researching Reading* and *Assessing Reading*." In: *English Language Teaching Journal* 57.3 (2003), P. 314–317.

WARD, Jerry W.: "Don' Be Fourteen (In Mississippi)." In: *Black Southern Voices. An Anthology of Fiction, Poetry, Drama, Nonfiction, and Critical Essays*. Eds.: J. O. KILLENS & J. W. WARD. NY: Penguin 1992. P. 296–297

WARSCHAUER, Mark: "Computer-Mediated Collaborative Learning: Theory and Practice." In: *The Modern Language Journal* 81. iv (1997). P. 470–481.

WARSCHAUER, Mark: *Electronic Literacies. Language, Culture, and Power in Online Education*. Mahwah, NJ: Lawrence Erlbaum 1999.

WARSCHAUER, Mark: "On-line Communication." In: CARTER/NUNAN 2001. P. 207–212.

◆ WARSCHAUER, Mark & Richard KERN (Eds.): *Network-based Language Teaching: Concepts and Practice*. Cambridge: Cambridge UP 2000 (= The Cambridge Applied Linguistics Series).

WERLICH, Egon: *Praktische Methodik des Fremdsprachenunterrichts mit authentischen Texten*. Bln.: Cornelsen-Velhagen & Klasing 1986.

WESKAMP, Ralf: „Selbstevaluation: Ein zentraler Aspekt schülerorientierten Fremdsprachenunterrichts." In: *Fremdsprachenunterricht* 40.49 (1996), P. 406–411.

WHITE, Goodith: *Listening*. Oxford: Oxford UP 1998.

WIDDOWSON, H.G.: "Directions in the Teaching of Discourse." In: *The Communicative Approach to Language Teaching*. Eds.: C. J. BRUMFIT & K. JOHNSON. Oxford: Oxford UP. 1979. P. 49–60.

◆ WILLIS, Jane: *A Framework for Task-based Learning*. Harlow: Longman 1996.

WILLIS, Dave & Jane WILLIS: "Task-based Language Learning." In: CARTER/NUNAN 2001. P. 173–179.

WOLFF, Dieter: „Einige Anmerkungen zur Curriculum-Entwicklung im bilingualen Sachfachunterricht." In: *Neusprachliche Mitteilungen aus Wissenschaft und Praxis* 55.2 (2002), P. 66–75.

◆ YULE, George: *The Study of Language*. Cambridge: Cambridge UP 1998.

ZIMMERMAN, Cheryl Boyd: "Historical Trends in Second Language Vocabulary Instruction." In: COADY/HUCKIN 1997. P. 5–19.

ZYDATISS, Wolfgang: *Bilingualer Unterricht in der Grundschule. Entwurf eines Spracherwerbskonzepts für zweisprachige Immersionsprogramme*. Ismaning: Huber 2000.

Journals

Applied Linguistics
Der fremdsprachliche Unterricht Englisch
Die Neueren Sprachen
Englisch
English Journal
English Language Teaching Journal
Fremdsprachen Frühbeginn
Fremdsprachen lehren und lernen
Fremdsprachenunterricht
Grundschule Englisch
Language Learning and Technology (http://llt.msu.edu)
Language Teaching
Language Teaching Research
Language Testing
Modern Language Journal
Neusprachliche Mitteilungen aus Wissenschaft und Praxis
Primary English
System
TESOL Journal
TESOL Quarterly
Zeitschrift für Fremdsprachenforschung
Zeitschrift für interkulturellen Fremdsprachenunterricht
(http://www.ualberta.ca/~german/ejournal.htm)
Zielsprache Englisch

Pressestimmen zur Reihe UNI-Wissen

„Generell scheinen die Bücher der ›UNI-Wissen Reihe‹ eine neue Generation von ›Schulbüchern‹ einzuleiten, da sie endlich mal mit der Zeit gehen und nicht der Zeit hinterherhinken." ***Amazon.de*** **(1999)**

„In den [...] Bänden dieser Reihe hat Professor Ansgar Nünning, einer der profiliertesten Vertreter dieser nun die Lehrstühle neu besetzenden Generation, als Herausgeber eine ungewöhnliche Homogenität in Form, Darstellung und Inhalt erreicht. [...]
Diese Reihe wird über Jahre hinweg der inhaltliche und finanzielle Maßstab von Konkurrenzbänden sein. [...] Die Bände sind rundweg zu empfehlen. Der erfreulich niedrige Preis [...] lässt das sonst leider gängige Kopieren zur unnötigen Zeitverschwendung werden." ***Der fremdsprachliche Unterricht*** **(1999)**

„Die Bände der Reihe vermitteln auf wissenschaftlich solider und verständlicher Weise grundlegende Informationen und Überblickswissen zu ausgewählten Standardthemen der Literatur- und Sprachwissenschaft. Sie eignen sich sehr gut für die effiziente Einarbeitung in Teilgebiete der Anglistik/Amerikanistik, die Auffrischung bereits erworbener Kenntnisse ebenso wie die zielgerichtete Prüfungsvorbereitung. Besonders hervorzuheben ist die methodisch transparente Strukturierung der Bände und das übersichtliche layout." ***Archiv für das Studium der Neueren Sprachen und Literaturen*** **237, 152 (2000)**

Pressestimmen zu einzelnen Bänden

Uwe Baumann: ***Shakespeare und seine Zeit***
„[...] Darüber hinaus vermitteln Baumanns Analysen einen informativen Einblick in eine Vielzahl thematischer [...] und formalästhetischer [...] Innovationen, die – trotz der erheblichen künstlerischen Unterschiede der vorgestellten Dramen – die Studierenden und auch Lehrenden auf ein leider noch immer marginalisiertes Gebiet der Ausbildung in unserer Anglistik aufmerksam machen." ***Archiv für das Studium der neueren Sprachen und Literaturen,*** **237, 152 (2000)**

Vera und Ansgar Nünning: ***Englische Literatur des 18. Jahrhunderts***
„Die in flüssigem Stil geschriebene Geschichte der englischen Literatur des 18. Jahrhunderts führt auf anschauliche Weise in die vielfältigen Formen, Gattungen und Entwicklungen der englischen Literatur des 18. Jahrhunderts ein. Dabei ist den Verfassern daran gelegen, nicht nur den Höhenkamm auszuleuchten, sondern sie steigen auch in die Niederungen der weniger bekannten Autoren und weniger populären Gattungen hinab. Alles in allem ergibt sich so ein sehr komplexes Bild der englischen Literatur des 18. Jahrhunderts, in dem sich nichtsdestotrotz noch klare Entwicklungslinien abzeichnen." ***Sprachkunst*** **30,2 (1999)**

Gottfried Krieger: ***Das englische Drama des 20. Jahrhunderts***
„[...] Krieger gelingt es in seiner Einführung, die Entwicklungszusammenhänge einer Gattung in einem Jahrhundert sowie deren spezifische Ausprägungen interessant und fundiert zu vermitteln." ***Arbeiten aus Anglistik und Amerikanistik*** **24,2 (1999)**

Ansgar Nünning: ***Der englische Roman des 20. Jahrhunderts***
„Die Leserin/der Leser gewinnt einen ausgezeichneten Überblick über inhaltliche wie formale Entwicklungsstränge des englischen Romans in diesem Jahrhundert. [...] Das Buch ist eine wertvolle Bereicherung für jeden, der sich aus beruflichem oder privatem Interesse mit englischen Romanen dieses Jahrhunderts befassen möchte oder schlicht mit der Qual der Wahl konfrontiert ist, welchen Roman er mit seinem Oberstufenkurs lesen möchte." ***Neusprachliche Mitteilungen aus Wissenschaft und Praxis*** **53,1 (2000)**

Herbert Grabes: ***Das amerikanische Drama des 20. Jahrhunderts***
„Mit dem Ziel, ›einen Überblick über die Grundformen und die Geschichte des amerikanischen Dramas im 20. Jahrhundert‹ (S. 5) zu geben, legt Herbert Grabes mit dem vorliegenden Band eine überzeugende Darstellung der Entwicklung dieser literarischen Gattung in den USA vor. [...]
Dem vorliegenden Band ist zu bescheinigen, daß er eine bemerkenswerte und in ihrer Argumentation überzeugende Einführung in das amerikanische Drama des 20. Jahrhunderts darstellt." ***Archiv für das Studium der Neueren Sprachen und Literaturen*** **237,152 (2000)**

John F. Davis: ***Phonetics and Phonology***
„... bei diesem Titel kann von einer überragenden Leistung, auch in didaktischer Hinsicht, gesprochen werden." ***Anglistik*** **11,2 (2000)**

Richard Aczel: ***How to Write an Essay***
„Die zahlreichen Beispiele erleichtern später auch die Umsetzung in die Praxis und nehmen gerade den Schülern/Studenten, die zum ersten Mal ein essay schreiben, die Hemmschwelle zum ersten Schritt." ***Amazon.de*** **(1999)**

Richard Humphrey: ***Grundkurs Übersetzen Deutsch–Englisch***
„Der Autor behauptet zwar im Vorwort zu diesem Band sehr bescheiden, er würde ›nichts grundlegend Neues‹ (S. 6) bieten, doch einige Elemente des Übungsbuches sind durchaus als unkonventionell einzustufen." ***Anglistik*** **11, 2 (2000)**
„Das Buch ist [...] optimal fürs Selbsttraining. Es ist gerade für Erstsemester eine hilfreiche Anschaffung, die auch bestimmt ins studentische Budget paßt." ***Amazon.de*** **(1999)**

Richard Humphrey: ***English Idioms for University***
„[...] eine äußerst kurzweilige Lektüre [...] In der Breite der berücksichtigten Themen und der abwechslungsreichen Fülle des Materials wird dieses Übungsbuch seinem eigenen Anspruch mehr als gerecht. [...] Ein bescheidenes Büchlein, dabei aber mit offensichtlichem Spaß an der Sache zusammengestellt und von immensem sprachlichen Gebrauchswert – von den literarischen und landeskundlichen Nebeneffekten ganz abgesehen." ***Mitteilungsblatt des fmf Westfalen-Lippe*** **19,1 (2001)**